SHOCK, MEMORY ,
THE UNCONSCIC
IN VICTORIAN FIC1

CW01499315

Jill Matus explores shock in Victorian fiction and psychology with startling results that reconfigure the history of trauma theory. Central to Victorian thinking about consciousness and emotion, shock is a concept that challenged earlier ideas about the relationship between mind and body. Although the new materialist psychology of the mid nineteenth century made possible the very concept of a wound to the psyche – the recognition, for example, that those who escaped physically unscathed from train crashes or other overwhelming experiences might still have been injured in some significant way – it was Victorian fiction, with its complex explorations of the inner life of the individual and accounts of upheavals in personal identity, that most fully articulated the idea of the haunted, possessed and traumatized subject. This wide-ranging book reshapes our understanding of Victorian theories of mind and memory and reveals the relevance of nineteenth-century culture to contemporary theories of trauma.

JILL L. MATUS is Professor of English at the University of Toronto.

CAMBRIDGE STUDIES IN NINETEENTH-CENTURY LITERATURE AND CULTURE

General editor

Gillian Beer, *University of Cambridge*

Editorial board

Isobel Armstrong, *Birkbeck, University of London*
Kate Flint, *Rutgers University*
Catherine Gallagher, *University of California, Berkeley*
D. A. Miller, *University of California, Berkeley*
J. Hillis Miller, *University of California, Irvine*
Daniel Pick, *Birkbeck, University of London*
Mary Poovey, *New York University*
Sally Shuttleworth, *University of Oxford*
Herbert Tucker, *University of Virginia*

Nineteenth-century British literature and culture have been rich fields for interdisciplinary studies. Since the turn of the twentieth century, scholars and critics have tracked the intersections and tensions between Victorian literature and the visual arts, politics, social organization, economic life, technical innovations, scientific thought – in short, culture in its broadest sense. In recent years, theoretical challenges and historiographical shifts have unsettled the assumptions of previous scholarly synthesis and called into question the terms of older debates. Whereas the tendency in much past literary critical interpretation was to use the metaphor of culture as "background," feminist, Foucauldian and other analyses have employed more dynamic models that raise questions of power and of circulation. Such developments have reanimated the field. This series aims to accommodate and promote the most interesting work being undertaken on the frontiers of the field of nineteenth-century literary studies: work which intersects fruitfully with other fields of study such as history, or literary theory, or the history of science. Comparative as well as interdisciplinary approaches are welcomed.

A complete list of titles published will be found at the end of the book.

SHOCK, MEMORY AND THE UNCONSCIOUS IN VICTORIAN FICTION

JILL L. MATUS

CAMBRIDGE
UNIVERSITY PRESS

CAMBRIDGE UNIVERSITY PRESS
Cambridge, New York, Melbourne, Madrid, Cape Town,
Singapore, São Paulo, Delhi, Tokyo, Mexico City

Cambridge University Press
The Edinburgh Building, Cambridge CB2 8RU, UK

Published in the United States of America by Cambridge University Press, New York

www.cambridge.org
Information on this title: www.cambridge.org/9780521310253

© Jill L. Matus 2009

This publication is in copyright. Subject to statutory exception
and to the provisions of relevant collective licensing agreements,
no reproduction of any part may take place without the written
permission of Cambridge University Press.

First published 2009
First paperback edition 2011

A catalogue record for this publication is available from the British Library

ISBN 978-0-521-76024-9 Hardback
ISBN 978-0-521-31025-3 Paperback

Cambridge University Press has no responsibility for the persistence or
accuracy of URLs for external or third-party internet websites referred to in
this publication, and does not guarantee that any content on such websites is,
or will remain, accurate or appropriate.

Contents

vii

Acknowledgements

I have incurred many debts of gratitude and appreciation over the last decade in which this book was being researched and written. Along the way, several friends and colleagues generously agreed to take time out from their own work to read portions of the manuscript. Special thanks to Audrey Jaffe, Heather Glen, Cannon Schmitt and Henry Auster. Keith Oatley kindly offered instruction and reading lists on contemporary developments in emotion theory. Meredith Skura invited me to visit her Mellon Graduate Seminar on the Emotions at Rice University, and Heather Glen twice invited me to talk about my research at the Nineteenth-Century Graduate Seminar at Cambridge University. Thanks also to Jason Camlot and Teresa Mangum for invitations to present work at Concordia University and The Dickens Universe. Helena Michie and Jim Adams encouraged me at the early stages of the project by soliciting my work on Dickens and railway accident for *Nineteenth-Century Geographies* and *Victorian Studies*, respectively. For their suggestions, comments and stimulating conversation, I thank also Suzy Anger, Mary Jacobus, Sally Ledger, Ruth Leys, Teresa Mangum, Clare Pettitt, Rick Rylance, Dianne Sadoff, Simon Stern, Marjorie Stone, Jenny Bourne Taylor and Athena Vrettos.

I owe much to the audiences who responded to the various presentations related to the project at MLA conferences in Philadelphia and San Diego, NAVSA conferences at Virginia and Purdue, NVSA conferences at Queens and Drew, a VSWAC conference at University of British Columbia and The Dickens Universe, Santa Cruz, as well as talks at Cambridge, Concordia, Alberta and Rice Universities. I have on several occasions taught a graduate seminar on "The Victorian Unconscious" at the University of Toronto and an undergraduate senior seminar on "Victorian Fiction and Psychology." Thanks to the successive generations of bright and challenging students who helped me think through and refine my approach to many of the topics around which this book is organized.

As I prepared various aspects of my research for publication as essays, I benefited from the editorial comments and criticism of Andrew Miller,

Nicholas Dames, Anne Stiles, Joe Bristow, John Maynard and Adrienne Munich. Carolyn Dever's report for Cambridge University Press was most helpful in the final stages of revision, as was the other, anonymous report for the Press. Linda Bree provided sensible and incisive editorial advice. It has been a pleasure to work with her and Maartje Scheltens at Cambridge. Special thanks to my able research assistants on the project: Sara Malton, Natalie Rose, Lisa Smith, Emily Simmons and, most recently, Alisha Walters, who aided enormously in the preparation of the final manuscript.

I am most grateful for the fellowships and research grants that supported my work: a Social Sciences and Humanities Research Council of Canada (SSHRC) grant (2002–6) and, in 2005, a Chancellor Jackman Fellowship in the Humanities at the University of Toronto, which allowed six months of teaching release, thus providing valuable time to write.

Earlier versions or parts of several chapters have already been published as articles: "Historicizing Trauma: The Genealogy of Psychic Shock in *Daniel Deronda*," *Victorian Literature and Culture* 36 (2008): 121–40; "Victorian Framings of the Mind: Recent Work on Mid-Nineteenth Century Theories of Consciousness, Memory, and Emotion," *Literature Compass* 4:4 (2007): 1257–76; "Emergent Theories of Victorian Mind Shock: From War and Railway Accident to Nerves, Electricity and Emotion," in *Neurology and Literature 1860–1920*, ed. Anne Stiles (Houndmills, Basingstoke: MacMillan Palgrave, 2007), 163–84; "*Mary Barton* and *North and South*," in *The Cambridge Companion to Elizabeth Gaskell*, ed. Jill Matus (Cambridge: Cambridge University Press, 2007); "Trauma, Memory and Railway Disaster: The Dickensian Connection," *Victorian Studies* 43:3 (2001): 413–36. I thank the publishers for permitting me to draw on this material.

As always, I owe the greatest debt of gratitude to my family – my husband Geoff, and our daughters Lauren and Hayley, who have all been expected to show more interest in psychic distress and train wreckage than is generally thought conducive to good health. Their love and support has sustained me in this and all else in more ways than I can say.

Introduction: the psyche in pain

The famous "red room" episode in *Jane Eyre* (1848) ends with Jane experiencing a species of fit and passing out of consciousness. Describing the aftermath of her terror, she explains that for many weeks "and even to this day," she suffers the tremors of the mental anguish she was made to endure:

No severe or prolonged bodily illness followed this incident in the red-room; it only gave my *nerves a shock*; of which I feel the reverberation to this day ... Next day, by noon I was up and dressed, and sat wrapped in a shawl by the nursery hearth. I felt physically weak and broken down; but my worst ailment was an unutterable wretchedness of *mind*: a wretchedness which kept drawing from me silent tears; no sooner had I wiped one salt drop from my cheek than another followed. Yet, I thought, I ought to have been happy, for none of the Reeds were there; they were all gone out in the carriage with their mama ... but, in fact, my racked nerves were now in such a state that no calm could soothe, and no pleasure excite them agreeably. (Emphasis added)[1]

Jane goes on to describe how the servant Bessie brings her a tart on a "brightly painted china plate, whose bird of paradise, nestling in a wreath of convolvuli and rosebuds, had been wont to stir in me a most enthusiastic sense of admiration; and which plate I had often petitioned to be allowed to take in my hand in order to examine it more closely."[2] Allowed now to examine the plate and eat the circlet of delicate pastry on it, she can find no pleasure in it. Even the plumage of the bird seems strangely faded. Bessie asks if she might not like a book, books of course being Jane's great delight. She asks for *Gulliver's Travels*, but when this "cherished volume" is placed in her hand, she finds all "eerie and dreary" and closes the book and puts it on the table beside the untasted tart. The account is a poignant representation of the aftermath of overwhelming emotional shock. Brontë makes use of the language of nerves here as a hermeneutic through which to understand Jane's experience of psychic suffering. Her pointed distinction between bodily illness and "wretchedness of mind" emerges in the description of what we would call dissociation and lack of affect.

Jane is not herself, we might say, and can relish none of the things that used to delight her. Few readers today would quarrel with the pronouncement that Brontë's heroine is traumatized by her experience in the red room. But to what extent are contemporary concepts of trauma similar to Brontë's formulation of a "shock to the nerves," the reverberations of which continue to be felt in permanent aftershocks?

In *Little Dorrit* (1857) Dickens describes the latent effects of William Dorrit's long imprisonment as a final and painful hallucinatory return to the Marshalsea. Now liberated from debtors' prison, wealthy and living in the style that behooves a gentleman, Dorrit is attending a society dinner at the Merdles when he is suddenly mentally transported back to debtors' prison. He asks for Bob, the turnkey, and then makes his humiliating speech to the assembled company requesting alms, standing upon his shabby dignity as a fallen gentleman, and claiming his position as The Father of the Marshalsea. "They got him up to his room without help, and laid him down on his bed. And from that hour his *poor maimed spirit, only remembering the place where it had broken its wings, cancelled the dream* through which it had since groped, and knew nothing beyond the Marshalsea" (emphasis added).[3] The shift in Mr. Dorrit's consciousness so that he is oblivious to his present circumstances and surroundings but lives again in the past dissociates him from the present "unreality" of wealth and status. In returning to the place where his spirit has broken its wings, Mr. Dorrit returns also to a reality that his daughter Amy can share. Her father's delusion, with its refusal of the present, Dickens implies, is both a return to the overwhelming experience of debtors' prison – the place that broke his spirit's wings – and, paradoxically, a recognition of what is real and valuable in his life – his daughter. A life of riches has been unable to erase the wounding past; but worse, it is a "dream" that has replaced the painful reality of prison life. What is extraordinary about the passage is that one would expect the prison experience to be the dream or nightmare from which Mr. Dorrit awakens through his miraculous reversal of fortune. But the pretentious world of monied society is, in the Dickensian twist, the real delusion.

As Dickens creates a scene involving hallucination, memory erasure and confusion of time and place, he registers an interest in the latent effects of past crisis and the dysfunctions of memory and consciousness it can produce. It is not unknown for characters in Victorian novels to relive and inhabit happier, childhood memories in the passage from life to death. In *Mary Barton* (1848), for example, the dying Alice readily returns to the loving memories of her mother. But the painful return is less usual. In the representation of Mr. Dorrit's final days, we see Dickens broaching questions of the temporality of the unconscious and of memory. His grasp of psychic temporalities that defy the movement of linear time implies a sense of belatedness – the unbidden return of a painful, self-annihilating, yet paradoxically "real" past. From the vantage point of the twenty-first century both the episodes from *Jane Eyre* and from *Little Dorrit* appear to be in some ways about trauma, the aftermath of psychic shock and suffering, yet our use of the term "trauma" to mean psychic injury was quite unknown to Brontë or Dickens and their contemporaries. Did the Victorians have similar concepts for which other terms were used, or rather different ideas about the structure of mind and the nature of a mental wound?

In attempting to answer these questions, this book is about the cultural formation of trauma as a concept, the changing representations of mental, nervous or psychic shock in the mid- to late-Victorian period, and the various ways in which Victorian authors render the tangle of physiological and psychological effects that attend on great emotional upheaval, strain or terror. "[T]he fact is, I was a trifle beside myself; or rather *out* of myself," Jane Eyre explains, when trying to convey her damagingly transformative experience in the red room. Interested in the narration of those occasions on which we are "not ourselves," or "beside ourselves," this book explores in fiction of the period the threat to self-possession and governance that a non-unitary model of mind entailed, and how that threat implicated the already fragile illusion of an individual subject in possession of itself. It is interested also in the kinds of narrative rupture occasioned by those fictional occasions of not being oneself. While valuable contributions to our understanding of Victorian theories of consciousness and unconsciousness have been made by literary and cultural critics and historians of science, there has been no sustained exploration of how Victorians construed the effects of psychic shock or pain and how such investigations shaped a cultural context whose legacy is detectable in late-modern theories of trauma, memory and unconscious processes.[4] *Shock, Memory and the Unconscious in Victorian Fiction* works in two directions: from the vantage point of late-modern theories of trauma, I look back to the Victorian moment to uncover a pre-Freudian genealogy; from that vantage point I look forward to see how this longer history might inflect our understanding of the direction that trauma studies has taken in the last few decades. I will argue that theories of shock formed a crucial aspect of the way Victorians attempted to think through the relations between mind and body, and that changing conceptions of the emotions during the period were central in shaping mid-nineteenth-century theories of consciousness and memory.

Shock has been distinguished from trauma in current criticism in terms of an opposition between physical and psychical. Shock and trauma have also been differentiated in terms of a "decisive *break* between medical and psychoanalytic conceptions of the wound." Such a view consequently posits "a radical *discontinuity* between a modernist culture of shock and a post-modern culture of trauma."[5] Mark Seltzer argues that these "distinctions and periodizations have their place" but also rightly disputes their purely oppositional nature. In Freud's terms, as Seltzer points out, trauma remains a borderland concept between the physical and the psychical. In "Two Types of Shock in Modernity," Tim Armstrong seems to support this formulation. He represents Freud as insisting that "there is a wound attached to the traumatic situation; a wound which is at first neurological, then fantastic, and finally located somewhere between the two." However, Armstrong does not see pre-Freudian conceptions of shock as having a psychical component. In his view, Freud saved the "notion of trauma from the materialistic and historically specific neurasthenic paradigm, with its attachment to the 'actual,' the quotidian." Freud dispensed with the "economic notion of 'actual' shock" in order to develop the idea of an internal trauma. In place of accounts of actual shock, "Freud substitutes family melodrama, and the timelessness of the unconsciousness."[6] Armstrong cites Freud himself as dismissing "the old naïve theory of shock" in favor of his own notion of trauma. Armstrong thus sets up an opposition between "the *economic* model of shock, in which experience is conceived as a succession of stimuli which must be processed in time," and "the timelessness of the unconscious wound."[7] Before Freud we have what he calls a "'neurasthenic paradigm,' in which shock is seen in terms of processing *speeds*, (excitation, activation), rather than in terms of wound."[8]

In questioning Armstrong's opposition, I would emphasize along with Seltzer that opposing shock and trauma has the effect of rewriting the tensions within the two concepts: "*[S]hock*, for example, refers both to the impact of the event and to its effect, the concept already encrypts the deferrals, or 'afterwardness,' of cause and effect that, in part, defines the trauma."[9] Similarly a distinction between shock as pointing to the world or the collective order, and trauma to the subject or individual, erases the complex interactions and dependencies between world and subject. Furthermore, the psychical effects of shock, and the relation between the psychic and the physiological, are the subject of increasing scrutiny and competing formulation in the period under consideration. To see trauma rather than shock as a "sort of switch point between bodily and psychic orders" is to discount (if not ignore) the rich variety of Victorian thinking about the relationship between somatic and psychic registrations of shock.[10] It is that rich variety that this book seeks to explore.

An interesting borderland between bodily and psychic orders in the Victorian novel is that suitably undefined ailment, "brain fever," which functions as a loose and catch-all diagnosis for many kinds of mental crisis and is especially often related to emotional shock. The condition is of ancient origin, having arisen from the Greek "phrenitis," meaning "frenzy," but also translated as "brain fever." Hippocrates defined it as an inflammation or affection of the mind.[11] Historians focusing particularly on the nineteenth century characterize it as an inflammation of the brain, caused by either emotional shock or overuse of the brain.[12] Not usually contagious, the Victorian versions of this disorder were rather different from the conditions of encephalitis or meningitis to which the term may refer today. Patients were warned to avoid shocks to the system and the experience of strong emotion, since these were often the putative causes of the problem.

In *Mary Barton* (1848) the eponymous heroine develops a brain fever after the strain of defending Jem in the dock while still trying to keep secret her father's identity as a murderer. She raves deliriously for weeks. In *Great Expectations* (1861), Pip falls into a fever and experiences nightmarish delirium after the death of Magwitch, awakening at last to find Joe nursing him. Although he explains that the "late stress upon me had allowed me to put off illness, but not to put it away," the illness itself seems related to his overwrought emotional state and functions as a kind of purgation of his moral shortcomings.[13] In Charlotte Yonge's *The Daisy Chain* (1856), Dr. May's son Norman experiences great shock in witnessing his mother's death in a carriage accident, an experience that brings him perilously close to brain fever. The boy cannot sleep and suffers horrific dreams. In Gaskell's *Cousin Phillis* (1864), the disappointment and shock of being quietly jilted by the lover she thought was hers plunges Phillis into a dangerous brain fever. Even well into the next century, the label "brain fever" to denote "brain symptoms of great severity" occurs in Sherlock Holmes' "The Adventure of the Cardboard Box" (1917). In this case, the symptoms are the result of a distressing shock that implicates Miss Sarah Cushing in the death of her sister. Unsurprisingly, women seem more susceptible to such fever as a form of purification or refeminization after acts of self-assertion. Like neurasthenia, a diagnosis of the nerves that was named in the late 1860s, brain fever could be caused by too much studying. Periodicals such as *Girls' Best Friend* provide abundant examples of foolish young women who have carelessly overtaxed their brains.[14] Nevertheless, as the example from *Great Expectations* shows, brain fever was a less conventionally gendered category than either hysteria or neurasthenia.

What is significant about the examples I have just discussed is that they all *imply* emotional or psychological rather than purely physiological causes for the imperiled condition. In many instances the sufferer undergoes a cleansing of sorts, even a form of expiation (as can readily be seen in Pip's case) for past mistakes. Even as occurrences of brain fever suggest that mind and brain are intimately related, they also declare fever and delirium to be the guarantees of serious illness; shock and its "merely" psychic after-effects could be dismissed as malingering, hysteria or, worse yet, madness. To be really commanding of sympathy, illness must be bodily. At the same time, because brain fever is associated with fever and delirium, it is potentially an opportunity to explore altered states of mind, and to recover memories and knowledge inaccessible to ordinary consciousness. A case in point is that of an uneducated young woman who "during the delirium of fever, continually repeated sentences in languages unknown to those around her, which were found to be Latin, Greek and Hebrew."[15] She had unknowingly memorized what she had overheard as a child when in the care of a pastor who recited Rabbinical texts. The delirious mind ramblings of Pip or Esther Summerson, for example, are thus ways of gaining access to interiority and psychic realities of which the subject may be unaware. While brain fever is a serviceably capacious but vague category in Victorian fiction that can be used to represent shock, I focus particularly on aberrations of consciousness, affect and memory, which, although linked in materialist science to the physical, are more generally associated with the psychological.

Twentieth-century concepts of trauma imply a model of mind in which cognition and experience are severed. According to the dominant interpretative paradigm, knowledge of the experience is unavailable to ordinary consciousness, but in some other part of the mind, a record, as it were, of the overwhelming event is stored away. In much contemporary theory, dissociation rather than repression is the process which best describes the mind's response to overwhelming experience. Inaccessible to conscious recall, memories of the experience obtrude nevertheless in flashbacks and hallucinations and wreak damage unconsciously. The attempt to "apply" trauma theory to literary texts raises a number of problems, not the least of which is that trauma theory is not a unified or stable set of propositions describing a timeless, historically transcendent condition. Psychoanalytically inflected theory differs in important ways from the definitions of psychological trauma (Post-Traumatic Stress Disorder [PTSD]) offered since 1980 in the *Diagnostic and Statistical Manual of Mental Disorders*, for example. Moreover, trauma theory, as it has been taken up and applied in literary studies, differs greatly in assumptions and emphasis from the now large body of psychological literature devoted to the diagnosis and therapy of trauma and dissociative disorders. On the one hand, I am critical of attempts to apply trauma theory as a set of transcendent truths about the way the mind functions, and would resist privileging or reifying trauma theory. On the other, I think it may, in its various incarnations, usefully open up a range of questions that shape historical and literary inquiry. I thus approach Victorian texts with the questions about self and consciousness that animate trauma theory from Freud to the present in order to recover and illuminate the array of specifically Victorian ideas about the mind and its operation in the aftermath of emotional shock.

The term "trauma" emerged in the late nineteenth century when the label for a physical wound came to be associated with a mental state. A precondition of that shift was that the mind had to be conceived of as physical, material and physiological – and therefore vulnerable – like the body. It could be argued that the rise of a discourse of trauma is concomitant with the establishment of psychology itself as a discipline, and more particularly with the emphasis in physiological psychology on mental shock as the basic unit of consciousness. But, of course, trauma is not just a concept formulated by medical and psychological discourse in isolation. It is highly dependent on social and cultural ideas about suffering, accountability, responsibility, reparation and victimhood, which is to say that its social, legal and cultural implications are far-reaching. What may be useful about the history I attempt to trace is that it illuminates the culture of belief, values and ethical codes that produced shifts in perceptions and explanations about the effects of emotional shock. Pondering the eminence (and yet abidingly controversial nature) of trauma theory today, we may recognize that it speaks to a "wound culture" in which relief or healing is sought for haunting psychological injuries, and along the way accountability established for their perpetration; evidence of wounding and its perpetrators is found in the unwitting witnessing, inaccessible to memory except through hypnosis and therapeutic recovery.[16] Debates in trauma studies continue to swirl around precisely this question – the reliability of witnessing, and the extent to which the traumatic experience is recorded in the brain as "a reality imprint" or subjected to unconscious fantasmatic reordering. Given the current debates in trauma theory, we may ask what similar or different cultural imperatives produced Victorian formulations of psychic suffering, and what social, professional and political ideologies they served or resisted.

As an exploration of the categories and languages available to the Victorians for articulating the idea of a psychic wound, this book focuses on the period 1850–86 and traces the emergence of trauma as a concept and object of knowledge in an array of disciplinary formations: pre-eminently literature, medicine, mental physiology and psychology, but also mental philosophy and epistemology of mind, as well as religion and law. I examine the growth of a cluster of ideas about the effect of shock on consciousness and memory; the psychology and physiology of emotions; the nature of will and susceptibility; theories of dreams and trance; the corporeality of thought; and the involuntary or unconscious aspects of psychic life.

The initial impetus for this study came, on the one hand, from my sense of the limitations of an unhistoricized and presentist use of trauma theory in relation to Victorian literature, and, on the other, from the omission of literature's role in histories of the conceptualization of trauma.[17] A recent trend in literary criticism deploying trauma theory is the retrospective diagnosis of anguished fictional subjects as suffering from trauma, as if trauma were a timeless and historically transcendent category. It is seldom that critics invoking the concept of trauma reflect on the history of its discursive development and provenance or attempt to read Victorian novels in the context of nineteenth-century theories of psychic shock or wound. As an alternative to the application of contemporary or Freudian formulations of trauma (themselves vexed and continually under interpretative revision), my project is to explore what Victorian novelists and mental physiologists understood by psychic shock and what valence and social meanings that concept had in mid- to late-Victorian culture. Historians of psychology have noted that developing nineteenth-century scientific areas of inquiry (physiology, medicine) and so-called "pseudoscientific" areas (mesmerism, phrenology) propelled "the puzzle of the mind–body relation" to the forefront of public debate.[18] By attending to the literary text not only as an index of cultural reactions to scientific concepts, but also as an agent in developing discourses of the mind and body, we may at once broaden our sense of the complexity of Victorian formulations of emotion and its potential to disrupt consciousness and memory, and provide further historicization of contemporary theories of emotion and of trauma.

It may be argued that literary representations have always been in the business of representing suffering subjects, irrespective of changing medical and psychological ideas about how the brain and mind work. There is obviously some truth to this contention – Mr. Dorrit's reimagining of himself in the Marshalsea is as clearly a representation of his present dislocation as Lady Macbeth's derangement is of hers. But beyond the broadly similar terms in which literature speaks of psychic suffering across time, there are important ways in which literary and psychological discourse at any period are interlinked and mutually influential. While broadly interdisciplinary, this book aims to explore in particular the participation of fictive narrative in what has been assumed to be the province of emergent psychology and memory science, and to offer new readings of a range of Victorian texts through a focus on mid-Victorian conceptions of emotional injury and the psychic wound. This study focuses, therefore, on the extensive traffic between literary and psychological discussions of the way the mind functions in the aftermath of overwhelming experience.

In so doing, *Shock, Memory and the Unconscious in Victorian Fiction* offers a corrective to studies of the genealogy of trauma that have largely disregarded fictive writing. It is curious that this gap should exist, since the contemplation of imagination and the powers of the creative mind were influential in spurring early-nineteenth-century investigations into the mind's architecture, and trauma as a concept is closely bound up with ideas about unconscious knowledge and conscious recall. We have only to turn to the Romantic poets, and writers such as Hazlitt and De Quincey, to recognize that it was not uncommon to think about the unconscious mind as the source of poetic creation.[19] This is an idea repeatedly echoed in the psychological discourse of the period and in theories of artistic creation from E. S. Dallas's accounts of the workings of imagination to R. L. Stevenson's witty attribution of literary work to his "Brownies." When Dallas described the action of the imagination in *The Gay Science*, he drew on the notion of the "hidden soul," by which he meant the creative capacity of the absent or unwitting mind. The study of this "soul" was to be a science of aesthetics, of pleasure – the "gay science." His work can be situated in the context of a burgeoning interest in unconscious processes, the puzzle of how we can know things of which we are not conscious, and the secret stores of memory.

In a metaphor of the traffic between the dark (unconscious regions) and the light (consciousness) Dallas sought to probe the strange ways in which the unconscious mind worked creatively. Whereas Dallas was fascinated with the pleasure, aesthetics and creativity in the transmission from "the light into the dark, and back from the dark into light,"[20] models of unconscious thinking more frequently provoked disquiet. If thinking could go on outside of the control of the will, did that mean that human beings are essentially governed by automatic processes over which they have little control? Dallas's idea of the hidden soul as associated with pleasure and play can be strikingly contrasted with the focus in literature and psychology on the more painful aspects of transmissions from darkness to light.

Towards the end of the century, the psychologist William James wrote an essay entitled "The Hidden Self" focusing on Pierre Janet's investigations into memory and alternate consciousness, the study of which was a science of pain – trauma. James himself is cited in the *Oxford English Dictionary* (*OED*) as one of the first to use the term "psychic traumata" to explain psychic injury: "Certain reminiscences of the shock fall into the subliminal consciousness, where they can only be discovered in 'hypnoid' states. If left there, they act as permanent 'psychic *traumata*', thorns in the spirit, so to speak."[21] Dallas too writes about shock, but from his point of view the shock that art produces is indefinable and wondrous:

The poet's words, the artist's touches, are electric; and we feel those words, and the shock of those touches, going through us in a way we cannot define ... Art is poetical in proportion as it has this power of appealing to what I may call the absent mind, as distinct from the present mind, on which falls the great glare of consciousness, and to which alone science appeals.[22]

From Dallas's emphasis on shock as pleasure to James's recognition of its painful aftermath, from secret association to unremembered dissociation, the trajectory I trace in this book follows shifts in models of the unconscious at work in literary representations of a self whose wounds are invisible, but detectable in disturbances of memory, affect and consciousness.[23]

That is not to say, of course, that a discourse of memory disturbance and mental pain did not exist before the period on which I focus. Schopenhauer writes that:

[e]verybody carries in his memory a general yet cohesive reminiscence of his earlier life that reaches into unconscious childhood. True health of the mind consists in complete recall ... [T]he object of great mental pain lies invariably in our memory, ... thus we can explain how such pain becomes madness (King Lear, Ophelia, etc.), because people cast away excessive pain just as they cast away memories and thus find relief in madness.[24]

The quotation suggests the contours of a history of thinking about the relationship between mental pain and memory, and, in cases where memory is torturous, resultant madness. What I wish to explore are Victorian attempts to understand the effects of great emotion and painful memory that do not depend on a stark opposition between madness and sanity but focus rather on changes in ordinary consciousness. As Joel Peter Eigen has shown in the case of legal rulings, the year 1876 marked an important

moment in which a state of absence or "missing," a state of unconsciousness, became the grounds of a "not guilty verdict." Prior to this, the idea of
unconscious behavior as a legal defense was always coupled with some
form of insanity. If one could be "not oneself" to the extent of being
innocent of acts committed in another state, and yet not insane, then ideas
about the fragmentation or splitting of self were clearly changing.[25]
"Pathology" was once, as its etymology suggests, simply the study of
feeling, the branch of knowledge having to do with the emotions (which
the *OED* lists as now a rare and obscure meaning). But it has come to
mean the study of disease, abnormality or malfunction, and, by the nineteenth century, the malfunctioning or disease of mental states, as in Henry
Maudsley's title, *The Physiology and Pathology of Mind* (1867). I focus
mainly in this study on Victorian ideas of emotional aftermath as a shift
in the continuum of ordinary, rather than pathologized, states of mind.
As a result of feminism and gender theory, and in the wake of Foucault,
a great deal of research has been carried out on Victorian constructions
of insanity, especially in terms of gender, hysteria and social power. But
ideas about trance, wandering attention, the mind's capacity to hold
knowledge latently and the nature of unconscious agency are, in the
period under scrutiny, the province of mental philosophy and physiology.
These are discourses that attempt to describe the ordinary mind and those
alterations of the mind from its ordinary state that are not extreme enough
to warrant the diagnosis of insanity. William Carpenter's *Principles of
Mental Physiology* (1874), for example, moves from an initial account of
attention, habit, perception, ideas, the emotions and the will to a second
section tracing a spectrum of "special" physiological states: memory,
imagination, unconscious cerebration, reverie, dreams and somnambulism, mesmerism, delirium, all the way to insanity.

The trajectory I follow certainly reaches a crux with the work of Freud,
Janet and Charcot, to which I refer, but which does not form a major part of
my focus. In part, this book is written to counter the tendency in studies of
trauma to historicize no further than these putative originators. Nor do
I wish to suggest an evolutionary or progressive narrative: how embryonic
Victorian ideas grew up to become mature Freudian ones. One of the aims
of this book is to provoke a critical assessment of contemporary trauma
theory's dominant focus on memory and the importance of making traumatic memory the subject of narrative. Victorian theories of emotion and
the kind of knowledge or "intelligence" conveyed by emotion are important
to the way in which mid-nineteenth-century texts understand the aftermath
of psychic shock. Although disorders of affect are included in the official

definitions of PTSD in the *Diagnostic and Statistical Manual of Mental Disorders*, emotion has been eclipsed or subsumed by memory in influential contemporary accounts of trauma both in psychoanalysis and in literary criticism.

It is an increasingly disputed assumption that literature simply follows or reflects what medical science makes available conceptually. As the work of Gillian Beer, George Levine and many others has shown, literature is not just a passive receptor of scientific ideas, but a participatory agent in their formation, able not just "to parallel developments in the sciences, but on occasion to anticipate them by virtue of its willingness to let the imagination, and the language itself, be a guide."[26] Literary texts are not supplemental illustrations but primary cultural documents. They shape culture profoundly and "frequently offer a more complex picture of cultural manifestations than many other written documents."[27] The history of the concept of trauma provides a useful example of this capacity. Far from merely following along and reflecting scientific advancements, literary narratives helped to shape and influence the cultural practices and narratives out of which the concept of trauma developed.[28] A key assumption of this study is that the relation between literary production and medical and psychological writing is a reciprocal one. Victorian fiction, especially, I will argue, participates in the debates of its day about the nature of emotions, unconscious processes and memory, and shapes the way mental physiologists write about the powers and mysteries of the mind.[29] So, for example, William Benjamin Carpenter cites Dickens on the force of the imagination when he writes about latency and memory.[30]

It is often asserted that, during the period under discussion, interiority and individual psychology became the stuff of novelistic material. As D. H. Lawrence remarked, "You see, it was really George Eliot who started it all ... And how wild they all were with her for doing it. It was she who started putting all the action inside. Before, you know, with Fielding and the others, it had been outside."[31] One may argue with Lawrence about whether George Eliot was indeed the first novelist to put all the action inside, but his point about the shift that Victorian fiction marks is well taken. One of the distinctive characteristics of the Victorian novel with its third-person, often omniscient, narrator is to explore the interior life of characters in an unprecedented way. The narrator, able to move in and out of her characters' minds, has a unique opportunity to provide imaginative access to their subjectivity and to probe questions of consciousness and memory. In a great many Victorian novels, inner life is an object of extreme interest and detailed representation.[32] As Ronald

Thomas has astutely pointed out, Freud himself admitted that the "narrative forms of fiction provided the explanatory models that led to his own shift from a physiological to a psychological understanding of hysterical symptoms."[33] Freud remarked that his case histories read like short stories and that he found enabling the works of imaginative writers with their detailed description of mental processes.[34] Although an interest in unconscious processes of the mind meant looking inward at the hidden and mysterious workings of the psyche, this focus was not, however, necessarily a turning away from social representation. Rather, many Victorian writers saw it as quite the opposite. George Henry Lewes, for example, insisted that "to understand the Human Mind we must study it under normal conditions, and these are social conditions."[35]

It is well known that nineteenth-century psychological discourse is highly dependent on metaphor and analogy to communicate conceptions of the mind. This book explores the relationship of this analogical reliance to literary representations of the mind's workings, locality and architecture – a cultural exchange in which it is less important to talk of originators than of a shared discursive matrix that shapes both "scientific" and novelistic representations. One of the sub-themes of this book is the powerful effect of the languages of technology on literary and psychological conceptions of the unconscious. Trauma has been described as "one of the signal concepts of our time"; taking the epithet "signal" literally, one might argue that trauma is indeed a concept about signaling, its overt rupture and breakdown, and its covert reconstruction.[36] The railway runs through several chapters, not only as a thread that structures the narrative of how injury from shock came to public attention but as an exemplary progenitor of vocabulary. Dickens writes in *Dombey and Son* (1848) of the urban upheaval created by the construction of the railway lines and station, describing the effect as akin to the "shock of a great earthquake."[37] The idea that shock comes in waves and may have diffused effects is the basis of Alexander Bain's theory of emotions; knowledge about batteries and Faradic current shape ideas about what may occur in mind and body after a shocking event.[38] Historians of the nerves and emotion record the shift in brain research at the end of the eighteenth century when people began to realize that nerves worked not by hydraulics but by electricity.[39] Ideas about transport, transmission, communication, signals, disruption, linkage and travel accrue in relation to discoveries of electricity, magnetism and telegraphy, and undergird the related speculative discourses of mesmerism and telepathy. An emergent discourse of psychic shock is hardly separable from current technologies – in particular, discoveries in the fields of electricity, steam, wave theory and magnetism. As one respondent to a debate about spiritualism in the *Cornhill Magazine* (1863) wrote, if we are skeptical about spiritualism, then we should be skeptical about "the results produced by steam engines, electric telegraphs, the use of chloroform," which "are as great a shock to all antecedent experience as any sensible phenomena which it is possible to imagine." Distinguishing his skepticism about spiritualism, Fitzjames Stephen countered:

I am told on good authority that there is an invisible and imponderable agent in nature which is called electricity and this is illustrated by a number of sufficiently familiar facts and experiments. By degrees I am taught to see that currents of electricity may by appropriate means be transmitted instantaneously to remote places, and so, step by step, I am led up to the electric telegraph, and when the matter is so put before me, I believe it as firmly as any one.[40]

While my focus on literary texts is restricted to Victorian Britain, the terrain of scientific, psychological and medical literature relevant to this study is at times Continental and American. The history of mesmerism and hypnotism cannot be invoked without reference to Mesmer, Puységur and Charcot; similarly, the history of ideas about electricity as nerve force must move from Italy to Germany. Conceptions of emotional injury in war emerge not only from the Crimean War and Indian Uprising but from the Napoleonic Wars, the Franco-Prussian War, the American War of Independence and the American Civil War, while concepts of neurasthenia and trance travel transatlanticly from George Beard and Silas Weir Mitchell; histories of emotion cannot be told without the work of William James.

The first chapter sets out some of the debates animating current trauma theory in order to introduce a series of questions and topics that are also pertinent to Victorian thinking about unconscious processes. To study Victorian theories about the architecture of the psyche means examining the entanglements of materialist and spiritualist discourse about body and soul in the period. A common characterization of the period is that materialist explanations were increasingly privileged over spiritualist ones. Yet it would be reductive simply to oppose secular, evolutionary and physiological thinkers to spiritual, creationist and metaphysical ones. Without a growing acceptance of the physicality of the mind, the localization of the mind in the brain, the idea of a psychic wound is not possible. Yet paradoxically, the more the psychic wound is literalized, the more magical seem the powers of mind now not attributable to external, supernatural agencies – god, ghosts, spirits, specters and the like – but to internal functioning. The greatest mystery, and one that seems only to grow as more about it is discovered, is the unfathomable nature of the corporeal mind. After surveying ideas of the unconscious and altered states of mind, memory science and emotion theory, the chapter considers Victorian discourse on the psychological effects of war and accident, and the extent to which shock features in accounts and narratives of war. I then turn to conceptions in physiological psychology of consciousness as itself a form of shock. Ideas about the electrical nature of nerve-force help to construct profound emotional experience as a jolt or shock, but also raise questions about the purely physical rather than cognitive nature of emotion. I suggest that a genealogy of trauma focusing on Victorian emotion theory as well as memory science may help us to understand the increasing nineteenth-century medical and literary interest in mental shock.

Subsequent chapters address a series of apposite literary texts by Elizabeth Gaskell, Charles Dickens, George Eliot and R. L. Stevenson. There is a very wide range of Victorian fiction that engages in one way or another with questions of the structure of mind and its response to overwhelming emotions such as fear, grief and shock. It is not, of course, the aim of this project to provide an exhaustive taxonomy of such fiction. I have chosen texts that pay significant attention to aberrations of consciousness and memory, dream, trance and hallucination, doubling or fragmentation of identity, haunting and the effect of powerful emotion on subjectivity and cognition, the topics around which chapters are organized. All the texts chosen reflect on similar questions under debate in psychological texts, and in all cases I read them in relation to the relevant psychological discourse of their moment.

I particularly want to avoid the association of a discourse of psychic shock with any specific subgenre of fiction, and, most obviously, with the rise of the sensation novel in the 1860s. Purveyors of sensation fiction were assuredly interested in writing about (and provoking) intense emotion and shock, and the novels of Wilkie Collins, for example, are engaged with questions of altered states of mind, the unconscious and memory erasure. To claim that this subgenre has greater purchase on ideas about emotion, shock and the unconscious, however, would limit the more generalized and diverse interest in the mind to which I wish to draw attention in this study. In making selections among fictional texts, I have attempted a balance between realist and non-realist fiction. The engagement of narrative with the secret, inner workings of the mind can be readily shown in *North and South* and *Daniel Deronda*, realist novels whose third-person narrators move in and out of their characters' minds exploring shifts and aberrations in ordinary consciousness and making transparent even unconscious transactions. But also important in this study are fictive creations that imagine the implications of theories of the mind in more stylized and fantastic ways. Ghost stories such as Dickens's "The Signalman," and gothic science fiction such as Stevenson's *The Strange Case of Dr Jekyll and Mr Hyde*, also engage with ideas about the architecture of the mind and different states of consciousness. Even in the realist texts chosen, I pay special attention to the importance of imagery, forms and conventions associated with the gothic as a means of expressing ideas about haunting, possession, phantoms and the otherworldly.

Since I will be suggesting in several chapters that ghost tales and gothic fiction provide Victorian authors with a ready conceptual, linguistic and formal arsenal for the representation of psychic distress, I want to say a few words about critical views on the development and deployment of these forms in the nineteenth century. The rise of ghost fiction is often linked to the assumption that materialist explanations trump belief in the super-natural as the nineteenth century progresses. So Robert Tracy has remarked that gothic fiction arose (with Walpole's *The Castle of Otranto* in 1764) only when "the educated classes ceased to believe in ghosts and witches and so began to find them entertaining."[41] According to Terry Castle's influential study *The Female Thermometer*, which focuses on the invention of the uncanny, the end of the eighteenth century marks the demise of a belief in the externality of specters, hauntings and terrors and the rise of the phantas-mal.[42] Arguing for a later shift, Ronald Thomas sees the Victorian period as the one in which the psychologization of the supernatural takes place:

[a]t the outset of the Victorian age, dreams belonged as much to the supernatural world as to science ... As a result of the dramatic movements in intellectual history which have come to be called "natural supernaturalism," "religious humanism" or "secularization," the nineteenth century reassigned more and more phenomena hitherto considered supernatural to a new but as yet undefined place in the human psyche.[43]

Similarly, in their account of the progress of the ghost story in the Victorian period, Smith and Haas suggest that the supernatural progresses "from an exterior, often physically manifested force acting upon characters to an interior, psychological power causing characters to act upon others."[44] The spiritual become material could still, however, be used to represent the psychic. Stories of ghosts and hauntings at the mid-century often look both ways, offering psychological or physiological explanations but preserv-ing the possibility of supernatural occurrences.

By the same token, retrospective summaries of the Victorian period need to be rethought in terms of the period's interest in ghosts, dreams, spirits and the conundrums of the mind. Looking back on the Victorian age in his study of the Edwardian, Samuel Hynes highlights a sharp contrast between the social realism of novelists from Dickens to George Moore and the "mysterious and the unseen" in Edwardian literature, suggesting that the literature changed "just as ... researchers turned from the natural sciences to spiritualism." Hynes dismisses Victorian psychology as a "biological science, concerned with the physiology of the nervous system and subject to the laws of evolution; the limitations of this approach had retarded the progress of psychology in England, and the further resistance of the universities to what seemed an irreligious treatment of mind had left psychology out of the late-Victorian scientific picture."[45] This is a view in need of qualification, given both the array of Victorian fiction outside the genre of social realism and the diversity of psychological writing in the period.

The second chapter focuses on dream and trance in Elizabeth Gaskell's *North and South* (1855), a condition-of-England novel whose abiding interest in emotional shock and the aftermath of grief and pain has been largely overlooked. Reading her references to dream and trance in relation to mid-century views about psychic states, I show how thoroughly the novel dramatizes the idea that violent shifts of emotion precipitate shifts in consciousness, at times to the extent that a reigning self may be abdicated. Moreover, I argue that the model of self she implies in the novel is more open to the destabilizing effects of emotional aftermath than that adumbrated by physiologists such as William Carpenter. Disruptions in ordinary consciousness, while fearful and threatening to self-governance, are also occasions of potentially beneficial self-alteration as knowledge from a hidden part of the self reconfigures, rather than incapacitates, self-understanding.

Exploring the context of railway disaster so important to the conception of psychic shock from the 1860s, the third chapter focuses on Dickens and discourses of memory and aftermath in his enigmatic ghost story "The Signalman" (1866). I argue that Dickens's story uncannily apprehends significant aspects of what will later be defined as trauma: the uncoupling of event and cognition, belatedness, repetitive and intrusive return, a sense of powerlessness at impending disaster. I explore the story in relation to medical discourses of railway shock, Victorian theories about memory function, and Dickens's own fascination with altered states of mind, concluding that Dickens's understanding of the literary possibilities of the ghost story helped him to articulate what the medico-psychological discourse at this time was not yet poised to formulate.

Moving from the traditions of the ghost story to realist fiction, I then discuss Dickens's last and unfinished novel, *The Mystery of Edwin Drood* (1870), published four years after Wilkie Collins's *The Moonstone,* and in some ways a riposte to it. Both novels are intimately concerned with the self in states of altered consciousness, and the discontinuity of memory from one state to the next. The chapter compares the different ways in which these texts imaginatively engage with questions of memory and dissociation. While I do not offer to solve the mystery of who killed Edwin Drood, my focus on shock and memory enables a new reading of John Jasper's changing psychological state.

The fourth chapter, on George Eliot, focuses initially on *The Lifted Veil,* a text exploring aberrations of consciousness and the effects of feeling or affect on what we know and how we know it. As an interrogation of vulnerability and defense – the inability to regulate powerful and unbidden feelings and thoughts that obtrude into consciousness – it offers a nineteenth-century meditation on how the subject processes overwhelming stimuli. Contextualizing George Eliot's work in relation to mid-century emotion theory, I argue that *The Lifted Veil* can be read as an affective memoir exploring the profound importance of emotion in cognitive processes. Governed by loss, fear, jealousy, desire and irritation, Latimer's narrative can be seen as an experiment in tracing what Martha Nussbaum has called "the intelligence of emotions." It is not only the *thoughts* of others to which Latimer is reluctantly subject, but, as George Eliot repeatedly writes, their emotions and feelings. While there have been many studies of the novella in relation to the question of *sympathy,* my reading focuses more broadly on a wide array of emotions – particularly negative ones – and explores George Eliot's developing understanding of the inextricability of thought and feeling, body and mind. Latimer's reluctant powers allow George Eliot to explore the subject's response to unregulated and overwhelming stimuli and the ways in which the self develops defenses against painful emotional engagement.

The chapter then considers the representation of terror and clairvoyance in George Eliot's *Daniel Deronda.* The narrator's representation of Gwendolen's troubled consciousness, stunned memory and hallucination in the aftermath of Grandcourt's drowning is read in relation to Mordecai's clairvoyant sensitivity in order to suggest George Eliot's engagement with contemporary views on consciousness in the writings of Herbert Spencer, Alexander Bain and, particularly, George Henry Lewes. I trace the conjuncture of a physiological genealogy of psychic shock and the conventions of gothic fiction, which play a significant role in the novel's articulation of terror.

The final chapter examines the findings of the Society for Psychical Research on multiple personality and the discourse of dissociated memory. Placing Robert Louis Stevenson's *The Strange Case of Dr Jekyll and Mr Hyde* in this context, I explore his correspondence with F. W. H. Myers and the implications of the concept of multiplicity for Stevenson's classic fantasy of the split self. To read Stevenson's tale in the context of Myers's discussion of multiple personality, particularly in response to the landmark case of Louis Vivet, is to see that both psychological discourse and literary creativity are responding to the idea that the unitary self is illusory; both ponder the consequences of the idea that will and knowledge may be split and undermined as one state of consciousness gives way to another. Both question what implications the notion of a fragmented self may have for ethics, responsibility, self-possession and self-governance. What is interesting about their correspondence is that Myers advised Stevenson to bring his representation of memory in the novella into line with recent psychological findings. Stevenson politely resisted the changes Myers suggested. Whereas Stevenson's novella has been read in terms of mid-nineteenth-century theories of the double brain, and is often considered in terms of duality, I explore it in relation to research on conscious and unconscious or automatic processes and the concept of "multiplex personality," particularly as it was articulated in the 1880s by Myers, whose concern with discontinuous selves and self-modification Stevenson shares.

A brief "Afterword on Afterwards" suggests that the emergence of trauma theory is less about developments in the science of mind than it is about cultural attitudes to responsibility and accountability. Victorian culture was less a "wound" culture than a "blame" culture. In particular, censorious attitudes to perpetrators, rather than sympathetic ones to victims, partly explain why Victorian culture stopped short of developing a fully formulated theory of trauma.

CHAPTER I

Historicizing trauma

I CONTEMPORARY TRAUMA THEORY

In the last few decades, trauma theory has achieved great saliency in an array of disciplines. It has been widely applied in studies of twentieth-century forms of testimony and the capacity of literature to bear witness to traumatic experience, not just individual but generational and national. From the uniquely personal repercussions of childhood abuse to the wide-scale reverberations of colonial rupture, the concept of trauma has come to cover a wide range of suffering.[1] E. Ann Kaplan remarks that "it is partly because of accumulated twentieth-century traumatic events that psychologists, sociologists, and humanists are investigating trauma."[2] Although no one could claim that the twentieth century has the monopoly on horrific experience, trauma theory, it has been suggested, emerged as a response to "modernity." This view arises in large measure from the influential work of Walter Benjamin, which identified modernity with a rupture in experience and a break in consciousness.[3] But, as Benjamin himself understood, the material conditions and technologies we associate with modernity began well before the twentieth century.[4] Large-scale cataclysmic accidents, experiences of near death and miraculous survival were certainly part of the Victorian industrialized world. How did Victorians understand the effect on consciousness and memory of events and experiences that "went beyond the range of the normal" – events so overwhelming and inassimilable that the ordinary processes of registration and representation were suspended or superseded? And what proposed architecture of mind would support a theory of ruptured or suspended registration? At the same time that factory and railway accidents and war experience produced psychic effects demanding medical and legal attention, Victorians were also attentive to other kinds of shocks to the mind, which were less dependent on external cataclysm and more closely related to private, individual disruptions of consciousness and composure. Moreover, as I discuss below, at least from the mid-century,

Victorian physiologists exploring the nature of consciousness and the conundrum of nerve transmission came to figure the basic unit of consciousness itself as a kind of shock. Before turning to Victorian formulations of mind, the unconscious and psychic shock, I want first to offer a survey of the current state of trauma theory and the debates which continue to characterize it.

Given official recognition for the first time in the third edition of the American Psychiatric Association's *Diagnostic and Statistical Manual of Mental Disorders* (DSM-III), in 1980, PTSD continues to be a vexed concept, though one would not know that from the tidy categorizations of the manual. The clusters of symptoms described by the *Diagnostic Manual*, which have all to do with disorders of emotion and memory, are divided into three groups: the first focuses on re-experienced symptoms, such as recurrent, intrusive recollections, dreams about the experience, and "flashbacks," which make one act and feel as if the experience were re-occurring. A second cluster is made up of "numbing symptoms, such as blunted emotion, feelings of estrangement from others, and loss of interest in previously enjoyable activities." The third cluster includes fear of impending doom, sleep disturbance, memory and concentration impairment, guilt about survival and "avoidance of distressing reminders of the trauma."[5] Not only do some of these characteristics seem contradictory, the composite definition is inevitably characterized by an ahistoricism, which not only gives the impression that trauma is a timeless condition but also flattens out the disputes and disagreements with which the field of trauma studies is riven.[6]

In her genealogy of trauma theory from Freud to the present, Ruth Leys has argued that "far from being a timeless entity with an intrinsic unity, as its proponents suggest, PTSD is a historical construct that has been 'glued together by the practices, technologies, and narratives with which it is diagnosed, studied, treated, and represented and by the various interests, institutions, and moral arguments that mobilized these efforts and resources.'"[7] While Leys is particularly interested in recuperating aspects of trauma that have been overlooked by the dominant interpretative paradigm as it developed post-Freud, I would suggest it is important to look back to the pre-Freudian roots of trauma theory because, as Leys rightly emphasizes, trauma is a concept whose line of development is neither linear nor continuous and whose genealogy throws light on the vexed question, even today, of how we define and understand trauma.[8] Dubious herself about the validity of Bessel van der Kolk's influential neurobiological explanations for traumatic memory, Leys suggests that "there is no consensus in the field of memory research" for the claim that "precisely because the victim is unable to process the traumatic experience in a normal way, the event leaves a 'reality imprint'... in the brain that, in its insistent literality, testifies to the existence of a pristine and timeless historical truth undistorted or uncontaminated by subjective meaning, personal cognitive schemes, psychosocial factors, or unconscious symbolic elaboration."9

Leys's critique is characterized by a strong resistance to the emphasis placed by Cathy Caruth and others on the event itself, pristine and unchanged, a kind of snapshot recorded by the victim without mediation and hence contamination by unconscious processes. Leys, for example, finds it ironic that Caruth, a critical theorist and, more specifically, a deconstructionist, should turn to the neurobiological explanations of Van der Kolk to underwrite the claim that the experience of trauma is never encoded as memory and escapes therefore the potentially distorting, subjective processes of assimilation and narrativization. It is the bypassing of these last factors that provokes the criticism of a range of critics, who have argued that although the memories of traumatic experiences may be unassimilable, their formation ought still to be considered in terms of the agency of the unconscious.10 Leys locates an irreconcilable contradiction at the heart of Freudian trauma theory, which persists in theories that succeed it. The contradiction arises out of an oscillation between so-called "mimetic" and "anti-mimetic" views. In the former, the subject of overwhelming experience is, like one under hypnosis, in an altered state of consciousness – dazed, in a trance, unable to make conscious, willed decisions. The subject imitates the will of another. Against this notion of mimetic identification, Leys argues, there was also advanced an antimimetic theory, which is characteristic of positivist or scientific interpretations of trauma – i.e. neurobiological approaches. The antimimetic theory claims that the trauma is a "purely external event coming to a sovereign if passive victim."11 The two approaches provoke the questions: Does the trauma come simply from the outside or is it also a product of what lies within? Is the mind a passive registrant or an active participant in the process? According to Leys, all trauma theory oscillates between these two poles.

A perennial question in trauma studies is why trauma theory has become so important in the last few decades. Many critics have pointed to the late-twentieth-century focus on the victim – of postcolonial rupture, genocide, sexual abuse. It has been suggested that in the wake of deconstructionist theory, so intent on revealing the ideological basis of truth claims or the relativity of values, humanist scholars have found a way through trauma theory to reintroduce the real, emotion and the body. Thus Ann Kaplan argues that "[a]ddressing the phenomena of trauma must have seemed one way for critics to begin to link high theory with specific material events that were both personal and which implicated history, memory, and culture generally."[12] In this view, Caruth's emphasis on trauma as the outside going inside without mediation is itself a desire to short-circuit the agency of the unconscious, a desire to see only the "ontologically unbearable nature of the event itself."[13] Judiciously weighing up the claims of Caruth and the critique of her position by Leys and others, Ann Kaplan proposes a more flexible, multi-faceted conception of trauma that in fact accommodates all camps – neurobiological data, the interpretations of humanist critics, and the objections raised by those who insist on psychosocial factors and the agency of the unconscious. Whereas Leys expressed skepticism about the validity and general acceptance of Van der Kolk's neurobiological explanations of trauma, Kaplan cites newer work in this field by Joseph LeDoux demonstrating that, if at times the traumatic experience bypasses the cortex and therefore memory, there are also instances in which trauma is remembered.[14] Accepting a plurality of brain processes allows Kaplan to mediate between the overemphasized role of dissociation in Caruth and others, on the one hand, and the overemphasis on unconscious processes, which does not give enough credibility to neuroscience, on the other.[15]

Late-modern trauma theory speaks to a culture in which reparation is sought for collective or individual perpetration of psychological injury. The cultural stakes in opposing positions about what goes on in the traumatized mind cannot therefore be underestimated. Seeing the mind as an active participant in the experience of trauma may lessen the sufferer's claim of innocence, muddy the clarity of victim and aggressor positions, and reduce the possibility of legal compensation. The more passive the mind in registering trauma, the less implicated, responsible or contributory the victim: the greater his or her social, moral and legal status as victim. The more passive the mind, however, the more corporeal and less distinguishable from the body it becomes. Mind is reduced to a series of brain changes that seem to go on outside of any kind of agency, conscious or unconscious.

Fierce debates about the relations between mind and body and the agency or passivity that attend various kinds of mental process will sound familiar to scholars working in Victorian psychology, a developing field in which these contentions are ineluctably both cultural and scientific. What this history of Victorian theories of mind will explore is how wedded we are to the idea of agency, evident in the recurrence of "agency/passivity" as oppositional structuring terms and despite the shift in content of those terms since the nineteenth century. From Coleridge's famous refutation of

Hartley's associationism, which depended on an objection to Hartley's representation of a mind lacking in agency, to William Carpenter's resistance to T. H. Huxley's claims that we are all automata, nineteenth-century thinkers declare their investment in an active mind whose agency is intact and uncompromised, despite some necessary concessions to automatic mental process. Indeed, the explanation of what constitutes agency and where it resides is an abiding theme in the history of mental science itself. Although the agency/passivity formulation is recurrent in contemporary trauma theory, we need to ask how the frontiers of agency have shifted from their Victorian location. A century and a half ago, most Victorian mental physiologists balked at accepting the agency of the unconscious mind; today unconscious agency may look like a better offer than changes in the hippocampus or the heightened activity of the amygdala, conditions that recent affective neuroscience has associated with trauma.[16]

It may appear as though unconscious mental functioning has thus moved all the way from first line of assault on sovereign consciousness in Victorian mental science to last bastion of agency in current trauma theory. But of course such different attitudes are explained in part by differences in what is understood by the term "unconscious." Agency is the *sine qua non* of the Freudian unconscious; in Victorian terms, even if many mental physiologists were prepared to accept the creativity involved in unconscious processes, "agency" together with "unconscious" was a highly problematic conjunction. Whereas the Freudian unconscious is a repository of repression, fantasies and disallowed or taboo knowledge, the Victorian unconscious is part of a vision of government that suggests at best an enabling division of labor and at worst a consciousness that is merely the epiphenomenon of a material system doing its work automatically. Questions of agency and their relationship to conceptions of unconscious mental functioning need to be closely scrutinized in any attempt to examine the Victorian antecedents of trauma theory. They take their place in a larger context in which the newly forming discipline of psychology wrestled with questions about the relations of mind and body. Historicizing the contemporary impasse between neurobiological and psychoanalytic explanations for trauma allows us to apprehend the similar yet distinctive stakes in the Victorian tussle between automatic actions of the mind and willed agency.

II MINDS AND SOULS, BRAINS AND BODIES

In his 1874 essay "On the Hypothesis that Animals Are Automata, and Its History," T. H. Huxley famously remarked that "the consciousness of brutes would appear to be related to the mechanism of their body simply as a collateral product of its working, and to be as completely without any power of modifying that working as the steam-whistle which accompanies the work of a locomotive engine is without influence upon its machinery."[17] Similarly he argued that "the soul stands related to the body as the bell of a clock to the works, and consciousness answers to the sound which the bell gives out when it is struck."[18] If Victorians were outraged to hear that they were descended from apes, a popular distortion of Huxley's views, they must have found insult added to injury with the idea that consciousness should turn out to be a mere letting off of steam or sounding of a bell, a by-product of the important and indeed primary activity going on elsewhere. Huxley's metaphor conflates consciousness and soul, long regarded as the quintessential capacity of human beings, distinguishing them and placing them above all sentient creatures. As can be imagined, his epiphenomenalist claims occasioned considerable debate and resistance.

In the 1876 preface to his fourth edition of *Principles of Mental Physiology*, the influential mental physiologist William Carpenter places the question of "Human Automatism" at the forefront of its concerns. He begins by acknowledging that a "distinguished Biologist" (Huxley) has "brilliantly expounded" the doctrine that "Animals are Automata" and that

Man is only a more complicated and variously-endowed Automaton: his bodily actions being determined solely by Physical causes; the succession of his Mental states depending entirely upon the molecular activities of his Cerebrum; and the movements he is accustomed to regard as expressing his feelings, or as executing his intentions, having their real origin in Brain-changes, of which those feelings and intentions are the mere concomitant "symbols in consciousness."[19]

In opposition to this view, Carpenter argues for the phenomenology of agency and the importance of disciplining and educating "the Will," that great bulwark against claims of human automatism.

It has been suggested that nineteenth-century scientific psychology, which replaced mental philosophy, was based on an "alternative metaphysics" which was decidedly secular, whether it be termed "agnostic monism," an atheological system, or Herbert Spencer's "The Unknowable," or, later, in 1869, Huxley's "agnosticism."[20] Huxley certainly inclined towards the physicalist side with his provoking analogy of the conscious mind being like the steam whistle of a locomotive engine (the brain). But Carpenter, a Unitarian, who nevertheless drew charges of being a materialist, is far more difficult to categorize in this regard. Any account of Victorian theories about the architecture of the psyche must reckon with the entanglements of materialist and spiritualist discourse about body, mind, brain and soul in the period.

Though Victorian mental science, which replaced mental philosophy and depended on developments in physiology and, later, neurology, increasingly promoted materialist explanations of the mind, the field we know as psychology was shaped by debate about the place of spiritual explanations for material phenomena. Secular, evolutionary and physiological theories were not always aligned and nor were they always opposed to spiritual, creationist and metaphysical explanations. Evolutionary theory, at least at the outset, was not a primary influence in shaping ideas about the mind. While physiological explorations of the mind took place alongside the development of Darwinian views about human nature, the latter did not, as historian Roger Smith has discussed, make the nature and origin of mind central to its polemic. It was somewhere between 1868 and 1875 that the two became more closely allied and a greater integration of debates was achieved on the mind–brain issue and the theory of evolution.[21]

A newly forming discipline at the mid-century, psychology did not begin to institutionalize itself until fairly late in the century. In the early 1800s, psychology was conceived of as the study and knowledge not of the mind, but of the soul; that is, everything spiritual as opposed to corporeal. As Edward Reed explains in *From Soul to Mind*, although psychology moved from being a science of the soul to that of the mind it was still intended "to reinforce important religious beliefs."[22] While one of the main functions of "the discourse of the soul," as Rick Rylance terms it, was to invigilate against "materialistic trespass," the discourse was used in very different ways.[23] To the point here is that talk about the soul was not simply the defense of anti-materialists against materialists. One could accept the material, physical basis of the mind, and yet preserve the notion that the soul exists. As Reed argues, we need to guard against the assumption that a "propensity for placing the mind in the brain is a stepping stone to a secular materialist worldview and therefore is opposed to, or at least independent of, any religious view of human nature."[24] Although he has been criticized for overstating the case, Reed usefully cautions against flattening out the variety of attempts to reconcile religious views with the materialist tendency of scientific psychology.[25]

By 1850 the term "psychology" was for the first time in common use, though it did not denote a specific body of knowledge or refer to a specific science.[26] However, as most recent historians agree, public debates in what we may describe as mental science were taking place throughout the period. There was no hard and fast demarcation or boundary between scientific writing and its ambient culture in these debates. To cite a few examples: Catherine Crowe, the anti-materialistic author of a popular book on ghost stories, who dismissed psychology as a "name without a science" also wrote on the credibility of spiritualism.[27] In his *On Mesmerism and Spiritualism, &c.: Historically and Scientifically Considered* (1877), Carpenter discusses Crowe's views on the subject at some length in his attempt to quash what he characterized as an epidemic belief in the occult.[28] Carpenter also pays respectful attention to the essays of Frances Power Cobbe on "unconscious cerebration." The fact that Carpenter engages with the writings of Crowe and Cobbe illustrates an important feature of mid-Victorian discourse – the relatively unstratified nature of the discursive field in which journalists, respected physiologists and popular writers could and did all converse.

Roger Smith has argued that "the literature on mind and body at one and the same time formed a public discourse about science and reflected on central moral questions of human identity and agency."[29] As questions about body and mind, spirit and soul, were being discussed in scientific treatises, they were also widely aired in the popular press and fiction of the period. In the periodical press at mid-century, we find a "*shaping* of an area of discourse, known as psychology, rather than the *popularization* of knowledge of brain and mind." As with many other newly forming fields of enquiry in the Victorian period, "[t]he debate was not conducted esoterically and then transferred to a public domain"; the way psychology emerged as an area of inquiry "took place in the ... periodicals themselves."[30] Rather than a field, or a subject in its own right, "psychology" was an "open-ended set of themes and sensibilities" and was porous to an extent that surprises readers in today's world of highly specialized disciplinary and professional distinction.[31] Attention to the periodical literature rather than just published treatises allows us to recover the texture of debate, contestation and, importantly, *reassurance* which suggests anything but an uneventful materialist consensus.[32]

Since Descartes, the doctrine of "the ghost in the machine" as philosopher Gilbert Ryle termed it, has been remarkably persistent. It runs along these lines:

Every human being has both a body and a mind. Some would prefer to say that every human being is both a body and a mind. His body and his mind are ordinarily harnessed together, but after the death of the body his mind may continue to exist and function. Human bodies are in space and are subject to mechanical laws which govern all other bodies in space ... But minds are not in space, nor are their operations subject to mechanical laws.[33]

Contestations on the question of whether mind is an entity separable from brain, whether consciousness is the by-product of bodily machinery or not, and what can be said to constitute a "self" recur throughout the period. As physician Daniel Hack Tuke presciently noted at the outset of his 1872 study of the influence of the mind on the body, "It is more than probable that no amount of scientific knowledge will ever displace the time-honored phrases of 'Mind' and 'Body.'"[34] The new science of physiological psychology sought to explore the "intimate mutual dependency of mind and brain," but the nature of that dependency was variously conceived, a variety reflected in an array of new terminology that was "awkward, opaque, and unsettled."[35]

The science of mind in the Romantic era had already, as Alan Richardson has shown, addressed the high stakes of neuroscientific speculation at that time: "no less than the existence of the soul, the necessity of God, and the integrity of the self were in question. This is the ground that Coleridge's theory of imagination would set out to reclaim, implicitly taking up the challenge posed by a resurgent physiological tradition in psychology building upon Hartley but moving beyond his mechanistic approach."[36] The work of Cabanis, Erasmus Darwin, Gall and Spurzheim provoked powerful responses of outrage and condemnation early in the century. So, throughout the rest of the century, contestations continued on the materialist/spiritualist question, and attempts to reconcile the apparently irreconcilable Cartesian division shaped Victorian psychological discourse. The stakes of debate continued to be high at community, professional and personal levels: for example the claim that mental operations were mere physical forces was enough to trigger the resignation of several members of the Phrenological Association in 1842. Writers of psychological treatises, such as William Carpenter, sought continually to escape the damning label of "mere materialist," and Harriet Martineau, a great proponent of the healing powers of mesmerism, fell out with her brother James, a Unitarian minister, over his hostile review of her *Letters on the Laws of Man's Nature and Development*.[37]

While opposed to mind–body dualism, many physiological psychologists adopted the position of "dual-aspect monism" which did not reduce mental experience to mere brain activity or to the activity of a spiritual substance separable from the body.[38] George Henry Lewes, specifically, has been associated with this view.[39] Alexander Bain, Herbert Spencer and William Carpenter, all of whom were known to varying degrees as materialist physiologists, talked of the different aspects of consciousness and emotion: the physical side and its mental counterpart. They may have emphasized the physical, but none asserted that mind was nothing but body and all asserted that mental processes and physical ones were, as Carpenter put it, opposite sides of the same shield. In *Principles of Human Physiology* (1855) Carpenter dismisses the controversies of the materialist and spiritualist schools by calling attention to the fable of the two knights who each approached a shield from opposite sides. One maintained it to be made of gold, the other silver. Both were right; they were each speaking from a different perspective. Although he admits one cannot solve the mind/matter dichotomy, he argues that we should recognize that the mind and brain are "intimately blended in their *actions*."[40] Carpenter concedes that many actions are performed automatically, but regards the Will as a reigning power that proves we are greater and nobler than simply our material selves. He begins by agreeing that the influence of the body on the mind is indisputable, and continues by listing several instances of that influence: the ill-effects of poor nutrition, perversion of mental powers produced by intoxicating agents, the "extraordinary influence of local affections of the Cerebrum upon the normal succession of Intellectual operations, as is especially seen in the strange disturbances or 'dislocations' of the memory consequent upon blows on the head."[41] But, Carpenter continues, these phenomena must be set against "the facts of our own internal consciousness." It is important to remember that our Will "can rise above all the promptings of external suggestion."[42]

[W]e cannot but feel that there is something *beyond and above* all this, to which, in the fully-developed and self-regulating mind, that activity is subordinated; whilst, in rudely trampling on the noblest conceptions of our nature as mere delusions, the Materialist hypothesis is so thoroughly repugnant to the almost intuitive convictions which we draw from the simplest application of our Intelligence to our own Moral Sense, that those who have really experienced these, are made to *feel* its essential fallacies with a certainty that renders logical proof quite unnecessary.[43]

Spencer also characterized feeling as "the subjective aspect of objective nervous changes" and used a similar metaphor to Carpenter, arguing that feelings and correspondent nervous actions were "the inner and outer faces of the same change."[44] Others, like Marshall Hall, for example, argued for "a neural province within which the immortal soul enjoyed unquestioned sovereignty."[45] And Henry Holland interpreted human mental faculties as signs and products of the wisdom and benevolence of the creator.[46] In one of the period's most intelligent essays on dreams and unconscious thinking, Frances Power Cobbe writes astutely about the nature of unconscious cerebration but asserts the divide between our "Conscious Self" and the automatic action of the brain. Ultimately we are not wholly the stuff of which dreams are made: "O mighty poet, philosopher! for in that 'stuff' there enters not the noblest element of our nature – that Moral Will which allies us, not to the world of passing shadows, but to the great Eternal Will, in whose Life it is our hope that we shall live for ever."[47] The variety of attempts to reconcile physicalist understandings of the mind with religious beliefs is itself worthy of lengthy and sustained study.

Even if not resisted on religious grounds, explanations of the mundane materiality of the brain were never (and still are not) easy to reconcile with a sense of the wonders of consciousness. In *Problems of Life and Mind*, George Henry Lewes asks: "Who that had ever looked upon the pulpy mass of brain substance, and the nervous cords connecting it with the organs, could resist the shock of incredulity on hearing that all he knew of passion, intellect, and will was nothing more than molecular change in this pulpy mass?"[48] In similar vein, some 150 years later, Ian McEwan's neurosurgeon in *Saturday* (2005) feels sure that in years to come the brain's fundamental secret will be laid open, but "even when it has, the wonder will remain, that mere wet stuff can make that bright inward cinema of thought, of sight and sound and touch bound into a vivid illusion of an instantaneous present, with a self, another brightly wrought illusion, hovering like a ghost at its centre."[49] The opposition of "mere wet stuff" to "bright inward cinema" articulates the abiding problem. Where Lewes writes of shock, McEwan's neurosurgeon expresses wonder, echoing perhaps George Eliot's verdict on evolution – that in the face of scientific explanation one may still be struck with the sense that the process is a mystery and a wonder.[50] Victorian attempts to reconcile physical and spiritual may appear historically distant or outdated, but, as Steven Pinker has pointed out, the "ghost in the machine" is an idea that has remarkable persistence in the present.[51]

One way to reconcile the physiological and the spiritual was to allow the spiritual a material existence, while insisting on the new order of that materiality. Discoveries in the physics of light and electricity fuelled the sense that the invisible could yet be material. Robert Chambers declared in *Vestiges of the Natural History of Creation* (1844) that "electricity is almost as metaphysical as ever mind was supposed to be" and that "mental action may be imponderable, intangible, and yet a real existence, and ruled by the Eternal through his laws."[52] An ingenious reconciliation, but, as Alison Winter remarks about mesmerism, belief in a mesmeric current or fluid was fuelled by developing knowledge about the power of steam: "This generation, surrounded by astonishing changes wrought by science, set few limits on the powers that might be revealed in electricity, light, magnetism, and gases … The claim that an imponderable fluid could pass from one individual to another, altering the processes of thought, was astonishing, but just as worthy of serious evaluation as other great scientific assertions."[53] Similarly, the claim that a spiritual fluid could be material was not as far-fetched, in light of knowledge about electricity and steam, as it might previously have been.[54]

III VICTORIAN FRAMINGS OF THE MIND

In the last few decades, Victorian psychology and mental science has become the focus of burgeoning interdisciplinary interest. It is over fifty years since Walter Houghton published *The Victorian Frame of Mind* (1957), a magisterial survey of the outlook and prevailing attitudes of the period. At first sight, "frame of mind" in Houghton's title suggests a focus on interiority and psychology. But Houghton's treatment of anxiety, for example, focuses on fear of revolution and the danger of atheism; he writes about worry, fatigue and ennui as responses to social and political conditions. While the soul comes in to discussions of atheism and doubt, Darwinism and evolution, there is really no sense that psyche or theories of mind is a topic to be discussed. What strikes me forcibly now, by comparison, is the vigorous scholarly interest today in Victorian psychology, and, in particular, Victorian theories of mental processes. By "frame of mind," Houghton means (as did Jerome Buckley) "temper." By "framings of the mind," I invoke both the ways in which Victorians understood the psyche and the recent critical interest in this aspect of Victorian science and culture.

Research on Victorian sciences of the mind has been reconfigured in some measure as the result of changing theorizations of history and the kinds of historicizing work engendered by Foucault in the last generation. Foucauldian discourse analysis prompted us to think beyond disciplinary borders. It called for an interrogation of the ways various discourses formed and differentiated themselves. And it had particular impact on nineteenth-century studies, since Foucault singled out that century as one in which the human sciences organized themselves into the shapes they have today, and brought all aspects of human life into discourse.[55] Histories of psychology such as Kurt Danziger's *Naming the Mind: How Psychology Found its Language* (1997) are no longer a roll call of names that seem retrospectively to have contributed to the field, that is biographical and progressive histories – victors' histories, we might say – but accounts of discursive formations and genealogies. Danziger's attention is as much on historiography as it is on the history of psychology. In particular, he mounts a critique of ahistoricism as a deeply embedded feature of modern psychology, which he explains as the result in part of psychology's desired identification with the natural sciences. It is "committed to investigating processes like cognition, perception, and motivation, as historically invariant phenomena of nature" and not as historically determined social phenomena.[56] Danziger further suggests there is a potential danger in the keywords approach to history – focusing on terms or single words, such as "intelligence," "emotion," "motivation" or "psychology" itself, might "promote an excessively atomizing account of conceptual history." Terms take their meaning from a discursive matrix and "are always embedded in a network of semantic relationships" where meaning changes relationally.[57]

Impetus for the interest in Victorian mental sciences has gathered in part as a result of interdisciplinary work since the late 1970s on the relationship of literature and science. Earlier studies of this reciprocal relationship, such as Gillian Beer's *Darwin's Plots: Evolutionary Narrative in Darwin, George Eliot and Nineteenth-Century Fiction* (1983) and George Levine's *Darwin and the Novelists: Patterns of Science in Victorian Fiction* (1988), focused preeminently on evolutionary discourse and its complex effects on novelistic form. Subsequent explorations produced a range of research on literature in relation to biomedical discourses of the gendered body, health, disease and sexuality. If the 1980s and '90s, registering the influence of Foucauldian and feminist theory, were the "body" and "sexuality" decades, they did not ignore the mind, but rather explored how gender inflected the way in which Victorian culture constructed minds (often female minds), which were seen to be shaped, limited and even deranged by the reproductive, maternal, bodies in which they found themselves.[58] Sally Shuttleworth's *Charlotte Brontë and Victorian Psychology* (1996) thus pays particular attention to questions of gender, sexuality and insanity in the psychological debates of the period and characterizes the new physiological psychology as a materialist science of the mind–body entity. While many of the recent studies on literary figures in relation to scientific and psychological contexts acknowledge the growing nineteenth-century emphasis on the interrelationship, even indivisibility, of mind and body, they also argue for focusing on the mind as a discrete and separate subject.[59]

Several recent anthologies have facilitated access to and provoked interest in primary Victorian psychological texts. Particularly noteworthy in its attempt to capture the range and subtlety of emergent, materialist science is Jenny Taylor and Sally Shuttleworth's *Embodied Selves: An Anthology of Psychological Texts 1830–1890* (1998), which offers excerpts of primary texts on social identity and emphasizes the embodiedness of the mind (there are sections on "The Sexual Body" and on "Race and Hybridity"). The anthology therefore draws attention to the thrust in Victorian mental science to dismantle the traditional Cartesian duality and demonstrates the variety of ways in which the new scientific psychology of the period explored the material and physical basis of mind and shifted mental science from philosophy and metaphysics to physiology. The editors' introduction contextualizes Victorian psychology in relation to earlier nineteenth-century theories of cerebral location and mental functioning, such as phrenology and associationism, and deftly charts psychology's mainstreams and tributaries in theories of dream, memory, consciousness, insanity, sciences of reproduction, and heredity.[60]

Because trauma theory from Freud to the present focuses on dissociation, affect regulation and, particularly, dysfunctions of memory, I have, as a way of introducing the Victorian psychological discourse pertinent to this project, demarcated four broad (though certainly overlapping and intertwined) clusters: on theories of unconscious mental processes; on altered states of mind; on memory science; and on the nature of emotions. Though later chapters will flesh out the areas sketched here, I want briefly to suggest the contours of each relevant area and the state of current scholarship that continues to shape investigations of it.

(a) The unconscious

The scope and nature of unconscious mental processing is, as we have seen, fundamental to conceptions of trauma. The unconscious mind is also a concept attracting fervent interest and provoking heated debate in the period under consideration. One of the most compelling examples of the mysterious powers of the unconscious mind derives from Coleridge: an illiterate young woman experiences a fever and begins suddenly to speak in Greek and Latin. On the face of it, this appeared to many an inexplicable miracle, evidence of spirit possession and supernatural haunting. But then it was discovered that, as a child, the woman had been looked after by a pastor who had knowledge of these languages and used to recite passages from the Latin and Greek fathers, and Rabbinical texts.[61] The explanation raised more questions than it answered. For many it was easier to believe in supernatural visitation than in the physiology of memory that the explanation supported. Again and again, this example of the apparently miraculous powers of mind recurs in Victorian discussions of the existence of the soul, the structure of the psyche, and the puzzling conundrums of memory and consciousness. Was it possible to store knowledge in a place inaccessible to ordinary consciousness? How, in an altered state of consciousness, occasioned by fever, could the mind turn up this cache of hidden knowledge? When William Hamilton invoked the case, it was to conclude sagely that "the mind may, and does, contain far more latent furniture than consciousness informs us it possesses" and, further, that consciousness is made up largely of unconsciousness.[62]

The recognition of a realm of feelings and memories that exists below or beyond ordinary consciousness certainly predates the nineteenth century; but as Nicholas Rand asserts in an essay on the hidden self, the nineteenth century saw a burgeoning of explanations and explorations of the unconscious:

The drawn-out attempt to approach and define the unconscious brought together the spiritualist and psychical researcher of borderline phenomena (such as apparitions, spectral illusions, haunted houses, mediums, trance, automatic writing); the psychiatrist or alienist probing the nature of mental disease, of abnormal ideation ... the physiologist and the physician who puzzled over sleep, dreams, sleepwalking, anaesthesia ... the neurologist concerned with the functions of the brain and the physiological basis of mental life; the philosopher interested in the will, the emotions, consciousness ... imagination and the creative genius, and last but not least the psychologist.[63]

While Rand's summary defines and separates out activities and agents that were often overlapping – the psychologist as physiologist, for example – and whose meanings changed historically in the latter part of the century, his account is nevertheless useful in drawing attention to the variety of enterprises involved in the pursuit of the unconscious. Eduard von Hartmann's magnum opus *The Philosophy of the Unconscious* (1869) is often cited as a landmark – the culmination of a century of interest and speculation on the subject. Hartmann's theories, however, are neither physiological nor psychological and probably best situated in the realm of metaphysics. As both Will and Reason, his unconscious is a form of Absolute, a blend of the metaphysics of Hegel and Schopenhauer. Nevertheless, the encyclopedic scope and subsequent expansion of the book, as well as its enormous popularity, signal the fascination of the latter part of the century with the concept.[64] The term "l'inconscient" entered French only after the publication of Hartmann's work, which was translated into French in 1877.

What distinguishes Victorian psychological discourse about the unconscious from earlier formulations? In this respect, developments in physiology and neurology seem significant, particularly the discovery of reflex response in 1833. This showed that a nervous impulse could be transmitted to the spinal cord resulting in an immediate action which the brain as such has neither chosen nor sanctioned. Jonathan Miller's lively essay, "Going Unconscious" (1988), emphasizes the "enabling" conception of the unconscious developed by Victorian mental physiologists. He points further to the currency of Victorian theories of automatic mental functioning in present-day concerns with artificial intelligence: "Experimental results from an ever-widening range of psychological functions tell the same story, that what we are conscious of is a relatively small proportion of what we know and that we are the unwitting beneficiaries of a mind that is, in a sense, only partly our own."[65] Miller unpacks the way Victorian thinkers negotiated evidence of the "reflex function of the brain," that vaguely defined area between "the unarguably automatic and self-evidently voluntary," and made concessions to automatic functioning.[66] Of pioneering neurophysiologist Marshall Hall, he writes:

Like Descartes, almost two hundred years earlier, Hall was prepared to make a large territorial concession to mechanism in exchange for a treaty which recognized the local sovereignty of the soul and the brain. The only difference was that whereas Descartes' soul was confined to the somewhat cramped premises of the pineal gland, Hall furnished the spiritual monarch with the large upholstered apartments of the brain as a whole.[67]

Whereas Hall had to limit automatic action to the spinal cord, Carpenter was prepared to "lose a few ganglia to the encroachments of mechanism" in order to secure the "sovereignty of the will."[68] The Victorians developed an "enabling" view of the unconscious as opposed to the "custodial" view that Freud would later articulate: "if consciousness is to implement the psychological tasks for which it is best fitted, it is expedient to assign a large proportion of psychic activity to automatic control: if the situation calls for a high-level managerial decision, the Unconscious will freely deliver the necessary information to awareness."[69] Rather than censorship and an edict against knowing, the situation was simply one of efficient delegation and storage. When Miller considers the question of accessibility, it is to contrast the "detention" in which the Freudian unconscious holds its mental contents with the free delivery that characterizes mid-nineteenth-century concepts of the unconscious.

Miller's characterization of the differences between Freudian and Victorian versions of the unconscious is illuminating, but he underplays the anxiety expressed in a wide range of Victorian psychological writing about the threat of automatism and the suspension of the will. The emphasis in Carpenter's later work, certainly in some respects in response to Huxley's argument that men are automata, as I discussed above, is firmly on the discipline of the will through exercise and the inculcation of habit.[70] The subtitle of *Principles of Mental Physiology* is "*with their application to the training and discipline of the mind and the study of its morbid conditions.*" As Jenny Bourne Taylor has shown in her study of Wilkie Collins, the shift in Carpenter's attitudes to will and his emphasis on the modifications that discipline and habit could produce is an important moment in the history of Victorian theories of the unconscious. Whereas he had earlier pronounced that an individual committing a crime reflexively or automatically could not be held responsible, he later revised that view during the 1840s, arguing that training and management could actually bring the unconscious mind under control of the will. Salutary habit was a prophylactic against susceptibility to mind-altering substances or mesmeric influence. It meant that in states of volitional suspension, the well-trained mind would still conform to its established moral principles and regulations.[71] Latent furniture or no, the well-trained mind was definitely the chief interior designer.

Despite the concessions to automatic function negotiated by mental physiologists such as Carpenter, developments in physiology and neurology on automatic and unconscious mental functioning pointed threateningly to an erosion of agency with its dark implications of a lack of social responsibility and accountability, an open door to unconscious and therefore unpunishable crimes.[72] A topic engaging Dickens, Wilkie Collins and, less sensationally, George Eliot, the unconscious perpetration of action (or the omission of action) raises urgent questions about the contradictory or congruent motives in the conscious self and its automatic or unconscious counterpart. As George Eliot remarks astutely in *Adam Bede* (1859):

Our mental business is carried on in much the same way as the business of the State: a great deal of hard work is done by agents who are not acknowledged. In a piece of machinery, too, I believe there is often a small unnoticeable wheel which has a great deal to do with the motion of the large obvious ones. Possibly there was some such unrecognized agent secretly busy in Arthur's mind at this moment … The human soul is a complex thing.[73]

The phrase "agents who are not acknowledged" humorously conjures a vision of serviceable minions who quietly perform important work, along the lines of Miller's enabling unconscious. The narrator does not suggest that this unobserved work is necessarily sinister or threatening. But what if the "unrecognized agent" is more powerful than its apparent lowly status suggests? As the narrator reveals, the effect on Arthur of an undetected "backstairs influence" turns out to be very serious in its consequences to Hetty Sorrel, the pretty milkmaid whom Arthur is planning, despite himself, to meet. Unconsciousness in George Eliot's fiction is not adequately accounted for in Miller's view of unconscious processes. While the minute play of unattended motive and feeling may go on unawares, this activity has a life of its own in the way it shapes and informs moments of decision and conscious thought.

Like Miller's "Going Unconscious," Jenny Bourne Taylor's excellent essay "Obscure Recesses: Locating the Victorian Unconscious" (1997) draws attention to the difference between Victorian and Freudian conceptions of the unconscious. Although we cannot repress our knowledge of the later framework of psychoanalysis, she argues, we can as Victorianists be aware of "the dangers of always reading one paradigm in the light of a later, dominant one" and of "reconstructing 'the Victorians' either as Others of our own more enlightened perceptions, or of mirror images of ourselves."[74] Taylor offers a fine introduction to different conceptions of the unconscious in the period and the deployment of trance, absent-mindedness and dreamy mental states in novels by Dickens, George Eliot and Wilkie Collins. One may note, however, the essay's implicit dependence on contemporary concepts of trauma and especially the association of trauma with memory dysfunction. Given the widespread adoption of "trauma" as a term now generally used to indicate painful experience, it is understandable that Taylor makes use of it. Yet it is worth pausing over the assumption that the response to a painful past is in some way going to involve dislocations of memory, intrusions of unconscious memory, or dissociation. Thus Smike in *Nicholas Nickleby* is constantly "reliving his *traumatic* early past through dreams ... Smike is not only recalling an event but a mode of consciousness which made that recollection possible ... Smike's problem is not so much that he cannot control his own associations but that the *trauma* which is continually relived has repressed the interconnecting links" (emphasis added).[75] Similarly, the discussion of *Silas Marner* focuses on the cataleptic trance "during which the traumatic events in Silas's life take place." The trance is also described as a powerful trope for "a process of amnesia, or *unconscious forgetting of trauma*" (emphasis added).[76] The point I wish to make here is that, even in the work of so historically attentive a critic as Taylor, the conceptual framework of trauma, memory dysfunction and dissociation is assumed.[77] Trauma has become so much part of late-twentieth-century thinking about consciousness and unconsciousness that it structures the interpretation of texts written at a time when concepts of trauma were, as subsequent chapters will show, formulated in rather different terms, terms about which it is important to think historically.

(b) Altered states of consciousness

Dissociation and trauma, linked in some contemporary theory, seem closely related to nineteenth-century conceptions of altered states of mind (such as those induced by mesmerism, magnetic sleep and hypnosis, or those evident in states of trance, double consciousness, dreams and hallucinations). A source of cultural fascination and scientific investigation throughout the Victorian period, unusual or aberrant forms of consciousness raised a slate of questions about the unitary nature of the self. Subjects in a state of altered consciousness seemed to possess knowledge of which they were not ordinarily conscious and to behave in ways that their conscious selves might not sanction. If one could be in possession of knowledge unavailable to the conscious self, then how was it possible to speak of an integrated or authoritative self? "Unconscious cerebration" was a term William Carpenter coined for the operation of the mind when the governing will was suspended. It referred to largely reflex or habitual action. But was it possible to think, memorize and reason in a state of altered consciousness? And if so, who or what was doing the thinking? Was such knowledge relevant to the study of interiority or was it evidence of other worlds?

De Quincey saw animal magnetism as "a discovery which opens nothing less than a new world to the prospects of Psychology, and, generally speaking, to the knowledge of the human mind" and looked forward to its further development.[78] The great apologist of mesmerism, Dr. John Elliotson defended his controversial demonstrations of the mesmerized O'Key sisters, saying that he brought an opportunity to the public to "exploit a mighty engine for the regeneration of humanity 'comparable in importance and power to that of the steam engine.'"[79] As Ekbert Faas has noted in his study of Victorian poetry and the rise of psychiatry, "the phenomenon of double consciousness ... had long been familiar to an age as obsessed with the self and its ever-threatening disintegration as the nineteenth century. Now mesmerism offered the possibility of subjecting this split consciousness to systematic analysis."[80] Mesmeric research also promised to solve the riddle of how memory and imagination, both in sleep and in certain nervous conditions, accomplish feats that they could never manage in normal consciousness. Entranced patients gave evidence of an "extraordinary revivification of memory at a certain stage of mesmeric and hypnotic sleep."[81] But if, for some, mesmerism was "the means par excellence for demonstrating the essentially psychological nature of spiritualist phenomena," for others it was "the royal road to the supernatural."[82]

If mesmerism and hypnotism produced excitement because of what they could reveal about the mind, they also provoked fear of manipulation and the abdication of agency. As many fictional examples of the period show, the control of one's will by an outside and possibly malevolent agency was a titillating and horrifying possibility. Sir Edward Bulwer Lytton's "The House and the Brain" (1859) and *A Strange Story* (1862) turn upon the machinations of an evil mesmerizer, but the apotheosis of this fear is surely realized in *Trilby* (1894), George du Maurier's popular novel about a controlling and possessive will that is also racially and anti-semitically inflected.[83] As Harriet Martineau, herself a great proponent of mesmerism, argued in her *Letters on Mesmerism*, however, such fears were overblown. One was more likely to experience derangements of self-possession as a result of narcotic drugs sold over the counter, she averred, than at the hands of a mesmeric charlatan. Martineau addressed the objection to mesmerism that "there should be no countenance of an influence which gives human beings such power over one another," by arguing that it was too late – the power was already abroad and should be monitored as an apothecary possessing narcotic drugs is regulated and controlled: "If the fear is of laying victims prostrate in trance, and exercising spells over them, the answer is, that this is done with infinitely greater ease and certainty by drugs than it can ever be by Mesmerism."[84]

The resurgence of critical interest recently in the social and cultural contexts of phrenology, mesmerism, spiritualism, telepathy and the findings of the Society for Psychical Research is testimony to the significance of the "pseudo-" or quack sciences in raising important questions, even if they did not answer them in a creditable, scientific way. Alison Winter's *Mesmerized: Powers of Mind in Victorian Britain* (1998), Pamela Thurschwell's *Literature, Technology and Magical Thinking* (2001) and Roger Luckhurst's *The Invention of Telepathy* (2002) are all important studies in this regard. No doubt it is entertaining to consider the wackiness of some Victorian thinking in these areas, but along with misconceptions about cerebral localization, magnetic fluids, travelling minds and memories, automatic writing and rapping tables, we also encounter in these histories of discarded science significant debates about the nature of volitional or reflex response and the meaning and mechanisms of shifts in states of consciousness.[85]

The widening association of shifts in consciousness with internal changes as opposed to external possession is an important movement in the history of the psyche. Writing about the phenomenon of double consciousness, Adam Crabtree explains how shifts in conceptualizations of psychic states helped to produce the manifestation and articulation of psychic malaise. He argues that

until the emergence of the alternate-consciousness paradigm the only category available to express the inner experience of an alien consciousness was *possession*, intrusion from the outside. With the rise of awareness of a second consciousness intrinsic to the human mind, a new symptom language became possible. Now the disordered person could express (and society could understand) the experience in a new way ... This means that when Puységur discovered magnetic sleep, he contributed significantly to the form in which mental disturbance could manifest itself from then on.[86]

The crucial phrases here are "new symptom language" and "form in which mental disturbance could manifest itself." Crabtree is saying that before Puységur and the discovery of magnetic sleep, mental disturbance could only be explained as external or extrinsic possession. With the knowledge that the unconscious mind could know things and cause actions of which the conscious mind was unaware or which it did not intend came new possibilities for expressing mental disturbance. What we think the mind does is capable of affecting the way we think.

(c) Memory science

If discarded or discredited sciences are nevertheless instructive, research into the dominance of inordinately powerful science, such as memory science, may uncover the genealogy of our own current investment in memory and its dominance in contemporary theories of trauma. Ian Hacking's *Rewriting the Soul* (1995) explores medical professionalization in the last quarter of the nineteenth century as a bid for authority over the soul. Late-twentieth-century interest in memory and forgetting, in Alzheimer's disease, trauma and commemoration has spawned studies of the histories of memory and the nineteenth-century sciences that paid attention to it. Hacking suggests that, during the latter part of the nineteenth century, a "new science, a purported knowledge of memory, quite self-consciously was created in order to secularize the soul."[87] Prior to this, science had been excluded from the study of the soul itself. But at this time, "[m]emory, already regarded as a criterion of personal identity, became a scientific key to the soul, so that by investigating memory (to find out its facts) one would conquer the spiritual domain of the soul and replace it by a surrogate, knowledge about memory."[88] The ascendancy of memory science, argues Hacking, following Foucault, meant that individuals could be ordered, subjected and disciplined. In this bid for control, concludes Hacking, lies the genealogy of recent debates about False Memory Syndrome and repressed memory. Even granting Hacking's approach to the history of memory science, we would still need to complicate and keep nuanced his claims by noting the ambivalence and contradiction that characterize Victorian definitions of body, soul and mind in discussions of the relationships among these phenomena.

Careful to distance himself from religious explanations of the soul or insistence on its perdurability and unity, Hacking argues that the soul has something in its largest sense to do with inwardness, the consciousness of being a self.[89] What the nineteenth-century sciences of memory sought to take over, then, were explanations and narratives of interiority – how people explained themselves to themselves. And if that is indeed so, surely literature, so occupied with representations of interiority, should be more thoroughly acknowledged alongside religious discourse as a competitor in Hacking's analysis of the colonizing tendencies of memory science. If memory science usurped the domain of the soul, how, we might ask, did literature participate in or resist that domination? In a very general way, Hacking's history of concepts such as trauma and multiple personality acknowledges the power of literary and cultural representations:

[T]he whole language of many selves had been hammered out by generations of romantic poets and novelists, great and small, and also in innumerable broadsheets and feuilletons too ephemeral for general knowledge today ... [T]he literary imagination has formed the language in which we speak of people – be they real, imagined, or, the most common case, of mixed origin. When it comes to the language that will be used to describe ourselves, each of us is a half-breed of imagination and reality.[90]

Yet when it comes to the specific details of how ideas about memory assumed cultural priority, Hacking seems to resort to the assumption that medical science produces, literature responds. On the question of amnesia, he remarks that loss of memory produced by charms and drugs "is as old as the hills" but "amnesia produced by shock was a new theme for penny dreadfuls. An intermediary case is perhaps found in the first and finest English detective novel, Wilkie Collins's *The Moonstone* (1866) ... Fictional amnesia produced by a fall or a blow followed soon after Collins's novel, in the wake of the new medical enthusiasm for the topic."[91] In *Amnesiac Selves: Nostalgia, Forgetting, and British Fiction 1810–1870* (2001), however, Nicholas Dames has disputed that formulation, arguing that "Collins's amnesiac sensations, and the plots of amnesia, are the signs of a genesis: the *birth of amnesia* as a cultural and scientific fact. Amnesia itself had yet to become a topic of psychology, physiology, or mental philosophy and was far from being considered the key to the mind's dynamics: as a word it scarcely existed in English."[92] In direct opposition to Hacking, he suggests that Victorian medicine might have been indebted to Collins, whose

> stress on the conditions and possibilities of forgetfulness predates the psychological emphasis on amnesia that we find in the late nineteenth century. Collins's amnesiacs are not stock medical figures in the 1860s, straight out of physiological textbooks, but are instead *new cultural formations*, rearrangements and refashionings of the earlier Victorian amnesiac self in the light of an emergent physiological concentration on "nervousness," "shock," and what came to be called "biological memory." ... Collins's role in this regard was to produce, more than a decade before psychological research could fully catch up, the new cultural category of "amnesia."[93]

Hacking's genealogy is through what he describes as a French rather than British focus on memory in discourses of double consciousness: according to him, there was virtually no interest in memory in the symptom language of double consciousness in Britain. In France, however, a growing awareness of different memory streams in medical descriptions of double consciousness flows, towards the end of the century, into Charcot's revived use and understanding of hypnotism. While there may indeed have been a stronger emphasis on memory in France, Hacking's dismissal of British discourses of double consciousness does not take into account the work of Henry Holland, for example, who, as early as 1839 in his *Medical Notes and Reflections*, drew attention to the "*double-dealing* [of the mind] with itself" and who later explored the phenomenon of "double consciousness," in which "the mind passes by alternation from one state to another, each having the perception of external impressions and appropriate trains of thought, but not linked together by the ordinary gradations, or by *mutual memory*" (emphasis added).[94] Like Holland, Dr. John Elliotson, the great proponent of mesmerism, also drew attention to alternations of memory and is invoked by both Collins in *The Moonstone* and Dickens in *The Mystery of Edwin Drood* for his famous example of a drunken porter who lost his watch and had to be drunk again to remember where he had left it.

Hacking's primary focus is memory science, a focus determined, arguably, by the moment and context within which he was writing – the emphasis on memory in clinical formulations of trauma and multiple personality disorder, and the crisis of False Memory Syndrome of the 1990s: "Trauma took the leap from body to mind just over a century ago, exactly when multiple personality emerged in France, and during the time when the sciences of memory were coming into being."[95] There is some irony, however, in the fact that, even as Hacking critiques the supremacy of memory science, he also helps to reinstall it as the key to syndromes such as trauma. In exploring a genealogy of trauma that reaches back into the mid nineteenth century, I would argue that it is worth looking less singularly at discourses of memory and more inclusively at theories of emotion. For Victorian physiologists and novelists, emotion – particularly in overwhelming forms – played a central role in conceptions of consciousness and its destabilizations.

(d) Emotion theory

[M]any novelists indulge [in] the description of minute changes in the *physical* expression in periods of deep feeling. This is, we are convinced, unartistic as well as false taste. The minute physical changes are not observed in themselves, but only in the change of expression which they produce, in all cases of deep emotion ... It would require a scientific man, intending to prepare "plates" of the different emotions to note these things. And the mind instinctively shrinks from the record of them. The grief and the love and the fear should absorb the attention, and not the resulting state of muscular action. It is uncomfortable, and always suggests the presence of an unparticipating spectator with a note-book.[96]

This rather testy 1855 review of Gaskell's *North and South* draws attention to the increasing focus in the period on the physiology of emotions. No longer seen as movements of the mind or soul, emotions were, according to historians of psychology, increasingly understood as visceral, bodily and physical states. The reviewer either does not have a finger on the pulse of such changes, or indeed does and means to imply that emotions are to be understood physically only in the realm of science. Objecting to descriptions of physical and muscular changes in the body in place of the analysis of feelings such as love, grief or fear, the reviewer contrasts the task of the "scientific man," preparing plates and taking notes, to that of the novelist. But novelists of the period – George Eliot, for example – certainly engage with shifts in conceptions of the emotions taking place in the new physiological psychology of the period and help to blur the lines demarcated here between artistic and scientific representation.

In *Naming the Mind*, Kurt Danziger's discussion of the history of emotion focuses initially on the discursive formation of the term "emotion," first regularly deployed by David Hume. At the time Hume was writing, the term was "a fairly recent derivative of *motion* that had been used to describe either a physical or a social agitation. By analogy it was also applied to mental agitation or excitement."[97] Danziger suggests that it was not until the second half of the nineteenth century that "emotion" replaced "passion" in ordinary usage. Emotion and desire emerged as the important categories, and passion came merely to mean an emotion that also raises desire. By the early nineteenth century, the term "emotion" was used to refer to non-intellectual states of mind.[98]

Thomas Dixon follows Danziger and Hacking in pointing to the physicalist and secularizing tendency of nineteenth-century psychology. He too asks why the physicalizing term "emotion" replaced more nuanced terms such as "passions," "affections" and "sentiments" around the mid nineteenth century. Dixon's study of the change in terminology – the shift from "passions" to "emotions" – seeks to situate the provenance of "emotions" as a category in the work of philosophers, moralists and especially theologians. He argues that while affective psychology changed a great deal during the same time, its categories remained largely constant. The "intellect," "will" and "senses" were adopted from the ancients; but the only new category was "emotions," which now signaled "a set of morally disengaged, bodily, non-cognitive and involuntary feelings."[99]

If, for Hacking, memory science of the last quarter of the nineteenth century was a means of scientizing the soul, for Dixon the soul was scientized and psychology secularized by the substitution of "emotion" for older terms. Like Danziger, Dixon urges that we redress victors' history, but whereas the former focuses on the discursive formation of psychological concepts, the latter draws attention to the bypassed anti-materialist, religious writers and advocates revisiting hierarchized concepts associated with a spiritualist philosophy of mind. A merely secularist history, he argues, delivers a category – the emotions – which is a rather blunt instrument when it comes to constructing histories of ideas about feelings and sentiments. "Emotions" is an over-inclusive category that obliterates distinctions between "primitive and organic" emotions, on the one hand, and "higher cognitive" and more culturally differentiated emotions on the other. Physicalist theory was initially intended to deal only with the coarser emotions, those that have a distinct bodily expression, but this restriction was rapidly forgotten and the physicalist theory was later applied to all emotions, so that emotion came to be synonymous with a distinct bodily expression.[100] The thrust of Dixon's argument is that contemporary emotion theorists might do well to take into account a more nuanced history of emotions and thereby save themselves from reinventing alternative emotion theories in ignorance of their past incarnations. It is not clear, however, that a return to the neglected religious writers of the period will indeed challenge the alleged hegemony of physicalist psychology in meaningful ways.[101]

In Dixon's view, all of Bain, Spencer and Darwin inclined towards an epiphenomenalist view of mind – that is, the real business of emotions went on at the physiological and neurological levels. Emotions appeared to be the mental side of what was really and objectively an activity of the central nervous system.[102] Thus Alexander Bain in *Mind and Body: The Theories of Their Relation* (1873) says: "When a shock of fear paralyses the digestion, it is not the emotion of fear, in the abstract, as a pure mental existence, that does the harm; it is the emotion in company with a peculiarly excited condition of the brain and nervous system; and it is this condition of the brain that deranges the stomach."[103] For Bain the bodily is of fundamental importance in producing the mental. In the line that Dixon traces from Bain to William James, the mind becomes increasingly passive as greater agency is attributed to the body. Dispensing with the idea of a substantial or immaterial will existing independently of passions, appetites and desires, emotion theorists viewed feelings as concomitants of physical change, or nervous disturbance and mental process as dependent on bodily organs.

Whereas Dixon sees the dual-aspect monism of Bain and others as a tacit epiphenomenalism, I think its distinction from Huxley's position (that human beings are simply more complicated automata than animals) is worth preserving. Significantly, Dixon does not discuss the influential work of William Carpenter in this regard. Since Carpenter addresses Huxley's views specifically in his preface (1876) to the fourth edition of *Principles of Mental Physiology*, and offers a pointed refutation of them, his work ought surely to be taken into account.

A brief survey of current histories and historiographies of emotion reveals that debates continue about whether emotions are automatic, involuntary and unwilled. In *The Navigation of Feeling* (2001), historian William Reddy offers an apt summary:

By the folk wisdom of the West, emotions are involuntary; they come over us irresistibly, or steal upon us when we least expect it. The will, aided by reason, must master them or be mastered by them. Psychologists have therefore looked for effects of emotion on "automatic," "subliminal" and "unconscious" cognitive processes. It must be stated at once, however, that the meaning of these terms is as much in debate as the meaning of the term "emotion" itself. It is hardly in dispute that attention is limited and that the range of things that can be attended to at any given moment is only a tiny fraction of what is available through ongoing sensory input or from the vast store of procedural and declarative memory. What has proved difficult is drawing a bright line between what lies in attention and what does not, what counts as voluntary or controlled, and what counts as involuntary or automatic. As attempts to clarify this distinction proceed, the place of emotion in the larger life of the self is necessarily being constantly reformulated by psychologists. There is currently no end in sight to this process of rethinking.[104]

Reddy reviews research suggesting that to the extent emotions are automatic they resemble "overlearned" cognitive habits; an example would be the way boys are socialized into controlling emotion and taught to keep from crying by substituting anger for sadness. Feelings can be regulated: "In this way, problem emotions, even though they feel automatic and uncontrollable, may be alterable." Notable in this research is "the likening of emotion to a form of cognition, and the dependence of both on the impact of conscious, intentional action – at least over the long run of an individual's life."[105] This does not seem far off the emphasis of William Carpenter on acquired habits and trained minds. The question of what kinds of knowledge emotions harbor – that is, the relations of emotion to cognition – enjoys a certain dominance in current Anglo-American research and continues to fuel a vigorous area of investigation.[106]

In addition to the study of cognition, and the development of cognitive therapies for dealing with emotional problems, there are several other areas of research informing contemporary emotion study. Ethnographers are developing techniques for grasping the cultural dimensions of emotions, and historians and literary critics are researching the social history of emotions. Reddy notes that

scholars working on the eighteenth and nineteenth centuries, in particular, have begun to trace out the rise and fall of an emotional revolution of the past, called "sentimentalism," or "the cult of sensibility" – a loosely organized set of impulses that played a role in cultural currents as diverse as Methodism, antislavery agitation, the rise of the novel, the French Revolution (including the Terror), and the birth of Romanticism.[107]

Also concerned with the social history of emotion, Barbara Rosenwein's informative review essay, "Worrying about Emotions in History," argues against an evolutionary explanation of emotion whereby the middle ages are seen as the violent and primitive precursor to more civilized eras. The hydraulic view of emotions persisted in Darwin and Freud despite discoveries about nerve force, and bequeathed a vocabulary for discussing emotion that, as Rosenwein rightly emphasizes, remains current today: emotions build up, overflow, overwhelm and need to be channeled. By the 1960s, the hydraulic view is to some extent displaced by a cognitive view of emotions, which emphasizes the appraising, evaluative aspect of emotional response:

"Although most cognitive psychologists believe that there are certain 'basic' emotions true of all human beings – fear and anger are on nearly everyone's list – it is clear that different perceptions by different individuals of what is relevant to their 'weal or woe' will produce very different sorts of emotions even in similar situations." In the next decade, social constructivist theories claim that

emotions depend on language, cultural practices, expectations, and moral beliefs. This means that *every* culture has its rules for feelings and behavior; *every* culture thus exerts certain restraints while favoring certain forms of expressivity. There can be no "untrammeled" emotional expression in this non-hydraulic view of the emotions because emotions are not pressing to be set free; they are created by each society, each culture, each community.[108]

In place of a grand, evolutionary narrative of progressive self-restraint, Rosenwein suggests the study of the historically specific shapes and styles – the emotional communities – that exist in any period. This view has potential for a history of trauma in that it prompts us to ask about the rules and restraints, and the forms of expressivity, for emotions of fear and terror at the mid nineteenth century. To what extent is the concept of overwhelming emotion itself a social construct of the period?

IV LOCATING A DISCOURSE OF SHOCK

Freud had been writing about the traumatic neurosis since the 1890s, but the case studies of shell-shocked soldiers in World War I prompted him to theorize the concept of trauma as overwhelming fright or shock. He noticed that the dreams of the traumatized were markedly different from those of ordinary dreamers in that they woke the patient up "in another fright," returning him to the scene of horror, and reproducing it repeatedly and literally. Ordinary dream work consisted of creating scenarios to express fears and desires, allowing ordinary patients to release anxieties and so keep sleeping; traumatic dreams woke the patient, and were therefore unable to appease anxiety. Since the effects of war were critical to the Freudian development of trauma as a concept, it seems logical to examine Victorian responses to war, which might yield a particularly Victorian discourse about the nature of overwhelming shock on the psyche. This section suggests two starkly different angles from which to approach the Victorian discourse of shock. It moves from the large-scale and cataclysmic events of the external world to the smallest and most invisible transactions and transmissions of the internal world – from narratives of Victorian war and other disasters to accounts of the physiology of feeling, sensation and emotion, and to new ways of understanding the nerves and how they receive and transmit messages.[109]

Both the Crimean War (1854–56) and the Boer War (1899–1902), in which numbers of British troops were involved, provide potentially useful starting points for an investigation of Victorian mind shock. Both involved large-scale suffering and casualties. Similarly, one might expect that the gruesome accounts of the so-called "Indian Mutiny" or Sepoy Rebellion of 1857, which horrified British subjects everywhere, would likewise document responses of shock to the slaughter and carnage experienced.[110]

There has been some recent research by medical historians Edgar Jones and Simon Wessely on the occurrence of psychological disorders such as chronic fatigue syndrome in the Crimean War and Sepoy Rebellion. Examining the pension files of the Royal Hospital, Jones and Wessely focus on the case of one Charles Dawes, a soldier who served both in the Crimea and then in India in the suppression of the uprising.[111] Dawes presented many symptoms that today would have qualified him for a diagnosis of chronic fatigue syndrome. The authors note too that "in the American civil war and the Boer war, soldiers exhibiting chronic fatigue syndromes, sometimes precipitated by the stress of battle, were occasionally diagnosed as suffering from the after effects of sunstroke."[112] They conclude that the "way we categorise symptoms and how we construct disorders is open to considerable variation, even if the clinical presentations are relatively stable."[113]

In a subsequent article on psychiatric battle casualties they compare Victorian to later World War I and II cases and conclude that Victorian incidences of psychosomatic disorder were either undiagnosed or somatized: "It appears, therefore, that unambiguous cases of combat fatigue were rarely identified in the Victorian period and that soldiers traumatised by the stress of battle appear to have somatised their fears often in the form of disordered action of the heart (DAH) or psychogenic rheumatism."[114] With the identification of shell-shock and neurasthenia, the number of cases diagnosed as psychological in World War I rose a great deal. One reason that the authors of this study give for the increased focus on psychological issues is the reduced number of battle fatalities: "Advances in medical science have progressively reduced the proportion of troops who die from their injuries, the rate falling from 20% in the Crimean War to 6.1% in the First World War, 4.5% in the Second World War and 2.5% in Korea."[115] Improved survival rates may have "increased the number of potential psychiatric casualties and allowed the focus of attention to move towards psychological issues."[116] Another reason, I would suggest, reiterating that trauma and, for that matter, chronic fatigue syndrome or PTSD are historically produced categories rather than timeless pathological entities, is that the articulation of shell-shock and neurasthenia as "syndromes" may have provided a symptom language for sufferers, a form in which their disturbances could be expressed. Certainly, the concept of PTSD or shell-shock was preferable to that of hysteria, a highly gendered concept associated with malingering, sexuality and madness.

An obvious factor inhibiting the recognition of psychological disturbance as a result of war is the determined stoicism with which soldiers recounted their war experiences. The glory of war and the heroism associated with enduring pain of any kind made the confession of mental symptoms unlikely, and yet from time to time the memoirist allows us a glimpse of the horror and psychological toll exacted by war and, especially in the case of the Crimean War, the ravages of the cholera epidemic, which killed more soldiers than were claimed by battle injuries. In his narrative of the Crimean War experience, *Kars and Our Captivity in Russia* (1856), the author writes movingly about the horrors of war as a "black and ghastly picture of horror and suffering that still clouds [his] ... memory like the hovering phantoms of some hideous dream."[117] The prevailing interpretation in the narrative, however, is that exertion and the stress of war are stimulants. Cholera thus abates from "the moral exertion and physical excitement, and all the fierce energies stirred by the perils of the battle-field" but it creeps again upon the troops "when the roar of our cannon was hushed into the sad silence of expectation, and the dreadful despondency of hope deferred ... The sights and sounds by which we were surrounded were not such as to inspire men with the strength which may sometimes shake off a dangerous epidemic."[118] Of his General he notes that "as soon as the intense mental excitement of Kars was over, the wear and tear which his health had undergone, having no longer any sustaining stimulant, began to tell on him."[119] And as a prisoner of war, when the author does feel released from trying responsibilities and "risks or terrors to be endured," he nevertheless cannot sleep. So habituated has he become to a state of alarm, that now, in a good state of health, he is disturbed by every slight sound.[120]

Alexander Kinglake's *The Invasion of Crimea* (1863) places considerable emphasis on the fatigue, exhaustion and suffering of the troops during the winter months, but Kinglake shapes the narrative in terms of stoicism and heroism, the soldiers "bearing cold and hardships of all kinds with obstinate pride." He writes that "Without extraneous aid men found strength, it would seem, in their own heroic qualities, found strength in that soldierly pride which forbids outward signs of disclosing self-pity or despair; and it is not, indeed, even certain that such of them as remained for the moment unstricken by illness were at all in a mournful humor."[121] "Misery ceases to be overwhelming when it is no longer solitary; individual loss is drowned in the feeling of common sympathy," writes James Gibson in his memoirs of the 1880s:

[W]e are roused from the slumber of a lengthened peace to activity and energy in a noble cause; one feeling, and one alone, pervades all classes in the United Kingdom; one subject, and one alone, is the theme on which we delight to dwell – how we can best promote the safety of, and show our admiration for, the bravest army that ever left England's shores.[122]

Moving from memoirists to medical discourse, we find similar convictions about the rousing and even salubrious effect of emotion in times of war. Daniel Hack Tuke focuses on emotional response to war in his 1872 treatise on the effect of the mind on the body in health and disease: "Stirring political events, demanding individual action, have a wonderful influence over nervous affections. This fact was exhibited in the first American war." He cites authorities who state that "many whose habits were infirm and delicate, were restored to perfect health by the change of place or occupation to which the war exposed them."[123] Similarly, Tuke claims that "the battle-field constantly affords examples of the influence of an engrossing emotion in blunting sensation." He quotes from an article on the battle of Monte Rotundo (1867) which was published in the *Cornhill Magazine*: "All day long the battle raged; the troops were fainting with hunger and fatigue. Certainly they were the liveliest, most patient set of sufferers I ever saw; *the certainty of victory chloroformed their pain*" (original emphasis).[124]

A different perspective on emotional, nervous or apparently non-physical injury is offered in *The Crimean Journals of the Sisters of Mercy, 1854–56*, which allows a fascinating glimpse into the tensions between Florence Nightingale and the Catholic Sisters with whom she had to work at the front. The various accounts of nursing rivalries include a contrast between the hardy, capable sisters, inured to shock, and their more delicate, less efficient secular counterparts, as well as a sense of psychological or spiritual injury in the troops. Sister M. Aloysius Doyle notes in a journal from Scutari that "the secular ladies" are unable to withstand the shocks of war which the Sisters can: "No wonder Miss Nightingale should have leaned on Mother Mary Clare, of Bermondsey, and her four Sisters."[125] Highly critical of Nightingale, Mother Francis Bridgeman implies in her journal that Miss Nightingale had no sense of injury beyond the physical: "Now at this time there were about four thousand patients in Scutari hospitals, from fifty to ninety were daily buried. We found the sufferers of *that year peculiarly prostrate in mind and body;* yet Miss Nightingale coolly affirmed they needed no nursing, as they were not wounded!" (original emphasis).[126] Andrew Ward notes that some of the more frail women involved in the conflict were reputed to have died of shock, but such statements speak more to gendered notions of emotional susceptibility than they imply any recognition of specifically psychic or emotional injury.[127]

If British sources on the Crimean War and the Sepoy Rebellion turn up relatively little overt discussion of psychological or emotional injury, there is somewhat more to be found on this subject in the medical discourse of the 1870s surrounding the siege of Paris during the Franco-Prussian War. On reflection, the reason for this becomes obvious. Since the valor and heroism of British troops are not at stake, observers are unconstrained in speculating about French susceptibility to emotional disturbance. Indeed, one might argue that national stereotypes of the French character as unstable and excitable (or worse) may even play into the numerous comments on the rise of psychological problems following the siege of Paris.[128] The author of an article on "The War" in January 1871 in the *Lancet* noted that "the number of those who have become insane since the war is very great; the asylums are quite full."[129] Later that year, a letter recorded that after the city's capitulation "the mental shock to some was such that they almost lost their reason!"[130] In the *Journal of Mental Science* (1872), an anonymous article entitled "Effects of Fright on the Mind" makes reference to the "late siege of Paris" as furnishing some interesting examples of the effects of a "profound shock on the mind."[131] He quotes a French medical source, which reported: "On July 14th last, about 1.45, a tremendous explosion resounded throughout Paris. The percussion cap manufactory at Vincennes exploded ... The next day a very intelligent lady, who had witnessed the whole affair, was found to have *no recollection whatever of the occurrence. A great emotional disturbance may then, in a state of health, be effaced from the memory* (original emphasis).[132] Looking back in 1892 at the history of "shock from fright," the railway physician Herbert Page, who was one of the first to draw attention to the psychical disturbance that terror in railway accidents could produce, noted that

[t]he siege of Strasbourg and the siege of Paris during the last Franco-German war [1870–71] were both productive of many examples of *grave nervous disorder,* even ending fatally, which clearly had their origin in the terrible circumstances to which the sufferers had been exposed – to wit, the constant bursting of shells, the ever-present sense of danger, the anxiety as to the safety of friends, the inadequacy of the

food supply. Happily in this country we have been spared such experiences, but like *sources of neurotic disturbance* are to be found very often in the events of an ordinary railway collision, where we have in combination everything which is likely to induce great terror – magnitude and violence of the forces, loud noise, shrieks of the injured and utter helplessness of individual passengers. (Emphasis added)[133]

Page's comparison of the French responses to war and the reactions "in this country" to railway collisions draws attention to the now well-documented discourse surrounding railway accidents from the 1860s to the end of the century. Railway accidents, even more than war, brought strange cases to medical attention and provoked a range of diagnoses (such as railway spine and railway brain). Indeed, it has not escaped the notice of historians of railway accidents that the medical discourse of shock was given a jolt by the railway disasters of the 1850s and '60s and the controversial injuries (and insurance claims) to which they gave rise. It is worth noting that one of the earliest specific treatises on the subject, Edwin Morris's *A Practical Treatise on Shock* (1867) was written in response to the phenomenon of railway shock. The full title of Morris's treatise is "*A Practical Treatise on Shock after surgical operations and injuries: with especial reference to shock caused by railway accidents.*" And in his preface, Morris warns that his chapter on the railways is included to "assist in unraveling those intricate cases in which there is every reason to believe the symptoms are simulated, and at the same time to put medical men on their guard against such cases."[134]

Though overtly suspicious of malingerers, Morris does, at the outset, place emphasis on both mental and physical forms of shock, and begins by describing shock as "that peculiar effect on the animal system, produced by violent injuries from any cause, or from violent mental emotions – such as grief, fear, horror or disgust."[135] Though he pays most attention to gunshot wounds and injuries both proximate to and distant from the brain, he returns in his conclusion to the way in which the brain and nervous system are paralyzed by shock, and "volition and sensation are temporarily suspended."[136] Morris may be hedging his bets with his inclusive sweep of all violent physical injury or emotional experience as possible causes of shock; yet his attention to emotional causes is part of a continuous thread in nineteenth-century scientific and pseudoscientific discourse giving at least cautious credibility to the power of emotions.

In a recent study of the law relating to liability for negligence resulting in psychiatric injury, Danuta Mendelson observes that, while medical discourse has evolved to produce an array of terms and concepts to express changing ideas of psychical injury, law has kept to the basic, one might say generic, term "nervous shock," which is still used in British, Australian and

Canadian law. This adherence produces some confusion because "nervous shock" is no longer a diagnostic category in contemporary medicine and psychiatry; nor does it carry the medical meanings that it once did. While, as Mendelson notes, this produces frustration in lawyers, it is instructive for historians of the psychic wound because it suggests that late-nineteenth-century jurisprudence, beginning to take account of the need to compensate sufferers for psychic harm, was looking for a terminology that indicated psychological injury but also implied a physical or bodily anchor. According to Mendelson, the first case in which a plaintiff was awarded damages for nervous shock involved the witnessing of a railway accident – *Coultas* v. *Victorian Railway Commissioners* (1888).[137] As I will show in chapter 3, the importance of railway disaster and consequent insurance claims and legal pronouncement to the development of conceptions of psychic injury cannot be underrated and has justly received critical attention.[138] What has been rather less explored, but is also significant, is an earlier, arguably preparatory discourse on the nature of consciousness, which conceptualizes shock at the micro-level of nerves and emotion.

V NERVES AND SHOCK

An example from George Eliot's novel *Middlemarch* (1872) will serve to introduce some key issues in this discourse. Dorothea Brooke is on her unhappy wedding journey in Rome, where "underwhelmed" by the rector Edward Casaubon, her new husband, she is nevertheless overwhelmed by the carnival of sights and sounds that Rome represents. The "stupendous fragmentariness" of Rome heightens the "dream-like strangeness" of her bridal life.[139] Rome, the "city of visible history," is an experience whose effect on consciousness and memory George Eliot likens to that of an electric shock:

Ruins and basilicas, palaces and colossi, set in the midst of a sordid present ... : all this vast wreck of ambitious ideals, sensuous and spiritual, mixed confusedly with the signs of breathing forgetfulness and degradation, at first *jarred her as with an electric shock*, and *then urged themselves on her with that ache belonging to a glut of confused ideas which check the flow of emotion.* Forms both pale and glowing *took possession* of her young *sense, and fixed themselves in her memory even when she was not thinking of them*, preparing strange associations which remained through her after-years. Our moods are apt to bring with them images which succeed each other *like the magic-lantern pictures* of a doze. (Emphasis added)[140]

There are several elements in this phantasmagoric description relevant to the topic of mental shock: the conceptualizing of strong emotion as a jolt of electricity, which gestures towards the mid-nineteenth-century scientific context in which nerve force was increasingly understood in electrical terms; the ensuing imprint on memory and possession of the senses; the return of the pictures beyond conscious recall – a magical technology of the unconscious that produces a ghostly and marvelous parade of images succeeding each other in states of slightly altered consciousness, light sleep, doze or dream. George Eliot also refers to Dorothea's state as one of "inward amazement," which, coupled with the earlier description of the "dream-like strangeness" of her bridal life suggests that this profound experience is tantamount to an altered state of consciousness like dream or trance. In focusing on the shock of this experience, I am not suggesting that George Eliot presents Dorothea's experience here as a disabling injury or wound. There are ways in which this experience is a necessary shaking up of her heroine's narrow, provincial world. Nevertheless, it is a jarring experience that possesses her and controls her memory involuntarily – haunts her, we might say.

George Eliot's evocative account simultaneously draws on and helps to construct a particularly Victorian discourse of the way in which mind and body are affected by powerful emotional experience. Such discourse is the seed-bed (to invoke an Eliot-like metaphor) for the formulations of psychic trauma that emerge at the end of the nineteenth century. Literature is important to the historicization of ideas about trauma precisely because trauma is a culturally and historically constructed concept; the medical and psychological discourse that helped to produce it ought to be seen in relation to its ambient culture.[141] As Janet Oppenheim puts it in her history of the discourse of nerves, "[s]cientists and medical doctors, belonging integrally to the public ..., share many of its biases and expectations. Their pronouncements are not objective, or free of implicit moral judgment, for science and medicine are interpretative endeavors into which the surrounding social context constantly intrudes."[142] I would add "cultural" to "social" in drawing attention to literature's status as a complex cultural document and an influential shaper of public opinions and perceptions.

George Eliot's attention to the jolt Dorothea's consciousness receives from a powerful experience is consistent with the way physiological psychologists such as Herbert Spencer and Alexander Bain were thinking of consciousness itself. Indeed, both offer definitions of consciousness as a form of shock. In his *Principles of Psychology* (1855), Spencer argues that it is possible, "may we not even say probable – that something of the same order as that which we call a nervous shock is the ultimate unit of consciousness; and that all the unlikenesses among our feelings result from unlike modes of integration of this ultimate unit."[143] Such shocks, he goes on to explain, are faint pulses rather than powerful charges; if we felt each one of them consciously, we would not be able to cope: "Were our various sensations and emotions composed of rapidly-recurring shocks as strong as those ordinarily called shocks, they would be unbearable: indeed life would cease at once. We must think of them rather as successive faint pulses of subjective change, each having the same quality as the strong pulse of subjective change distinguished as a nervous shock." Spencer concludes that if "the subjective effect or feeling, is composed of rapidly-recurring mental shocks ... it corresponds with the objective cause – the rapidly recurring shocks of molecular change."[144] If sensation itself is conceptualized as a tiny unregistered shock, then it follows that a very powerful feeling would register as a palpable one. This point is explicitly made by Alexander Bain in *The Emotions and the Will* (1859). He writes that a

sudden shock of feeling is accompanied with movements of the body generally, and by other effects. When no emotion is present, we are quiescent; a slight feeling is accompanied with slight manifestations; a more intense shock has a more intense outburst. Every pleasure and every pain, and every mode of emotion, has a definite wave of effects, which our observation makes known to us.[145]

Bain's point is that emotion is itself a kind of shock that produces waves which transmit effects throughout the body in proportion to the intensity of the initial shock.[146] Reiterating this position in his later work *Mind and Body* (1873), he writes:

The simplest term we can employ for a mental state is a *shock*; a word equally applicable to the bodily side and to the mental side. A sudden stimulation of the eye, the ear, the skin, the nose, is called a shock, from its more outward or physical aspect; it is also called a shock mentally ... because there is a rapid transition from quiescence to excitement, in which circumstance there is an acute parallelism between the otherwise distinct physical and mental facts.[147]

The concept of shock articulated here is the great solvent of the divide between body and mind. Around the same time, Daniel Hack Tuke, who, as we have seen, focused on the relations of body and mind in the conception of disease and treatment, declared that

an emotion may also be conceived to cause structural change in the higher centres of the encephalon ... It is easy to see how, from Fright or sudden Joy, there may be a shock, more or less temporary, to the motor centres, by which some part is rendered unable to respond to the stimulus of the Will, or of ideas, or emotions, just as a man is sometimes deaf for days after firing a cannon, or is blind for a time after his eyes have been subjected to intense light.[148]

He concludes that "[p]robably all we can say with certainty is that the shock which the brain receives from a violent emotion like Terror disturbs the normal relative nutrition and vascularity of the volitional and motorial centres."[149] Common to all these examples is the underlying assumption that what we experience as mental effect always has a physiological correlative.

Shock in the texts I have been quoting is likened to tremor and earthquake, a violent disruption, a clash, or physical upheaval. Mechanical and climatic (as well as climactic), it can also be imaged in terms of electricity, as we saw in George Eliot's description of Dorothea. During the last half of the nineteenth century, especially in Germany, electricity was being established as the agent of nerve force. Up-to-date on recent discoveries in this regard, George Eliot writes in *Daniel Deronda* (1876) of the average man, unaware of many important facts about himself, and dark to those "even concerning the action of his own heart and the structure of his own retina. A century ago he and all his forefathers had not had the slightest notion of that electric discharge by means of which they had all wagged their tongues mistakenly."[150] The significant discovery in brain research at the end of the eighteenth century was that nerves worked not by hydraulics but by electricity.[151] But it is important to remember that electricity in this regard is still being thought of as a kind of fluid. By the end of the eighteenth century, the idea of "an electrical fluid flowing in nerve tubules was an attractive hypothesis as the agent of nerve action" though, as Sidney Ochs points out, it was far from universally accepted.[152] Still, the analogical force of the battery was powerful in physiological texts such as William Carpenter's *Principles of Mental Physiology*:

Just as a perfectly constructed Galvanic battery is *inactive* while the circuit is "interrupted," but becomes *active* the instant that the circuit is "closed," so does a Sensation, an Instinctive tendency, an Emotion, an Idea, or a Volition, which attains an intensity adequate to "close" the circuit, liberate the Nerve-force with which a certain part of the Brain, while in a state of wakeful activity, is always "charged." (Original emphasis)[153]

The history of how electricity came to be accepted as the agent of nerve action is a long one. It extends from the ancients, who noticed that when amber (the Greek name for electricity) was rubbed it would attract small objects to it, to the work of Galvani at the turn of the eighteenth century, "when electricity was generated as a static discharge and its potent effects on the body experienced."[154] Galvani's explanation was that the nerve fibers were so constituted that they were hollow internally or composed of material able to carry electric fluid, but were oily externally so that the electric fluid was prevented from dissipating. Galvani posited that electric fluid was produced in the cerebrum and extracted from the blood, entering the nerves and circulating within them. He suggested that this animal electricity was identical to animal spirits, and hoped that, if this were the case, there would at last be clarity on that opaque subject.

German physiologist Emil du Bois-Reymond, known as the father of experimental electrophysiology, posited that current flowed continually in the fibers of muscle and nerves.[155] Though this proposition was erroneous, as later research into the electrical nature of nerve and muscle potentials in the 1880s showed, du Bois-Reymond was on the right track and also made important strides in measuring the conduct velocity of nerve impulse. In *Mind and Body*, Alexander Bain refers repeatedly to "nerve-force" and occasionally to "nerve-electricity" and makes mention of du Bois-Reymond's computation of nerve impulse transmission from the location of a harpoon wound to the brain in a whale; he also refers to Hermann Helmholtz's attempts to calculate reflex action in frogs.[156] Even earlier, as the following example from Morris's medical treatise on shock (1867) illustrates, general acceptance of the nature of electricity as an agent of nerve action provided a way of understanding shock:

Of the active principle in the nervous system, we in reality know little or nothing; this, however, is a matter of no importance to us, and I only allude to it, in consequence of the important part it plays in the production of the train of symptoms called *shock*. I am inclined to think that it is of the same nature as electricity, and the nerves act as conductors. Faraday has propounded this idea, and Abernathy also advocated this doctrine; certain it is that this nervous agent has an action of a peculiar kind, and if not identical with electricity, is very analogous to it. (Emphasis added)[157]

Only towards the end of the nineteenth century was the electrical nature of nerve potential better grasped, when the properties of ions in electrolyte solutions were demonstrated by the Swedish physical chemist Svante Arrhenius.[158]

VI THE PHYSIOLOGY OF EMOTION

If electricity was the means by which nerves transmitted impulses, then was it possible literally to experience a powerful transmission of nervous energy as an electric shock? While George Eliot could effectively represent shocks to consciousness as electric, the question of what actually goes on inside the

body when emotions are experienced was one that greatly occupied physiological psychology at the mid-century. Indeed, as I have explained above,
the mid nineteenth century is often seen in histories of emotion theory as
the moment when emotion was conceived of as a bodily, physiological
process.

Time and again, however, Alexander Bain talks of the *interrelationship* of
mind and body, not the *reduction* of the former to the latter. Although he
does say that "the mind is completely at the mercy of the bodily condition,"
he formulates the relationship thus in order to show that "there is no trace of
a separate, independent, self-supporting, spiritual agent, rising above all the
fluctuations of the corporeal frame."[59] Whatever mind is, he implies, it is
thoroughly tied up with body. In this way, Bain attempts to dismantle the
dualism of mind and body, but not to reduce mind to brain, or to suggest
that mind is merely and passively body. I return in Chapter 4 to explore in
greater detail the way physiological psychologists such as Bain, Spencer and
Lewes conceptualize emotion. What I wish to emphasize here is that, as
with the position known as "dual-aspect monism," a commitment to the
physiology of emotion is not necessarily an abandonment of the cognitive,
evaluative capacity of emotion.

In a complex literary representation of shock, emotion and cognition,
drawn once again from George Eliot's *Middlemarch*, we see both the
physiological and cognitive aspects of strong emotional experience.

When Mrs. Casaubon was announced he started up as from an electric shock, and
felt a tingling at his finger-ends. Any one observing him would have seen a change
in his complexion, in the adjustment of his facial muscles, in the vividness of his
glance, which might have made them imagine that every molecule in his body had
passed the message of a magic touch. And so it had. For effective magic is transcendent nature; and who shall *measure the subtlety of those touches which convey the
quality of soul as well as body*, and make a man's passion for one woman differ from
his passion for another as joy in the morning light over valley and river and white
mountain-top differs from joy among Chinese lanterns and glass panels? Will, too,
was made of very impressible stuff. (Emphasis added)[160]

The passage is striking as evidence of the way emotion, internal feeling, is
rendered bodily and physical, read through its corporeal manifestations. In
this regard, George Eliot is very much in line with the way emotions
themselves in physiological psychology were being emphasized as a physical
process. But in conjunction with the bodily changes Will experiences, we
are encouraged to recognize the magical aspect of the transformation – even
as George Eliot details the physical process, she keeps alive a sense of the
miraculous, marvelous and inexplicable. And she preserves the language of

soul. This is not, however, a remystification. If Will's emotional response is visceral, it is also cognitive – the passage speaks of his evaluation and assessment of Dorothea's worth; his discrimination of her value among other women. To express the small but significant choices, preferences and discriminations that reveal our cognitive schemes, George Eliot contrasts a preference for natural light and natural scenery with that for artful light and manufactured materials. As in the passage I quoted earlier from *Middlemarch*, the lantern (here Chinese, there magic) is an important metaphor allowing George Eliot to draw on visual technologies to represent internal processes such as cognitive choice and involuntary memory. Finally, the statement about Will being made of impressible stuff – a good conductor of the emotional as electrical – is a light, slightly ironic, touch, bringing us (and him) down to earth after the sublimity and serious-ness of the previous remarks on body and soul.

Martha N. Nussbaum has recently argued in *Upheavals of Thought: The Intelligence of Emotions* that emotions have come to be regarded as "'bodily' rather than 'mental,' as if this were sufficient to make them unintelligent rather than intelligent." She continues:

Although I believe that emotions are, like other mental processes, bodily, I also believe, and shall argue, that seeing them as in every case taking place in a living body does not give us reason to reduce their intentional/cognitive components to nonintentional bodily movements... Certainly we are not left with a choice between regarding emotions as ghostly spiritual energies and taking them to be obtuse, non-assessing bodily movements, such as a leap of the heart, or the boiling of the blood.[161]

Anticipating Nussbaum's refusal of binary oppositions, George Eliot does not structure her representation of the power of emotion in terms of a dichotomy between physical and mental, bodily and cognitive, but attempts a kind of synthesis. Read in relation to the history of Victorian psychological discourse and the debates that continue in contemporary emotion theory, literary texts such as George Eliot's *Middlemarch* offer a richer and more complex representation of Victorian responses to the nature of emotions than historians of emotion have generally allowed.

The focus in this section on emotions and consciousness as nineteenth-century antecedents of a discourse of trauma may at first glance seem out of step with the preoccupations of much contemporary trauma theory, which places a great deal of emphasis on dissociated and dysfunctional memory. Nevertheless, there is a growing body of recent work in the neurosciences exploring the neurophysiological mechanisms responsible for emotional consciousness and mapping the effects of stress on the hippocampus and amygdala. While the limitations of scientific explanations of trauma continue to be mooted by humanist critics, an informed approach to trauma theory needs to take such developments into account.[162] Neuropyschoanalyst Allan Schore has described the most far reaching effect of trauma as the loss of ability to regulate feelings, yet affect regulation seems to have been eclipsed by memory in dominant and influential trauma theory over the past few decades.[163] Theorists, analysts and therapists such as Cathy Caruth, Dori Laub, Shoshana Felman and Judith Herman all emphasize unprocessed memory as the key element of trauma. And in his history of multiple personality disorder, *Rewriting the Soul* – which is, along the way, also an account of how trauma was constructed as a syndrome – Ian Hacking traces the rise of memory science in the last quarter of the nineteenth century. On the literary front, Nicholas Dames's remarks about trauma in *Amnesiac Selves* suggest that its hallmark is memory disturbance. He has argued that the Victorian novel (certainly before 1870) evinces an "amnesiac self" in the sense that memories deemed unproductive are expunged or absent from the narrative. Only after memory becomes nervous, a result of the burgeoning physiological psychology in the latter half of the century, do we find evidence of what Benjamin has called the "traumatophile."[164]

The emphasis on memory as somehow the key to trauma arises understandably out of the puzzling question: how are cognitive processes affected in the event of overwhelming experience? As that question is answered in terms of unconscious rather than conscious registration, involuntary rather than voluntary recall, so the domain of trauma becomes the domain of memory. But in nineteenth-century discourse, disturbance of memory as the result of overwhelming or shocking experience is only one aspect of a network of related ideas that later cohere (albeit uneasily) as the concept of trauma.[165] In exploring that "seed-bed" of discourses, I would argue that, in addition to discourses of memory, important as these are, we need to attend to theories of consciousness and emotion. To the extent that emotions are cognitive, they do the work of memory in mid-nineteenth-century discourses of the wounded mind. Understood to carry intelligence (that is, knowledge) that may not be consciously available, emotions provide evidence of the thorns in the spirit. What today we would call "unregulated affect" is in the Victorian period the royal road to the hidden self. It is within the context of mid- to late-Victorian medical and psychological discourse on emotion, memory and the unconscious that I turn now to a range of fictional texts, all of which imagine states of emotion, dissociation and disruptions of consciousness that contribute to conceptions of psychic shock.

CHAPTER 2

Dream and trance: Gaskell's North and South as a "condition-of-consciousness" novel

One of my mes is, I do believe, a true Christian – (only people call her socialist and communist), another of my mes is a wife and mother, and highly delighted at the delight of everyone else in the house ... Now that's my "social" self I suppose. Then again I've another self with a full taste for beauty and convenience whh is pleased on its own account. How am I to reconcile all these warring members? I try to drown myself (my *first* self,) by saying it's Wm who is to decide on all these things and his feeling it right ought to be my rule, And so it is – only that does not quite do.

Gaskell to Eliza Fox 1850

As a social problem novel, or a novel of industrial life, *North and South* has traditionally received much critical attention for its purchase on questions of political economy and the relations of labor and capital.[1] It is also, I will argue in this chapter, a novel with a sustained focus on interiority and consciousness. From the opening pages, where Margaret Hale, now a stately girl of eighteen and about to leave her aunt's home, recalls her early "wild passion of grief" at being separated from her parents, the narrative pays close attention to painful feelings – their expression, censorship and transformative potential. More specifically, *North and South* is interested in the effect of very powerful feelings on psychic functioning and in the haunting aftermath of intense emotional experience.[2] In its attention to dream and the power of unconscious processes, the novel seems as interested in the nature of the psyche as it is concerned with social problems. Indeed, as I hope to show, the two are closely related. Attentive to social change, Gaskell envisions social conditions in an industrialized world as involving a fair amount of turbulence, upheaval and disruption, all of which affect the mind in various destabilizing ways. Studying the human mind under social conditions in mid-century England, *North and South* suggests, we may learn more about both. I want in this chapter to revise its most common categorization as a condition-of-England novel, and suggest that it is equally

61

a condition-of-consciousness novel. Concerned with shock at many levels, *North and South* not only captures the psychic and physical exhaustion of constant stimulus and change, but, through its use of dream and trance, explores the altered states of consciousness consequent on emotional upheaval.

Again and again, *North and South* explores how people cope with shock and pain – the "heart ache and the thousand natural shocks" that the mind and, through it, the flesh are heir to. Gaskell is abidingly concerned with interiority – states of mind that alter under the pressure of social and psychic causes, producing effects such as "languor," mental fatigue and stunned consciousness. For the most part, Gaskell's concern with heightened affect has been seen as a melodramatic excrescence. As I will argue, however, the novel has a significant place in the Victorian history of affect and consciousness.

Gaskell's foray into novel writing has often been linked to her own acute experience of grief at the loss of her young son, Willie, from scarlet fever. Emotional anguish and suffering inform her first novel, focused as it is on the plight of the working classes in a period of economic privation. Gaskell's avowed subject in *Mary Barton* is working-class woes "which come with ever-returning tide-like flood to overwhelm the workmen." In *Mary Barton* (1848), psychic suffering is a prelude to potential madness and unhinging, so that Mary's extreme emotional stress after her public appearance in court sends her into a brain fever, which has Jem worrying that she may remain "a poor gibbering maniac all her life long."[3] In *North and South* Gaskell deliberately avoids pathologizing strong feelings and their effects, rather seeing the negotiation of painful feelings occasioned by love, death and moral crisis as ordinary, even daily, business.[4] In *Mary Barton*, the toiling, suffering, working classes are continually being brought before the reader's attention in the novelist's attempt to evoke readerly sympathies. Death, often from starvation and disease, is there the cause of pain and suffering, and the novel seems almost relentless in detailing a succession of deaths. Though *North and South* is not similarly focused on working-class poverty, its death toll is similarly high – Mrs. Hale, Bessy Higgins, Mr. Hale, Boucher, his wife, Mr. Bell. Indeed, Gaskell wrote to Charles Dickens in December 1854: "I think a better title than N & S would have been 'Death & Variations.' There are 5 deaths, each beautifully suited to the character of the individual."[5] Gaskell was at this point in the process of writing the novel serially for *Household Words*, and Dickens had chosen the title "North and South." While many readers have criticized Dickens's choice, suggesting that its dichotomy does not adequately reflect Gaskell's complex view of England, there are few, one imagines, who would opt for the suggestion Gaskell offers here. Still, her comment does serve to highlight her own, possibly self-ironic, awareness of the centrality of death in this novel. "Beautifully suited to the character of the individual," the deaths also frequently say something about the social conditions in the industrial North. Mrs. Hale dies because of the upheaval of the move to Milton and its insalubrious climate. Mr. Hale is bowed down and depressed by the ructions attendant on his departure from the Church and his sorrow at his wife's death. Boucher commits suicide as a result of the strike failure, poverty and lack of work. Bessy dies because hazardous working conditions at the factory have ruined her lungs. The deaths are often occasions of sentimentality and pathos, but also – in so far as they affect Margaret – spurs to independence, and moments of education and instruction. They offer the novelist opportunities for observing the aftermath of powerful emotional experience.

In *North and South*, death is, however, only one among several events that produce emotional upheaval and provoke a response of shock and pain. There is also Mr. Hale's decision to leave the Church; Frederick's discredited and fugitive status; Margaret's encounter with the mob; her lie to protect Frederick; the cruel local superstition that involves the roasting of a live cat, which she hears about on her return to the South. There are further, less obviously eventful, more private, even undetected, experiences that are equally painful: Margaret's responses to the proposals by Lennox and Thornton; Thornton's experience of rejection in love. Furthermore, the experience of and response to powerful emotion is not conventionally gendered in this novel. Gaskell was quite prepared in *Mary Barton* to show working-class men as emotional and feeling, but the gender differences in the experience of mental anguish are in *North and South* even further blurred. Mr. Hale's face is marked by "habitual distress and depression" as a result of his crisis of faith; when Frederick arrives back to see his dying mother, Mr. Hale begins to "cry and wail like a child."[6] Frederick sobs in the night after his mother's death, and the painful effects of passionate love on Mr. Thornton leave him stunned and dizzy, with a violent headache and a throbbing intermittent pulse. Although some critics have pointed to Mr. Hale's effeminacy in contrast to Mr. Thornton's masculine power and control, a close look at the text's rendering of emotion suggests that it is not necessarily unmanly for men to experience powerful feelings over which they cannot always exert control.[7] "I am a man. I claim the right of expressing my feelings" (195), declares John Thornton. And even Nicholas Higgins momentarily expresses profound emotion at the death of his daughter before he heads out to the gin palace where he will take a "sup o' drink just to steady me again sorrow" (220).

Men in *North and South* seem even more prone than women to excessive and destabilizing emotionality. After Mrs. Hale dies, Dixon the maid is concerned that Margaret's father will suffer a stroke as a result of grief, and indeed he seems unhinged as he keeps talking to his wife as if she were alive: "I was really afraid for master, that he'd have a stroke with grief ... I've heard him talking to her, and talking to her, as if she was alive ... he ought to be roused; and if it gives him a shock at first, it will, maybe, be better afterwards" (253). As if to bring home the double standard of her culture's way of coding overwhelming emotion as feminine, Gaskell describes Mr. Hale's fear of breaking down entirely at his wife's funeral and therefore wanting Mr. Thornton to accompany him. When Margaret asks to go with him, he says "You! My dear, women do not generally go" (266). Margaret explains that she knows that is the case and it is so because "[w]omen of our class ... have no power over their emotions and ... are ashamed of showing them. Poor women go, and don't care if they are seen overwhelmed with grief" (266–67). From Margaret's point of view poor women have it right in not caring if they are seen exhibiting emotion; she should accompany her father and if they are both overcome, so be it. The implicit critique here of emotional control broaches what will be more strongly suggested elsewhere – that the expression of powerful emotion may be an important way of knowing and understanding the self. It suggests too that the social injunction to keep strong feelings in check is a class convention, which may be as bad in its way as the inability (culturally coded as female or working-class or both) to avoid surrendering to excessive emotion.

MENTAL AND PHYSICAL EXHAUSTION

Time and again *North and South* describes the aftermath of powerful emotion as exhaustion and depletion. Exhaustion is certainly associated with the working-class body, fatally fatigued not so much by depression-era starvation, as it was in *Mary Barton*, as by the tedium and unhealthy working conditions of factory life. The dying Bessy exemplifies this vital collapse: "If yo'd led the life I have, and gotten as weary of it as I have ... oh, wench! I tell thee thou'd been glad enough when th' doctor said he feared thou'd never see another winter" (89). But alongside the physical tedium of life in the Milton (Manchester) cotton mills, Gaskell's industrial novel also represents, particularly in its middle-class subjects, the effects of affective or emotional overload.

Margaret's father's decision to leave the Church reduces him to a state of "mental and bodily languor" (47); Mrs. Hale's illness leaves the family "exhausted by their terror" (169); and, Hale as she is, Margaret finds herself, in the vicissitudes of Milton life, often giving way to "listless languor" (288). When caught out in a lie by Mr. Thornton, Margaret collapses and lies on the floor "too much exhausted to think. Half an hour or more elapsed before the cramped nature of her position, and the chilliness, supervening upon great fatigue, had the power to rouse her numbed faculties" (283). Even the energetic and commanding Mr. Thornton suffers fatigue of this kind. When his declaration of love is rejected by Margaret, he is "so languid that he could not control his thoughts; they would wander to her; they would bring back the scene" (213).

The emphasis on languor and fatigue suggests a condition that in later decades came to be known as neurasthenia, and is most often associated with Silas Weir Mitchell and the rest cure. The term was coined in 1869 by the American physician George Beard, about whom I shall have more to say later, but well before the late 1860s "a language of 'nerves,' a popular bodily economy of nervous energy, an expanding medical culture of nerve management, and a belief that civilisation produced nervousness were all in place in Britain," as Roy Porter and Janet Oppenheim have shown, long before the term "neurasthenia" came into use.[8] A condition that was figured as a disease of modern life, neurasthenia was essentially an over-stimulation of the nerves and hence a sapping of nerve force, or vital nerve power. In the North/South distinction, Gaskell seems to invoke the idea of neurasthenia: "It is the town life," says Margaret; "Their nerves are quickened by the haste and bustle and speed of everything around them, to say nothing of the confinement in these pent-up houses, which of itself is enough to induce depression and worry of spirits" (301). And Mrs. Shaw, Margaret's aunt visiting from London, whose pressured city life was itself well known to cause all manner of depletions and prostrations, fears that Milton will bring on "one of her old attacks of the nerves" (363). These two references illustrate the different poles of "luxury" and "labor" that medical historians such as Roy Porter have seen in the constituencies of neurasthenic sufferers as the century progressed and in the way the condition was manifested in Britain and America.

From Margaret's point of view, London is enervating in a different way from the North. It is a kind of Lotus land: "[Margaret] was getting surfeited of the eventless ease in which no struggle or endeavour was required. She was afraid lest she should even become sleepily deadened into forgetfulness of anything beyond the life which was lapping her round with luxury" (373). If there are "toilers and moilers" in London, Margaret never sees them as the servants seem to live "in an underground world of their own" (373). Also part of the South, Helstone is associated, from a working-class point of view, with the exhaustion of hard physical labor and a stagnation of spirits. While the novel offers contrasts between North and South, it allows no easy or fixed opposition between them.

North and South may be opposed in various ways, but it is significant to note that in this newly industrialized world they are readily accessible of each other. Railway transport connects all parts of the country. There is certainly a contrast between the railway stations of the North and those in the South, but the point is that the country is traversed with lines of communication:

> There were few people about at the stations, it almost seemed as if they were too lazily content to wish to travel; none of the bustle and stir that Margaret had noticed in her two journeys on the London and North-Western line. Later on in the year, this line of railway should be stirring and alive with rich pleasure-seekers; but as to the constant going to and fro of busy trades-people it would always be widely different from the northern lines. (384–85)

The slow carriage rides of Jane Eyre or Pip give way to the railway journey, whirling travelers to and fro across the countryside. As I shall discuss more fully in the following chapter, the railway is an important aspect of Victorian modernity and a marker of industrial change. The railway was also a crucial site of accident and the exploration of its aftermath. The medical discourse of shock proliferated in response to the railway disasters of the 1850s and '60s and the controversial injuries to which they gave rise. The reason for many railway accidents, years after tracks had been installed, was itself a question of fatigue – metal fatigue, a subject about which Victorian engineers did not know very much when the railways were built and which was first documented in 1854. In a lecture at the London Institution of Civil Engineers, "On the Fatigue and Consequent Fracture of Metals," Frederick Braithwaite proposed that "there are many reasons for believing, that many of the appalling, and apparently unac-countable accidents on railways, and elsewhere, are to be ascribed to that progressive action which may be termed, the 'fatigue of metals.' This fatigue may arise from a variety of causes, such as repeated strain, blows, concussions, jerks, torsion or tension."[9] The description of metal fatigue is strikingly similar to accounts of "railway spine" and mental shock con-sequent on railway accident that began to accrue in the 1860s: both railway lines and bodies were thought to be subject to similar kinds of onslaught.

The occurrence of accidents meant that traveling by rail involved some risk. Insurance companies thus commenced insuring passengers against accident. Highly topical in this regard, Gaskell has Mr. Bell promise to bring Margaret home safely after their train visit to Helstone. "I'll give you back safe and sound, barring railway accidents," he says, "and I'll insure your life for a thousand pounds before starting, which may be some comfort to your relations," he adds with dark humor (383). Passengers insured against accident began to claim for injuries that were shock-related, psychological or not obviously physical. Doctors were called on to pronounce on the validity of such invisible wounds. Hence medical debates about the somatic or psychological basis of shock increased. Indeed, as Wolfgang Schivelbusch and others have pointed out, it is only in the 1860s, when the question of damages for shock became pressing, that medical attention to the question began in earnest.

Although there are no train crashes in the novel, it is not insignificant, I suggest, that the railway station is associated with accident and its aftermath – shock. Margaret's fugitive brother Frederick is sighted at the railway station by one Leonards, who would like to turn him in for the reward. In an ensuing confrontation Leonards trips and hits his head, which concussion turns out to be fatal. It is as a result of Leonards's death that the police begin to investigate whether Margaret was at the station, as had been reported, prompting her spontaneous lie about her presence in order to protect her brother. As we shall see, the accident at the railway station raises questions of guilt and responsibility and entails important consequences for Gaskell's exploration of consciousness.

EMOTIONAL SHOCK AND ALTERED CONSCIOUSNESS

The medical discourse of shock in the latter half of the nineteenth century was provoked and developed in response to physical or surgical shock, but "great mental emotion" is almost always recognized as a cause of shock, along with surgical or purely physical factors. Edwin Morris's treatise on shock states that "nerves may become paralyzed by being stimulated too much; or by a state of excitement continued too long, exhaustion of the nervous susceptibility may ensue. Men overworked, or animals overdriven, will ultimately succumb and lie down and die, being deprived of all nervous power, which would enable them to make further effort."[10] Shock is the ultimate, the fatal, exhaustion. It is also a mystery since the sudden collapse of vitality is not attributable to any "apparent pathological changes in the animal structure."[11] Morris makes reference to "the specific influence which the nerves have over the heart's action," which accounts for its "sudden cessation following violent injuries, or great mental emotion."[12] Shock, in Gaskell's novel, is often followed by bodily collapse. Thus, Margaret's response to her father's unexpected death:

The shock had been great. Margaret fell into a state of prostration, which did not show itself in sobs and tears, or even find the relief of words. She lay on the sofa, with her eyes shut, never speaking but when spoken to … her physical exhaustion was evidently too complete for her to undertake any such fatigue [a journey] – putting the sight that she would have to encounter out of the question. (353)

If shock doesn't kill, Morris warns, it exerts a remarkable effect on "volition [which] becomes suspended," a condition followed by "great exhaustion, with a strong tendency to sleep."[13] This emphasis on the suspension of volition directs our attention to conceptions of mesmeric or hypnotic trance, in which volition is also suspended and consciousness altered. Shock then is an agent inducing a state of altered consciousness.

The connection between shock and altered consciousness is explicitly explored in George Beard's professionally interested essay on trance as a state in which responsibility is abdicated. Beard argues that in legal cases where responsibility and culpability have to be determined, it is only the qualified medical professional who can pronounce on blameworthiness. Along with his coinage of the term "neurasthenia," for which he is best known, Beard was much captivated by the phenomenon of trance, which he described as much like other "functional nervous diseases," in that it may be induced physically or psychically; that is, by influences that act on the nervous system, or on the mind, or on both. Among the physical causes are injuries of the brain, the exhaustion of protracted disease or of starvation, or of over exertion, anesthetics, alcohol and many drugs, and certain cerebral diseases. Under the psychical causes are included all conceivable influences whatsoever that may powerfully excite any emotion, or group of emotions:[14] "Under emotional trance are included cases that are caused by the so-called mesmeric performances, or through the feelings of fear, wonder, reverence and expectation, however excited."[15] Everyone has these emotions, he continues, and they undermine the authority of reason. Beard furnishes several examples of self-entrancement or fascination by terror: standing on a height, on a track as a train is approaching, or being paralyzed by the outbreak of fire in a crowded building:

The one fact common to all these conditions is, that they exert some one or several emotions ... to such a degree that the *activity of the rest of the brain is suspended while these emotions are abnormally active*, and consequently *the will loses control, and the subject acts automatically in response to external or internal suggestion*, doing the very things he wishes to avoid doing, and unable to do what he most desires. (Emphasis added)[16]

The idea of the powerful effect of emotion as a state of entrancement akin to that produced by hypnosis is even more specifically taken up in medical writing towards the end of the century. Herbert Page, in an article entitled "Shock from Fright," to which I have referred in the previous chapter, likened the state of unconsciousness that may follow the shock specifically to the state of altered consciousness to be found in experimental hypnosis: "[It] is now very commonly held that *the dazed condition which has been described is very closely allied to, if it be not indeed identical with, the state induced in purposive experimental hypnosis.*"[17]

Like Beard, Page clearly perceives the similarity between the effects of shock on the psyche and the hypnotic state. Both are altered states of consciousness which may compromise memory and self-possession. This discourse thus brings together the physiology of shock and fright, and a model of the mind as capable of a range of states of consciousness, each of which may have their own memory strands – a series of discontinuous selves. A trajectory can thus be traced from seeing shock and fright as productive of torpor and exhaustion through to the configuration, associated with Freud, of shock and fright as producing a psychic wound. But, whereas critics like Tim Armstrong have tended to associate the pre-Freudian discourse of shock with neurasthenia or physical exhaustion and characterized Freudian trauma as a new kind of shock, one that involves unconscious psychic elaboration, I am suggesting that an earlier Victorian discourse, of which *North and South* is part, goes well beyond understanding shock as a somatic response to overwhelming stimuli.

DREAM AND TRANCE

Turning from Beard and Page with their linkage of shock to a state of entrancement, of altered consciousness, I want now to explore Gaskell's interest in psychic states beyond the ordinary. Here I argue that the novel draws heavily on the language of dream and trance in order to express the shifts in consciousness that follow overwhelming emotion.[18] In *North and South*, the language of dream, fantasy, trance and somnambulism is often used analogically, as an explanatory mode of suggesting the subject's abdication of ordinary volition and consciousness. So, for example, "Mr. Hale came – as if in a dream, or rather with the unconscious motion of a sleep-walker, whose eyes and mind perceive other things than what are present" (252). And Margaret, lying insensible, a stone from one in the mob having grazed her temple, is described as one who lies "in death-like trance," unable to move or speak, yet fully aware of what is going on around her (183). Margaret likens the news of Mr. Hale's decision to leave the Church as "a night-mare – a horrid dream – not the real waking truth!" (40). So powerful is the experience of strong emotion, Gaskell implies, that it can distort our sense of reality and indeed our sense of ourselves. When Mrs. Hale is ill, Margaret spends the night watching over her:

She felt *as if* she could never sleep again; as if her whole senses were acutely vital, and all endued with double keenness, for the purposes of watching. Every sight and sound – nay, even every thought, touched some nerve to the quick ... Not more than thirty-six hours ago, she cared for Bessy Higgins and her father, and her heart was wrung for Boucher; now that was all *like a dreaming memory* of some former life; – everything that had passed out of doors seemed disseevered from her mother, and therefore *unreal*. Even Harley Street appeared more distinct; there she remembered, *as if* it were yesterday, how she had pleased herself with tracing out her mother's features in her Aunt Shaw's face, – and how letters had come, making her dwell on the thoughts of home with all the longing of love ... She would fain have caught at the skirts of that departing time ... It was *as if* from some aerial belfry, high up above the stir and jar of the earth, there was a bell continually tolling, "All are shadows! – all are passing! all is past!" And when the morning dawned, cool and gray, like many a happier morning before – when Margaret looked one by one at the sleepers, it seemed *as if* the terrible night *were unreal as a dream*; it, too, was a shadow. It, too, was past. (Emphasis added; 170)

The passage proceeds through a series of five comparisons indicated by "as if" and "like." While the sentiments of the passage are quite conventional, what is interesting here is the recourse Gaskell has to the language of dreams and unreality, which allows her to suggest the jolt that Margaret's perception of reality has suffered as a result of her mother's illness. The sense created here of living a nightmare or bad dream in troubled times is repeatedly evoked in the novel. On the other hand, Gaskell also uses the contrast and continuity between dreaming and waking worlds to suggest that reality may be worse even than bad dreams. After Margaret learns that her father can no longer in good conscience carry out his duties as vicar, Gaskell writes: "She awoke with a start, unrefreshed, and conscious of some reality worse even than her feverish dreams. It all came back upon her; not merely the sorrow, but the terrible discord in the sorrow" (43). On the occasion that she lies about Frederick, dreams exaggerate the horrible reality: "Even when she fell asleep her thoughts were compelled to travel the same circle, only with exaggerated and monstrous circumstances of pain" (283). At times, dreams are worse than reality: Mrs. Hale's old, recurrent dream about Frederick in stormy waters is so bad that she is "thankful to waken, sitting straight and stiff up in bed with my terror" (106).

The effects of shock and emotional upheaval are often described as stunning or numbing, which suggests a state of hypnosis and paralysis. Early in the novel, Margaret has two experiences that profoundly unsettle her: Henry Lennox's proposal, which leaves her "stunned, and unable to recover her self-possession" (30), and the news of her father's crisis of conscience that precipitates his leaving the Church, after hearing which she returns to the living room in a "stunned and dizzy state" (40). The latter seems to displace the former in her consciousness, but her encounter with Lennox returns to haunt her dreams. Not only does the report of the dream convey Gaskell's strong sense of psychic life beyond the conscious, but she indicates how experiences which seem to have been forgotten are accessible to recollection in a different state of consciousness. This is prefigured by Lennox's response to her suggestion that they "forget" he has ever proposed, and return to being friends as they always were: "That is all very fine in theory, that plan of forgetting whatever is painful, but it will be somewhat difficult for me, at least, to carry it into execution" (29–30). And, indeed, Margaret does not forget the proposal, much as it is marginalized by other concerns:

Mr Lennox – his visit, his proposal – the remembrance of which had been so rudely pushed aside by the subsequent events of the day – haunted her dreams that night. He was climbing up some tree of fabulous height to reach the branch whereon was slung her bonnet: he was falling, and she was struggling to save him, but held back by some invisible powerful hand. He was dead. And yet, with a shifting of the scene, she was once more in the Harley Street drawing-room, talking to him as of old, and still with a consciousness all the time that she had seen him killed by that terrible fall. (43)

Although many Victorians still held to the idea that dreams were produced by bad digestion, on the one hand, or were messages sent from departed souls, on the other, Gaskell's use of dream is revelatory of psychological states. Dreams are not here, as they are in many other novels of the period, prognostications of the future, or communications from denizens of another realm.[19] Gaskell can be placed in the company of mental physiologists such as Henry Holland, George Henry Lewes and

William Carpenter, who argued that dreams do replay experiences of the recent past, and "transform immediate physical sensations into vivid dramas which are ultimately determined by the character of the dreamer."[20] So Margaret's dream is not a message that Henry Lennox's life is in peril, but a replaying of troubled emotions in relation to his proposal. In it she revisits anxieties about wounding him and expresses a sense of powerlessness to prevent cataclysm. The effects of her refusal are translated into a physical realm, so that rejection becomes a fatal fall. He has gone out on a limb to save her bonnet, which signals her sense of responsibility for his vulnerability and her inability to save him from falling. Gaskell manages to capture the familiar strangeness, apparent contradiction, irrationality and incoherence of dream in the sudden scene shift to Harley Street, and the peculiar endurance of the previous part of the dream – a consciousness of his death – even though he appears in the drawing room "as of old." The dream reminds her that she can never return to being his friend as before. The knowledge of his feelings for her and her rejection of him will underlie all future interaction. There is no forgetting.

Similarly, Mr. Thornton's dream of Margaret after he learns she has lied about being with Frederick dramatizes to him his conflicting feelings of continued attraction to her and yet his sense of her duplicity:

He dreamt of her; he dreamt she came dancing towards him with outspread arms, and with a lightness and gaiety which made him loathe her, even while it allured him. But the impression of this figure of Margaret – with all Margaret's character taken out of it, as completely as if some evil spirit had got possession of her form – was so deeply stamped upon his imagination that when he wakened he felt hardly able to separate the Una from the Duessa, and the dislike he had to the latter seemed to envelope the former. (331)

Compounding the lie Margaret has told, her fantasized sexual involvement with this other man renders her loose and whorish, tainting her even as it confirms her seductive power. Furthermore, Margaret appears in the dream as "not herself," which Gaskell explains as possession by an evil spirit. The dream allows Gaskell to explore Thornton's feelings and shows her again, in her recognition of the way dreams impress themselves on one's imagination, drawing out the enigmatic relationship between one realm of consciousness and another.

Gaskell's challenge in *North and South* is to find a language that will be adequate to her interest in emotional states and will convey the nightmarish cast of interiority in moments of shock or distress. The kind of Victorian fiction that makes greatest use of nightmare in relation to emotions of fright and terror is the gothic. Gaskell was, of course, no stranger to the ghost story or the supernatural tale, and she does in this novel occasionally make use of the accoutrements of gothic horror to describe extreme states of mind. Margaret's eyes dilate with horror when she hears the news of her mother's illness, and a trance-like state of horror and thralldom, which is likened to a bad dream, is the aftermath of Thornton's proposal to Margaret. Gaskell deploys the most highly gothicized imagery in the novel in order to express the specter of sexuality and Margaret's repudiation of the taboo knowledge of her attraction to Thornton:

The deep impression made by the interview, was like that of a horror in a dream; that will not leave the room although we waken up, and rub our eyes, and force a stiff rigid smile upon our lips. It is there – there, cowering and gibbering, with fixed ghastly eyes, in some corner of the chamber, listening to hear whether we dare to breathe of its presence to any one. And we dare not; poor cowards that we are! ... Hitherto she had not stirred from where he had left her; no outward circumstances had roused her out of the trance of thought in which she had been plunged by his last words ... (198)

For the most part in *North and South*, the language of shock and horror is absorbed into the realist texture of the novel's narration so that it rarely produces a gothic or melodramatic effect; the inner world's nightmare and fantasy are not aberrations but come to seem co-extensive with the ordinary workaday world, and are often largely undetected by others.[21]

Still, it is not difficult to understand why critics have sometimes described Gaskell's work as melodramatic. Her descriptions of powerful emotional response, especially taken out of context, do have an air of melodrama or exaggeration about them. So when Mr. Thornton sees Margaret with a man he does not know to be her brother, Gaskell draws on a varied artillery of metaphor and simile relating to haunting, fantasy, dream, pain and death to capture his agonized interior space:

[h]e was *haunted* by the remembrance of the handsome young man, with whom she stood in an attitude of such familiar confidence; and the remembrance *shot through him like an agony*, till it made him clench his hands tight in order to subdue the pain ... his trust dropped down *dead and powerless*: and all sorts of *wild fancies chased each other like dreams* through his mind. (Emphasis added; 270)

This is a great contrast to the usual Mr. Thornton; more often Gaskell draws attention to his keen observation, sensual perceptiveness and emotional control. At one point the narrator invites us to decipher his strong emotional response to his mother's slighting remarks about Margaret by describing her uncertain reading of him: Mrs. Thornton was "not sure of the nature of the emotions she had provoked. It was only their violence that was clear ... she could not read it. Still, it made her uneasy, – as the presence of all strong feeling, of which the cause is not fully understood or sympathized in, always has this effect" (186). There is nothing melodramatic about the restraint Thornton (and the narrator) exercises here. The fact that Mr. Thornton is usually in command of his feelings serves only to underline how greatly he suffers when they overpower him.

Gaskell represents intense emotional experience as undoing the equanimity and balance of the self. Indeed, it is often likened to bodily suffering in its threat to wholeness and health: Margaret's mother cries out *"as in some sharp agony"* at the mention of Frederick's name (129). There are several further examples where comparison is abandoned and Gaskell blurs the line between physical and mental anguish. The mutual influence of mind on body and body on mind is also implicitly demonstrated in the way she writes about the effects of emotions. Thus she gives physical form to painful thoughts, feelings, consciousness, and other states of mind that are mental and therefore intangible and invisible. Describing her shock in response to the letter about Frederick's mutiny, Mrs. Hale says, "I could hardly lift myself up to go and meet him – everything seemed to reel about me all at once" (108). In line with the emergent physiological psychology of the 1850s, Gaskell seems to emphasize the correlation between physiological and mental states, and the importance of the former in elucidating the latter. The most cogent example of the representation of agonized consciousness in terms of its physical aftermath is Mr. Thornton's visceral reaction to rejection: he is almost blinded by baffled passion, feels dizzy, and develops a violent headache. Going further, Gaskell shows the destabilizing effects of strong emotion on identity and self-knowledge. Thornton experiences confusion about the apparent incommensurability of the cause of his suffering in relation to the consequences. It is as if such a palpable aftermath ought to have had a more obviously disastrous cause to precipitate it.

When Mr Thornton had left the house that morning he was almost blinded by his baffled passion. He was as dizzy as if Margaret, instead of looking, and speaking, and moving like a tender graceful woman, had been a sturdy fish-wife, and given him a sound blow with her fists. He had positive bodily pain, – a violent headache, and a throbbing intermittent pulse. He could not bear the noise, the garish light, the continued rumble and movement of the street. He called himself a fool for suffering so, and yet he could not, at the moment, recollect the cause of his suffering, and whether it was adequate to the consequences it had produced. (207)

For a time the overpowering experience dominates consciousness, but then seems to subside: "[i]t seemed as though his deep mortification of yesterday, and the stunned purposeless course of the hours afterwards, had cleared away all the mists from his intellect" (212). Yet, as Gaskell shows, Thornton's self-congratulation at dispelling the effects of the emotion is premature. Powerful feelings return, unbidden, to arrest the mind's focus once more:

It seemed as though he gave way all at once; he was so languid that he could not control his thoughts; they would wander to her; they would bring back the scene, – not of his repulse and rejection the day before, but the looks, the actions of the day before that. He went along the crowded streets mechanically, winding in and out among the people, but never seeing them, – almost sick with longing for that one half hour. (213)

The narrative focus here on Thornton's wandering attention, and his lack of control over his mind, raises a well-aired question in mid-nineteenth-century physiology – the role of volition or will in controlling psychical states. States in which the will is suspended include wandering attention, reverie, abstraction, absence of mind, and signs of functioning by rote or habit while the mind is otherwise occupied. But as William Carpenter averred, the will

can determine what shall not be regarded by the Mind, through its power of keeping the Attention fixed in *some other direction;* and thus it can subdue the force of violent impulse, and give to the conflict of opposing motives a result quite different from that which would ensue without its interference. This exercise of the Will, moreover, if habitually exerted in certain directions, will tend to form the Character, by establishing a set of *acquired habitudes;* which no less than those dependent upon original constitution and circumstances, help to determine the working of the "Mechanism of Thought and Feeling."[22]

Throughout Carpenter's discussion of abstracted states of mind, he draws reverential attention to "the Will" as the commander of the ship, in the absence of which it runs without steering or direction. Another frequent analogy to express the relation between the will and the emotions or unconscious mind is that of horse and rider. Thus Carpenter:

[T]he relation between the Automatic activity of the body, and the Volitional direction by which it is utilized and directed, may be compared to the independent locomotive power of a horse under the guidance and control of a skilful rider ... Now and then, it is true, some unusual excitement calls forth the essential independence of the equine nature; the horse takes the bit between his teeth and runs away with his master; and it is for the time uncertain whether the independent energy of the one, or the controlling power of the other, will obtain mastery.[23]

While Carpenter's focus on order and control and his advocacy of vigorous mental training has been linked to the Unitarian preoccupation with education and self-regulation,[24] Gaskell herself, also a Unitarian, seems more ready to explore what may emerge in states where self-control is destabilized. She is interested in why the horse takes the bit and runs away, as it were. The text is not quick to dispel those states in which the force of feeling precipitates shifts in ordinary consciousness. Rather more tolerant of such lapses in ordinary consciousness, Gaskell uses states of suspended will in order to explore what lies under the surface – who we are or what we feel when we are not ourselves. The difference between Gaskell and Carpenter is her implicit sense that the undermining of self-control and will can at times be useful and informative – a condition, even, for new growth and change.[25]

Gaskell would of course not dispute the importance of will and rational control. There are several examples in the novel of the dangers of intemperate response: Frederick's mutinous reaction to injustice; the ancestor, "old Sir John" Beresford, who shot his steward for insulting him; and, in an especially stereotypic representation of primitive, working-class mob mentality, the strikers who watch "open-eyed and open-mouthed, the thread of dark-red blood which wakened them up from their trance of passion" (179). While this collective "trance of passion" is a very dangerous thing, the many states of trance or abstraction that Gaskell evokes in the novel are not generally feared as dangerous paths to unreason and not seen as undermining the will in a threatening way. *North and South* undoes the familiar dichotomy of passion and reason, which are less dramatically oppositional in this novel (than say in Brontë's *Jane Eyre*) and more mutually informative. Recognizing the precariousness of the coherent and stable subject, as is evident in her lively epistolary account of her "many me's" (the epigraph of this chapter), Gaskell inflects Carpenter's model of selfhood so that it can less threateningly accommodate the displacement of a vigilant, governing consciousness.

Her open-mindedness is here literally that – an attention to the mind opened to its unconscious processes. Significantly, only after the torment of love has opened Thornton up to his capacity to feel strongly is he capable of responding to Higgins. It is not so much Margaret's beneficent womanly and emotional influence that is the cause of this transformation as the almost magical effect of Thornton's own powerful emotions that renders him receptive. That Thornton has always been shown as someone of keen and sensitive perception, highly attuned to his consciousness of those around him, prepares for his responsiveness to powerful emotional states.

He notices that the Hales don't like the wall-paper and instructs their landlord to alter it; he is struck by the contrast between Higgins's bent figure and determined way of speaking, which prompts him to find out that the worker had waited five hours to speak to him about employment. Immediately responsive to Margaret on a sensual level, he minutely observes the bracelet tightened about her flesh as she is pouring and serving tea, and the way her father uses her fingers pincer-like in place of sugar tongs; he is highly conscious when they do shake hands that this is the first time they have touched, a fact of which she is quite unaware. And when he brings the fruit to her ailing mother the day after he has declared himself to her, he is hyperconscious of her presence in the room, even though he never looks at her. Often described as unfeeling, he is less unfeeling than controlled.

Thornton's powerful feelings for Margaret destabilize his ability to check or compartmentalize emotional responses. After it strikes Thornton that Higgins must have been waiting five hours to speak to him, he spends two hours of his own time verifying Higgins's account of himself.

He tried not to be, but was convinced that all that Higgins had said was true. And then the conviction went in, *as if by some spell,* and touched the latent tenderness of his heart; the patience of the man, the simple generosity of the motive (for he learnt about the quarrel between Boucher and Higgins), made him forget entirely the mere reasonings of justice, and overleap them by a diviner instinct. (Emphasis added; 325)

Here Gaskell describes the change in Thornton's attitude to Higgins as the effect of a spell, as if some emotional alchemy has been at work. And though she uses the language of enchantment in describing the process, she is not being evasive or mystifying the nature of his changed attitude. There is some unknown and mysterious way in which feelings unconsciously act upon judgment and in so doing "overleap" justice with mercy and humanity. Thornton, the self-made man, must be slightly unmade by the ministration of tenderness and vulnerability. As Higgins aptly remarks to Mr. Hale, "He's two chaps. One chap I knowed of old as were measter all o'er. T'other chap hasn't an ounce of measter's flesh about him. How them two chaps is bound up in one body, is a craddy for me to find out" (339).

A further instance of Gaskell's interest in abstracted states that suspend will and volition occurs in relation to Thornton's delayed consciousness of Margaret's embrace of him in the mob scene. When Margaret throws her arms around Mr. Thornton to protect him from the strikers, he shakes her off without really thinking about what she has done. Absorbed in his thoughts about the threatening crowd, "he had pushed her aside, and spoken gruffly; he had seen nothing but the unnecessary danger she had placed herself in" (181). But later on, when he is no longer responding to the urgency of the situation with the strikers, he belatedly recalls the feeling of her arms being around him, at which point he cannot stop thinking about it.[26] The idea of delayed or belated recall, along with the concept of latent knowledge, is nicely articulated in this scene. Gaskell seems to be suggesting that an extreme state of emotion can prevent the subject from consciously registering aspects of the experience, but that, once the emotion has passed, the unnoticed elements may intrude upon consciousness to be experienced anew. In this perception are the seeds of what later psychologists will focus on as the belated witnessing or delayed recall of events too overwhelming to process as they are happening.

Gaskell thus looks forward to the examples of latency that begin to accrue in descriptions of survivors of shocking railway accidents, which provided examples of those who walk away from the train accident apparently unharmed, only to manifest psychical and physical symptoms at a later date. She clearly understands the gap between perception and cognition and the belatedness or latency of knowledge to which these examples allude. Recall is available after the fact, but the experience has been unrecognized at the moment of occurrence, suggesting that the violence of powerful feelings (falling in love, in this instance) is about breach and vulnerability.

As we have seen, mental physiologists wrote lengthily about the curious phenomenon of double consciousness in which the subject was able to remember things in an altered state of consciousness that he or she did not know under normal circumstances. Gaskell does not probe the conundrum of how we can know at some level what is beyond recall or conscious knowledge; nor does she enter contemporary debates about whether the mind is just a physical organ like others in the body, and, if so, how one accounts for "spirit" or soul. Nonetheless, her implicit model of a layered self – composed of conscious and unconscious elements – sheds light on her treatment of impulsive action, especially when it works to call into question the subject's governing self-image or undermine her sense of integrity. Several recent critics have written about Gaskell's refusal of absolutes and embracing of complexity and even contradiction in this novel: "We constantly witness the crumbling of absolutes, the clear becoming irresolute, the iron will a vulnerable flesh."[27] Deeply skeptical about solutions and abidingly interrogative, her scrutiny turns also in *North and South* to question the unitary and integrated nature of the self.

ACCOUNTABILITY AND THE DISCONTINUOUS SELF

By the late nineteenth century, the medical discourse of shock was firmly tied to the question of legal responsibility – who should pay damages and for what injury. Similarly, the discourse of trance, as George Beard summarized it, centered round the question of responsibility for action and required the expert testimony of doctors to pronounce on account-ability. What engages Gaskell in her exploration of shock and the dazed or entranced mind is likewise the question of responsibility, self-knowledge and coherence.

In particular, Margaret's two impulsive public responses – saving Thornton from the mob and lying to a policeman to save her brother – both involve actions which seem to arise from a part of the self that is not under conscious control.[28] "You forgot yourself in thought for another," explains Mr. Bell (396–97), who helps Margaret to rationalize the lie by referring to the "temptation" as "strong, instinctive motive" (397). The self forgotten or possessed is invoked to explain both these impulsive actions: Margaret wonders "what possessed" her to defend Thornton. And after she has told the lie to save Frederick,

> she tried to recall the force of her temptation, by endeavouring to remember the details which had thrown her into such deadly fright; but she could not. She only understood two facts – that Frederick had been in danger of being pursued and detected in London as not only guilty of manslaughter, but as the more unpardonable leader of the mutiny, and that she had lied to save him. (277)

Each of these occasions on which Margaret feels possessed or cannot recall what prompted her action is also accompanied by a scene of swooning or loss of consciousness. After Margaret has confronted the mob and lies injured,

> she could no more have opened her eyes, or spoken to ask for more bathing, than the people who lie in death-like trance can move, or utter sound, to arrest the awful preparations for their burial, while they are yet fully aware, not merely of the actions of those around them, but of the idea that is the motive for such actions. (183)

The death-like trance to which Margaret's state of insensibility is likened is a powerful image of apparent unconsciousness and powerless cognition. She may appear unconscious but she is aware of the "burial" of her reputation as she hears how her protection of Thornton has been (mis)construed. Later she struggles to maintain her precarious hold on consciousness:

Margaret's thoughts were quite alive enough to the present to make her desirous of getting rid of both Mr. Lowe and the cab before she reached Crampton Crescent, for fear of alarming her father and mother. Beyond that one aim she would not look. That ugly dream of insolent words spoken about herself, could never be forgotten – but could be put aside till she was stronger – for, oh! She was very weak; and her mind sought for some present fact to steady itself upon, and keep it from utterly losing consciousness in another hideous, sickly swoon. (185)

The "ugly dream" rather than the confrontation with a violent mob is what dominates consciousness here, and looks forward to the "gibbering" horror of a dream that follows Thornton's proposal. Often indicated by blushing and feelings of shame, Margaret's knowledge and awareness of herself as sexually attractive is repeatedly denied as it is simultaneously recognized and commented on by others. Lennox's proposal arouses her shame at being seen as a marriageable woman. The factory men who comment imperti- nently on her looks inspire "dread" and "fright," but also call up "a flash of indignation which made her face scarlet" (72). In Margaret's impulsive protectiveness of Thornton and subsequent question – "what possessed me?" – Gaskell attempts to unpack the nature of dissociated or inadmissible knowledge. Without using the term "subconscious," Gaskell is nevertheless drawing close to the idea it conveys of a part of the mind that is not fully conscious but is able to influence actions and behavior.[29]

The second of the two scenes that show Margaret abstracted from herself deploys much the same language of altered states, and takes place after she is forced to lie about Frederick's presence. While Margaret's lie is impulsive, springing up from a need to protect Frederick, its execution makes of her an automaton, a somnambulist, whose actions come from another place than ordinary consciousness: "'I was not there,' said Margaret, still keeping her expressionless eyes fixed on his face, with the unconscious look of a sleep-walker" (273). She later repeats the lie, again with a "glassy, dream-like stare" so that the policeman's "quick suspicions were aroused by this dull echo of her former denial. It was as if she had forced herself to one untruth and had been stunned out of all power of varying it" (274). When the policeman leaves, "[s]he kept her eyes upon him in the same dull, fixed manner, until he was fairly out of the house. She shut the door, and went into the study ... paused – tottered forward – paused again – swayed for an instant where she stood and fell prone on the floor in a dead swoon" (275). Margaret's swooning, loss of conscious- ness and stunned faculties put her in the company of many a fainting Victorian heroine. But in several other situations of crisis Margaret behaves with strength and fortitude where ordinary women might have succumbed. Confronted with Boucher's bloated and disfigured body, she covers his face, and sets about breaking the news to his family. On a prior occasion, the doctor who tells her about her mother's poor health says to himself: "[I]t's astonishing how much those thorough-bred creatures can do and suffer. That girl's game to the back-bone. Another, who had gone that deadly colour, could never have come round without either fainting or hysterics. But she wouldn't do either … And the very force of her will brought her round" (127). Such instances prompt us to look beyond the merely theatrical effect of her fainting fit in this instance.

While the narrator offers us the view that lying is so alien to Margaret that she is incapable of being inventive or varied, the text also suggests that, in lying, Margaret is "not herself." The sense of dissociated consciousness that is conveyed serves to exculpate Margaret (though she roundly condemns herself) from full responsibility for her actions. Both actions muddy the ideal of clear moral behavior, straightforward and beyond reproach. The incident recalls Mary Barton's crisis in court where she attempts to defend Jem without divulging her father's guilt. Gaskell is less probing of Mary's decision to shield her father and more dramatic in imagining the threat to sanity that her self-division entails. In place of Mary's brain fever, Margaret suffers the lesser collapse of a swoon, but only temporarily, so that the narrator can resume exploration of Margaret's mind in the aftermath of the lie. Although Gaskell does not resolve the question of moral responsibility for actions that seem to contradict one's avowed and consciously held principles, she does use the experience to unsettle Margaret by opening her up to her own fallibility.

The text's tacit knowledge is that, despite cultural anxiety about the work of the unconscious mind when it escapes from the control of a governing will, the self that acts when entranced or transfixed by powerful emotions may indeed be a force for good – an unlicensed agent but an effective one that does not necessarily leave one, as in Beard's examples, standing on the train tracks in the face of an oncoming train. In Gaskell, experiences of mental shock, pain and violence of feeling are disruptive but not debilitating. While they may numb or stun the faculties, they do not result in sustained loss of memory or identity and their haunting potential is harnessed as a possibility of growth. If her representations of stunned consciousness do anticipate later formulations of trauma, they are never simply or narrowly personal but always viewed in terms of their larger social implications. Reading the novel with attention to the movement of the narrator into the recesses of consciousness, reading with an ear for the language of dreams and abstracted states through which the narrator adumbrates the mysterious but influential realm beyond ordinary consciousness, we recover what a focus on external action and event cannot provide. Far from being formulaic melodramatic effects, the novel's crises of inner life and consciousness are an integral part of Gaskell's attempts to chart the social transformations of mid-century England and understand the forces of feeling and unconscious life that jolt the individual into self-scrutiny and renewed engagement with the outside world.

CHAPTER 3

Memory and aftermath: from Dickens's "The Signalman" to The Mystery of Edwin Drood

In 1865 Charles Dickens narrowly escaped death when the train on which he was traveling from Folkestone to London jumped a gap in the line occasioned by some repair work on a viaduct near Staplehurst, Kent. The foreman on the job miscalculated the time of the train's arrival; the flagman was only 550 yards from the works and unable to give adequate warning of the train's approach. The central and rear carriages fell off the bridge, plunging onto the river-bed below. Only one of the first-class carriages escaped that plunge, coupled fast to the second-class carriage in front: "It had come off the rail and was ... hanging over the bridge at an angle, so that all three of them were tilted down into a corner."[1] Dickens managed to get Ellen Ternan and her mother, with whom he was traveling, out of the carriage and then behaved with remarkable self-possession, climbing down into the ravine and ministering to the many who lay injured and dying. With further aplomb, he climbed back into the dangerously unstable carriage and retrieved his manuscript, a fear which is recounted in the memorable postscript to *Our Mutual Friend* (1865).

Once back in London, however, Dickens began to develop the symptoms that today we would recognize as typical of trauma.[2] He was greatly shaken and lost his voice for nearly two weeks: "I most unaccountably brought someone else's out of that terrible scene," he said. He suffered repeatedly from what he called "the shake," and, when he later traveled by train, he was in the grip of a persistent illusion that the carriage was down on the left side. Even a year later, he noted that he had sudden vague rushes of terror, which were "perfectly unreasonable but unsurmountable." At such times, his son and daughter reported, he was unaware of the presence of others and seemed to be in a kind of trance. His son Henry recalled that he got into a state of panic at the slightest jolt; Mamie attested that her father's nerves were never really the same again: he would "fall into a paroxysm of fear, tremble all over, and clutch the arms of the railway carriage." An uncanny repetition also characterizes his death, falling as it did on the anniversary of the accident five years later.[3]

It is well known that Dickens was engaged throughout his literary career in representations of the railroad and used it to various effects, often combining the "humorous and the horrific."[4] Most memorable perhaps is the personification of the engine in *Dombey and Son* (1848) as a bloodthirsty monster, Death itself. There the railway as a predatory fiend that licks up the tracks and whatever falls in its path not only is identified with the villain Carker, himself predatory and cat-like, but is his nemesis.[5] It would be unwise to claim, therefore, that the accident must have provoked his short story about railway disaster, "The Signalman" (1866), which appeared a year later as part of "Mugby Junction," the special Christmas issue of *All the Year Round*. Yet there is, I want to argue, an integral connection between Dickens's experience of the accident and its aftermath and this ghost story. While the fact of Dickens's own experience of the train crash has sometimes been acknowledged in discussions of "The Signalman," it is usually by way of a closing gesture to the grim and eerie irony that he died five years later on the same day as the accident. To read "The Signalman" in light of questions raised by current trauma theory, however, is to see that Dickens's story uncannily apprehends subsequent formulations of traumatic experience in its focus on the uncoupling of event and conscious cognition, on belatedness, repetitive and intrusive return, and on a sense of powerlessness at impending disaster. The question that this reading of the story then raises is what conceptions of shock and its aftermath could have provided Dickens in the 1860s with a hermeneutic through which to respond to his experience. That question draws us to consider both the pre-Freudian history of trauma and the relation between literature and the psychological and medical discourse of its day.

Freud himself remarked in *Beyond the Pleasure Principle* (1920) that there is "a condition [which] has *long been known and described* [and] which occurs after severe mechanical concussions, railway disasters and other accidents involving a risk to life; it has been given the name of 'traumatic neurosis'" (emphasis added).[6] As I have discussed previously, the technology of the railway not only revolutionized travel and conceptions of time and space but gave rise to large-scale, disastrous accidents. The damage to life and limb resulting from such accidents provoked claims against the railroad companies, and these in turn produced the need for insurance companies. Insurance companies were reluctant to pay damages for anything except demonstrable physical injury consequent on the accident. Medical practitioners called upon to verify injury found their attention focused on hitherto unexamined forms of suffering. As a result, the question of injurious effects not consequent on gross mechanical injury but apparently the result of the shock of the accident became a vexed and contentious one in mid-Victorian medicine. Exploring the effects of modernity in the form of railway travel, its disasters, and the statistical risks associated with indemnification and insurance, we encounter an emerging discourse of psychic shock that stands behind the development of trauma theory.[7]

Occupied as it is with trains and railway disaster, this section follows a number of different tracks. First I sketch out the development of a medical discourse about railway shock in the 1860s. Psychic shock, as we have seen in the previous chapter, was certainly a subject of literary and medical interest before the 1860s, but at this time it came to be viewed as a medical condition worthy of notice and study as a result of modern technology and its effects. (This position does not preclude the possibility that the technology was indeed responsible for an increased incidence of psychical disturbance.) Freud was interested in what happened to the traumatized patient's memory – whether shocking events were processed and available to recall in the same way as other experiences. The focus on memory and flashback enabled Freud to remark on the peculiar bypassing of conscious memory that seemed to characterize response to trauma. In contrast, the Victorian discourse of nervous shock focused mainly on the effects on the nervous system; the effect of shock on memory is not something that particularly occupies Victorian doctors probing the psychic damage of railway accidents. Why did the Victorians not turn their attention to the connection between shock and memory dysfunction? What conceptions of memory and particularly "unconscious" memory were prevalent in the mid-Victorian period?

In order to probe these questions, I then switch tracks to examine those psychological domains where the Victorians *did* study memory. Here I discuss Carpenter's emphasis on the automatic nature of memory, but also his recognition of emotional memory – the way emotions may make evaluations and carry ideas unavailable to the conscious mind. Victorian theories of latency, as well as the modification and fallacy of memory are also relevant, as are Victorian constructions of memory under extraordinary but not necessarily traumatic conditions – altered states, such as somnambulism, trance, mesmerism, hypnotism.[8] Under what circumstances is memory lost or retrieved? By what mnemonic mechanism can knowledge unavailable to the conscious mind emerge in unusual situations? How, in sum, did Victorians formulate the relationship between conscious memory and what Christopher Bollas has aptly called "the unthought known?" These two tracks connect Victorian psychology (in hindsight) to the discourse of trauma from Freud on to the late-twentieth-century theorizings of Cathy Caruth, Shoshana Felman, Dori Laub and others, which is preeminently focused on memory and its dysfunctions, on belatedness, repetition, flashback and hallucination. I will then turn to Dickens's story "The Signalman" to uncover a subterranean route or switch whereby these two apparently distinct tracks come together (and thus are more nearly resonant with current trauma studies). I will suggest that "The Signalman" provides a link between the Victorian discourse of nervous shock and Victorian conceptions of unconscious memory. The discursive development of shock in the mid 1860s may have provided Dickens with a hermeneutic through which he could respond to his own experience, but, more significantly, his sensitivity to altered states of consciousness and the literary possibilities of the ghost story – a favored genre – helped him to articulate what the nascent study of the psychic wound at this time was not quite yet poised to formulate.

Railway shock

In or around the mid 1860s, the medical concept of a psychic wound or injury began to percolate in Victorian Britain. And what brought it most forcibly to consciousness was the railway. To place the railway more squarely within the history of trauma, we may say that the railway accident was to Victorian psychology what World War I and shell-shock were to Freudian psychology. The railway accident was, as Ian Hacking points out, "the epic symbol of the psychologization of trauma"; it was the exemplary instance for Victorian medical discourse that propelled the prevailing pathological bias in relation to injury in the direction of a psychic interpretation of injury.[9] Industrialization and the rise of the insurance company were the twin economic factors in the development of medical interest in this subject. As Henri Ellenberger notes in his magisterial history of the discovery of the unconscious, "the development of industry and the multiplication of industrial accidents on the one side, and the development of insurance companies on the other," meant that "[m]ore and more 'official medicine' was on the search for new theories and new therapeutic methods for these neuroses."[10] Similarly, Wolfgang Schivelbusch's 1978 study of the railway journey, which lays the tracks for all future studies in this line, points out that in England by 1864 railroad companies had become legally liable for their passengers' safety and health; since only "pathologically demonstrable ... damage" qualified victims for compensation, those victims who suffered damages without a demonstrable cause created "a legal and medical problem whose solution in the courts depended on the medical profession."[11]

In the 1860s the "phenomenon of accident shock," the traumatization of a victim without discernible physical injury, became the object of systematic investigation by the medical profession.[12] Thomas Buzzard, for example, a doctor whose series of articles appeared in the *Lancet* in 1867, was very interested in cases where external injuries were negligible but effects on the nervous system were severe. In one case, he noted, the shock changed the very national constitution of an individual, who transformed from "the most thorough Englishman in all his habits to the manner of the most coxcombical Frenchman."[13] In the next decades, Herbert Page, whose work I have discussed in previous chapters, would focus more closely on fright or shock, but would pay attention largely to its effects on the nervous system – hysterical fits, spasms, vomiting, pulse rate and so on. And though he notes the effect of shock on memory, it is merely to say that it affects energy and concentration rather than the recall of events and incidents of past life.[14] He does, however, record that patients suffering from traumatic hysteria some- times have a "great dread of impending evil."[15] They usually sleep badly and are constantly troubled by distressing dreams: "Depend upon it that the man who can sleep naturally and well after a railway collision has not met with any serious shock to his nervous system."[16] He notes too the element of delay or belatedness which will become so important in the Freudian conceptualization of trauma: "Warded off in the first place by the excite- ment of the scene, the shock is gathering, in the very delay itself, new force from the fact that the sources of alarm are continuous, and for the time all prevalent in the patient's mind."[17] The emphasis on a "continuous" and "prevalent" source of alarm suggests the possession of the patient by the shocking event. William James explained delay by means of the following example in his 1894 review of Pierre Janet's work: "The fixed ideas may slumber until some weakening of the nervous system favors their morbid activity. E.g., Col. is victim of a railroad accident, and passes six months in the hospital with a grave abdominal injury ... [Six years later] if the old scar be touched, [he suffers] an hysterical attack ... consisting in hallucinations of the railroad tragedy."[18]

Even this very brief history serves to contextualize and explain Freud's references in *Beyond the Pleasure Principle* to "a condition [which] has long been known and described."[19] Having acknowledged the lengthy history of traumatic neurosis, Freud then proceeds to offer the recent war (World War I) as the defining moment for the diagnosis of psychic shock. On the one hand, Freud indicates a familiarity with the phenomenon of railway trauma; on the other, he seems not to acknowledge the medical studies that had already, for some decades, focused on the absence of gross mechanical force:

> The terrible war which has just ended gave rise to a great number of illnesses of this kind, but it at least put an end to the temptation to attribute the cause of the disorder to organic lesions of the nervous system brought about by mechanical force ... In the case of the war neuroses the fact that the same symptoms sometimes came about without the intervention of any gross mechanical force seemed at once enlightening and bewildering.[20]

Freud's study of shell-shocked soldiers' dreams provided him with an important insight into the nature of dreams. He noticed that the dreams of the traumatized were markedly different from those of ordinary dreamers, in that they woke the patient up "in another fright"; they returned him to the scene of horror, reproducing it repeatedly and literally, whereas ordinary dream work consisted of creating scenarios to express fears and desires.[21] Dreaming allowed ordinary patients to release anxieties and so keep sleeping; traumatic dreams woke the patient, and were therefore unable to appease anxiety. This insight in relation to traumatized soldiers allowed Freud to theorize what he had remarked in a less obvious way in his earlier work on traumatic neurosis. The hallmark of trauma, Freud decided, was the inability to possess memory, to make the event the subject of narrative. The memory seemed to possess the sufferer rather than the other way around. Hence Caruth's rearticulation of Freud: "to be traumatized is ... to be possessed by an image or event." It has been suggested that trauma involves the collapse of witnessing and understanding, in that the event can only be witnessed at the cost of recognizing oneself as a witness: "Central to the very immediacy of this experience, that is, is a gap that carries the force of the event and does so precisely at the expense of simple knowledge and memory. The force of this experience would appear to arise precisely ... in the collapse of understanding."[22] Trauma, then, comes to be theorized (albeit contentiously) as the experience in which knowledge and conscious cognition are disjoined. Geoffrey Hartman describes this as the missed encounter, the event "registered rather than experienced," in that the traumatic event bypasses "perception and consciousness, and falls directly into the psyche."[23] The knowledge that the traumatized subject stores is inaccessible to ordinary memory, but signals its presence in the form of intrusive return. It is as if the encounter, having been missed, demands recognition through reenactment rather than recall.

The latency and fallacy of memory

> If any one faculty of our nature may be called *more* wonderful than the
> rest, I do think it is memory. There seems something more speakingly
> incomprehensible in the powers, the failures, the inequalities of mem-
> ory, than in any other of our intelligences. The memory is sometimes
> so retentive, so serviceable, so obedient – at others, so bewildered and
> so weak – and at others again, so tyrannic, so beyond controul! We are
> to be sure a miracle every way – but our powers of recollecting and of
> forgetting, do seem peculiarly past finding out.
>
> Jane Austen, *Mansfield Park*[24]

Fanny Price's awareness of the vagaries of memory serves to indicate what,
by the mid nineteenth century, had become the focus of much scrutiny –
those aspects of memory that seemed "peculiarly past finding out": our
powers of "recollecting and of forgetting," and the operations of unconscious memory. From the first, Freud's work, unlike that of his Victorian
predecessors, emphasized the effects of shock on memory. In the review
mentioned earlier, James writes also of the studies of two "distinguished
Viennese neurologists" for whom hysteria "starts always with a shock, and is
a 'disease of the memory.'"[25] Victorian physiologists and psychologists
writing about memory are, however, little interested in the effect of
shock, though physical blows to the head prove perennially engaging.[26] In
his 1860 treatise, *On Obscure Diseases of the Brain, and Disorders of the Mind*,
Forbes Winslow does give some examples of the disruptions in memory
after shock, but these are in effect a cabinet of curiosities drawn from cases
reported in the previous century rather than a thoroughgoing investigation
of what makes one remember or forget in response to extraordinary stimulus. One case, for example, concerns a "lady of rank" who

experienced a severe shock consequent upon the receipt of the melancholy intelligence of the sudden death of an only and much-beloved child. She continued for
several days in a stunned and apparently dying state. She, however, recovered. For
many months afterwards her memory exhibited a singular defect. She appeared to
have no recollection of the cause of her illness, and of the severe loss she had
sustained. When she was informed of the death of her son, for the period of a
minute she appeared to realize the melancholy fact; but the impression almost
instantly passed away. About nine months from this time she was found dead in her
bed. Disease of the heart and brain was said to have been discovered after death.[27]

And as we have seen in Chapter 1, there are a few instances in medical
discussions of the Franco-Prussian war where memory loss is mentioned. In
Diseases of Memory (1881, translated in 1882), Theodule Ribot, well known
for his work in France on physiological psychology, cites cases in which

memory actually becomes more intense in abnormal states and undergoes permanent improvement after illness and shock:

[A] man with "a remarkably clear head" ... was crossing a railway in the country when an express train at full speed appeared closely approaching him. He had just time to throw himself down in the center of the road between the two lines of rails, and as the vast train passed over him, the sentiment of impending danger to his very existence brought vividly into his recollection every incident of his former life in such an array as that which is suggested by the promised opening of "the great book at the last great day." Even allowing for exaggeration, these instances show a superintensity of action on the part of the memory of which we can have no idea in its normal state.[28]

Ribot rehearses here the widely credited idea that all memory is stored and recoverable. He operates on the assumption that the "normal state" of memory is merely a less intense version of the "superintensity" occasioned by an extreme situation. The "normal state" of memory is a happy relationship of storage and retrieval, an archive under good management. If memory was thought of as a storehouse of previous thoughts, a klepto-maniac's secret hoard, an engraving or even a photograph, the assumption that unusual conditions could suddenly assist in bringing to light the further reaches of such stores is understandable in its appeal. Noting that others have already commented on the remarkable and permanent devel-opment of memory after shocks, attacks of smallpox and other diseases, Ribot concludes that "the mechanism of this metamorphosis being inscrutable, there is no reason why we should dwell on it here."[29] The case histories recited by Winslow and Ribot suggest that the erasure and recovery of memory are equally mysterious processes. Why the one occurs as opposed to the other is as inscrutable as the "mechanism of metamor-phosis" itself. What seems undisputed, however, is the miraculous latency of memory.

In *Principles of Mental Physiology* (1874), William Benjamin Carpenter, probably the most authoritative voice on memory in mid-Victorian mental physiology, sets out the prevailing view of the latency or dormancy of all memory:

It is now very generally accepted by Psychologists as (to say the least) a predictable doctrine, that any Idea which has once passed through the Mind may be thus reproduced, at however long an interval, through the instrumentality of suggestive action; the recurrence of any other state of consciousness with which that idea was originally linked by Association, being adequate to awaken it also from its dormant or "latent" condition, and to bring it within the "sphere of consciousness."[30]

Drawing on the image of the railway, which frequently crops up as an apt structuring metaphor in explanations of the relation between conscious and unconscious thinking, Carpenter continues:

And as our ideas are thus linked in "trains" or "series," which further inosculate with each other like the branch lines of a railway or the ramifications of an artery, so, it is considered, an idea which has been "hidden in the obscure recesses of the mind" for years – perhaps for a lifetime, – and which seems to have completely faded out of the *conscious* Memory ... may be reproduced, as by the touching of a spring, through a *nexus* of suggestions, which we can sometimes trace-out continuously, but of which it does not seem necessary that all the intermediate steps should fall within our cognizance.[31]

Similarly, E. S. Dallas's *The Gay Science* (1866) draws on the idea of traffic between related spheres. The railway being such a visible aspect of modernity in Victorian life, it is not surprising that railway tracks, networks, trains of thought, and lines of communication should come to the aid of those explaining the activity of invisible modes of thought, and, indeed, influence the very way in which the mind's operations could be visualized. A study of psychology and aesthetics, Dallas's text includes a discussion of imagination – the unconscious, or the hidden soul – in its evaluation of current theories of memory: "Between the outer and the inner ring, between our unconscious and our conscious existence, there is a free and a constant but unobserved traffic for ever carried on. Trains of thought are continually passing to and fro, from the light into the dark, and back from the dark into the light."[32] One might phrase the matter more succinctly, as Dickens has Mr. Toodle in *Dombey and Son* (1848) sagely remark: "What a Junction a man's thoughts is ... to be sure!"[33]

The idea of memory as a treasure house of stored and recuperable knowledge was notably challenged in the early 1860s by Frances Power Cobbe's emphasis on the fallacies of memory. What we remember – she argued in opposition to the idea of the permanent register, the engraved tablet – are layered reconstructions of memories, where each "fresh trace varies a little from the trace beneath, sometimes magnifying and beautifying it, through the natural bias of the soul to grandeur and beauty, sometimes ... distorting it through passion or prejudice; in all and every case the original mark is ere long essentially changed."[34] What Cobbe describes here is akin to that which trauma theorists such as Judith Herman (following Janet) would describe as normal, narrative memory. Narrative memory is simply memory that is available for recall and retelling. It can be made the subject of narrative. It is possessed by the subject who remembers and it is inevitably shaped by distortions and biases in the process of narrativization. In contrast, traumatic memory is that which lies inaccessible and unpossessed. It is not at the disposal of the subject, but rather able itself to possess the unremembering subject by obtruding on the present in the form of dreams, flashbacks and hallucinations. It was after all the very literalness of the traumatic memory or dream that alerted Freud to the fact that the process of registering traumatic events and experiences was out of the ordinary. On that basis, we might argue that what made it possible for Freud to recognize traumatic memory was the very normalization of distortion, or what Cobbe calls fallacy.

Until Cobbe's emphasis on the fallacies of memory, Victorian ideas about memory as an accurate if not always accessible inventory were dominant. As in the case of the young woman reciting Latin and Greek texts, memory was thought to be an archive of preserved and uncontaminated knowledge. It will not escape notice that this view of memory is what became Freud's literal, unchanged and therefore "traumatic memory." Moreover, the peculiar nature of "traumatic memory" is precisely what is in contention among the critics of trauma theory described in Chapter 1. Ruth Leys writes of the dominant but contested view of traumatized memory as that which in its "insistent literality, testifies to the existence of a pristine and timeless historical truth undistorted or uncontaminated by subjective meaning, personal cognitive schemes, psychosocial factors, or unconscious symbolic elaboration."[35]

As Victorian discourse on memory absorbs the idea of subjective or unconscious distortion, so it can be seen to till the ground of subsequent debates in trauma theory. Acknowledging Cobbe's views on the fallacies of memory, Carpenter also challenges the doctrine of memory's indelibility, suggesting that it has been too generally applied; it is questionable "whether *everything* that passes through our Minds thus leaves its impression on their material instrument."[36] Carpenter suggests that we sometimes visualize so strongly that we

realise … forgotten experiences, by repeatedly picturing them to ourselves, … the ideas of them attain a force and vividness which equals or even exceeds that which the actual memory of them would afford. In like manner, when the Imagination has been exercised in a sustained and determinate manner, – as in the composition of a work of fiction, – its ideal creations may be reproduced with the force of actual experiences; and the sense of personal identity may be projected backwards (so to speak) into the characters which the Author has "evolved out of the depths of his own consciousness," – as Dickens states to have been continually the case with himself.[37]

The process Carpenter outlines is the exercise of the imagination in creating something apparently fictitious that then assumes a life of its own and, in becoming that with which the author identifies, is able to show him what was hidden or covert within him. The author both creates himself and reveals himself through his characters, an intense form of the process detectable in all memory "creation." And, not unexpectedly, Dickens provides an example in Carpenter's explanations, coming to mind as the author most readily associated with imaginative intensity and creative memory. Like Cobbe's fallacies of memory, Carpenter's recognition of "the sense of personal identity projected backwards" contains the seeds of later conceptions of recovered and false memory.

While the tenor of Carpenter's discussion is to question how far the "doctrine of indelibility" extends, he does specify that certain categories of experience are indelible. One of these is especially pertinent to ideas about trauma: "Single experiences of peculiar force and vividness, such as are likely to have left very decided 'traces,' although the circumstances of their formation were so unusual as to keep them out of ordinary Associational remembrance."[38] Carpenter refers by way of example to a case (cited in the 1830s by John Abercrombie) involving a fifteen-year-old boy who, while suffering from delirium, recalled aspects of surgery he had undergone at the age of four. He was able to remember scenes he could only have "witnessed" while unconscious and very young. Carpenter's "single experience of peculiar force" indelible and yet unavailable to ordinary associative memory is not unrelated to Freud's traumatic event, the experience of which is unremembered yet belatedly, intrusively and literally asserted. The point of Carpenter's example is that the boy was not "there" in consciousness and hence one would not have expected him to be able to remember details of the operation; in the case of trauma, the subject is apparently "there" and conscious – so it was expected that physically unscathed victims of railway accidents be able to recall their experiences. It was only after the connection was made between accident shock and the absent state of mind associated with trance, mesmerism or hypnotism that the altered consciousness, and therefore altered memory, of the patient became important. After considering shell-shocked soldiers, Freud theorized trauma as a category of experience that was inaccessible to memory in a different way from the repressions of the unconscious. Whereas ordinary dreams were the royal road to the unconscious, the dreams and hallucinations of traumatized patients were too literal and self-referential to lead anywhere but back to the traumatic event itself. They were a reliving rather than a representation of the event, a snapshot rather than a symbology.[39] This is to say that the Freudian concept of trauma takes its meaning differentially from the related concepts of unconscious repression and symbolic elaboration.

While ideas about memory's distortions and the possibility of unconscious and latent modifications were seriously entertained by mental physiologists, the abiding emphasis in Carpenter's work is on memory as an
automatic process. By automatic, Carpenter means that the mechanisms of
memory go on beyond consciousness. Thus he explains that, if a long period
has elapsed since he last spoke French, he encounters difficulty in recalling
French words and phrases. After being in France for a few weeks, however,
he again finds himself starting to think in French: "The Physiologist would
say that the nerve-tracks which disuse has rendered imperfect, have restored
themselves by use; so that the part of the brain which has recorded the
Language, has been brought back into ready connection with that which
ministers to the current play of ordinary Thought."[40] Indeed, he suggests
that, because "there is no part of our Mental action, in which what the Will
can and what it *cannot* do is more clearly distinguishable, it will be worth
while to dwell somewhat on the subject."[41] Although we cannot through the
force of will summon memory, we can focus attention on associated ideas
and go back over the train of thought. Memory may be an automatic
function of the brain, Carpenter concedes, but the culture and discipline
that surround it are certainly volitional and it can be guided and disciplined
by the will. When memory functions automatically, the state of mind of the
subject is akin to other altered states of mind – dreaming, drunkenness and
delirium – in which "the directing power of the Will is suspended, while the
Automatic power of the Brain is in full play."[42]

Memory is furthermore closely linked to emotion, not in the more obvious
sense that "memory supplies the emotional glue which links past and present
together,"[43] but in the sense that emotions in the absence of conscious
memory nevertheless do the work of thinking and remembering. Citing a
case from the *Lancet* (1845), Carpenter touches on the role of unconscious
emotional memory. A young woman, who accidently fell into a river and was
nearly drowned, remembered nothing of her experience; indeed, she remembered nothing at all of her past life. Her entire memory appeared to have been
effaced. Although she took pleasure in embroidery and worsted work, she had
no recollection from day to day of what she had done, "and every morning
began something new, unless her unfinished work was placed before her."
What Carpenter points out, however, is that, while she remembered nothing
consciously, she did demonstrate considerable emotional memory:

When, however, she was shown a landscape in which there was a river, or the view
of a troubled sea, she became intensely excited and violently agitated; and one of
her fits of spasmodic rigidity and insensibility immediately followed. If the picture

were removed before the paroxysm had subsided, she manifested no recollection of what had taken place; but so great was her feeling of dread or fright associated with water, that the mere sight of it in motion, its mere running from one vessel to another, made her shudder and tremble.[44]

The young woman's ideas "manifested themselves chiefly in the form of *emotions*; that is, the chief indications of them were through the signs of Emotional excitement."[45] Furthermore, it was through the arousal of another emotion that her memory was once more regained. One day, after experiencing a powerful feeling of jealousy because a young man paying attention to her had begun to notice another woman, she had a kind of fit from which she awoke "no longer spell-bound." The case shows, says Carpenter, that "Memory is essentially an *automatic* form of Mental activity."[46] But what also clearly emerges from the narrative of the case is that automatic memory takes account of and is informed by emotion. Carpenter's primary concern may be the automatic/volitional opposition but what is important to my exploration is his recognition that the subject may make unconscious but cognitive assessments that express themselves in emotions. Emotions may thus carry the intelligence of cataclysm, even if conscious memory is inoperative.

In the chapter entitled "Unconscious Cerebration," Carpenter builds on the work of predecessors Henry Holland and William Hamilton in laying out the idea that the mind "may undergo modifications, sometimes of very considerable importance, without being itself conscious of the process, until its *results* present themselves to consciousness, in the new ideas, or the new combinations of ideas, which the process has evolved."[47] His presentation of the phenomenon conveys wonder and respect for the orderly and efficient operations of the mind in problem-solving or retrieval of information consciously forgotten:

It is often wonderful, on returning to the subject after such an interval, to find how unhesitatingly the Mind then gravitates, how distinctly the balance of judgment then turns. I feel convinced that, in the habitually well-disciplined nature, this unconscious operation of the Brain, in balancing for itself all these considerations, in putting all in order (so to speak), and in working out the result is far more likely to lead us to a good and true decision, than continual discussion and argumentation.[48]

This mode of action is also important in the processes of artistic and scientific invention. In this regard, he cites both Gaskell's *Life of Charlotte Brontë* as furnishing interesting examples of the hidden work of memory, and the account of the inventor of the centrifugal pump, "which attracted much attention in the International Exhibition of 1851."[49] Turning from intellectual to emotional work, he draws attention to the important modifications of feelings that go on without our conscious knowledge. Although his emphasis is predictably on habit and moral training, the power of early and forgotten feelings, conceptions and prejudices is certainly conceded, and he fully acknowledges that the mind is capable of many kinds of unconscious processes.

The emphasis on will and training in Carpenter's discussion of memory as a largely automatic process is of a piece with his defense of consciousness as anything but automatic or epiphenomenal. As we have seen in previous chapters, Thomas Huxley's provoking analogy of consciousness as the steam whistle, a mere side-effect of the body as locomotive, made epiphenomenalism the bone of contention in subsequent discussions of consciousness. In response to Huxley's address on automata, Carpenter's 1876 Preface to his fourth edition of *Principles of Mental Physiology* urged attention to the question of "human automatism." Engaging directly with Huxley's proposition that humans are just more complex automata than animals, Carpenter set out to show that, although many aspects of mind can be justly regarded as automatic, the question of volition and will is critical.[50] What is striking, especially in relation to Dickens's story of the signalman and train accident, is the extent to which Huxley's and Carpenter's explanations about the functioning of the mind rely on analogies drawn from a technological and industrial context. For example, Carpenter cites an account of telegraphers who transmit messages unconsciously, having become so habituated to the work. "'They read the words,' says my informant, 'pass them through their minds, and transfer them to the sending part of the apparatus, just as unconsciously and automatically as Wheatstone's transmitter does.'"[51] This is a case of secondary or acquired automatism, Carpenter explains. More importantly, his defense of volition as the basis of responsibility relies on the analogy of train accident: we do not blame "the self-acting points of a Railway" whose misdirection of "the train which passes over them ... causes a terrible sacrifice of life."[52]

If the machine proves to have been ill-constructed, or to have got out of order by neglect, we blame the man whom we believe to have been at fault ... [I]f the pointsman can excuse himself by showing that he had been on duty for eight-and-forty hours continuously, and did not know what he was about, we shift the blame on the Directors who wrongly overtaxed his brain; whilst, if it turns out that his inattention was due, neither to drunkenness nor to over-fatigue, but to sudden illness, we cannot say that any one was in fault.[53]

As William James remarks in his essay "Are we Automata?" (1879), "[a] locomotive will carry its train through an open drawbridge as cheerfully as to any other destination."[54] Such analogies provide an interesting context for Dickens's story, engaged as it is with accidents, missed signals and accountability. Bearing in mind the analogical power of the steam engine and the tracks in Victorian conceptions of the mind, I turn now to explore "The Signalman," a tale of unheeded steam whistles and accidents on the line, which seems to tell of the mind's response to cataclysm.[55]

Dickens: signaling trauma

Represented in Carpenter's work as a writer intimately engaged with the imaginative reconstruction of the self through memory, Dickens was also fascinated by mesmerism over a long period and in a variety of ways. Not only was he a close friend for many years of Dr. John Elliotson, the great pioneer of mesmerism in England, and witness to a large number of displays of animal magnetism, he was himself a practicing mesmerist. Fittingly, he took the role of the Doctor in Elizabeth Inchbald's eighteenth-century farce, *Animal Magnetism* (1788), a play that formed a double bill with *The Frozen Deep* (1857) and was performed in private theatricals.[56] According to Fred Kaplan, by the time Dickens departed on his Italian trip in 1844, he was able to magnetize a range of subjects and was primed to develop an intense relationship with Augusta de la Rue, helping to relieve her "convulsions, distortions of the limbs, aching headaches, insomnia, and a plague of neurasthenic symptoms" through frequent mesmeric therapeutics. He was in fact practicing a form of psychotherapy, and working on the assumption that her altered state revealed aspects of personality and psyche that were hidden from her ordinary consciousness. Dickens relied on techniques such as "sleep-waking" and mesmeric trance.[57] Through questions to his mesmerized patient, he formulated theories of what was causing her ailments and attempted to battle the dominating phantoms that surfaced when she was in a state of altered consciousness. Though Dickens never abandoned his belief in an independent fluid as the physical basis of magnetism, it was clearly the relation between conscious and unconscious selves that fascinated him about the magnetized state. He seemed to understand that the mesmerized state offered the prospect of finding out what it is we know, but do not know that we know. Later discussions of accident shock would propose that the psychically injured subject, though not somnambulist or mesmerized, was in a state akin to these "altered states." Shock or fright could produce the effect of making memory inaccessible;

trance, nightmare or flashback could return the victim to the unprocessed and terrible knowledge of the shocking event. We have seen in the previous chapter how Gaskell represents the aftermath of powerful emotion as a state of trance – a stunned state in which the self seems to be other or beside itself and acts in an automatic way. By the 1860s medical accounts of trance were suggesting similarly the fascination of terror and the abdication of volition as the result of powerful emotional experience. By the 1890s, Herbert Page was arguing *pace* Charcot that accident shock and hypnotism were similar states:

> To Charcot, it may be said, and to his disciples, more perhaps than to any others, it is that we owe a knowledge of the fact that *the phenomena of hypnotism are practically identical with the phenomena of the state which has been here spoken of as not uncommon after railway accidents where fright acts as an all-powerful cause of ill.* (Emphasis added)[58]

Although such propositions were not a familiar part of the discourse of nervous shock in the 1860s, I am suggesting that a creative writer like Dickens, attentive to the realm of the unconscious, could offer a powerful articulation of psychic effects of aftermath. Because Dickens was sympathetic to the possibility of unconscious knowledge, and because he was adept at manipulating the literary possibilities within the genre of the ghost story, his story is able to articulate more about the relations of memory to cataclysmic event than was available to him in the current discourse on psychic shock.

The genre of the ghost story and trauma narrative have much in common, since to be traumatized is arguably to be haunted, to be living a ghost story: it is "to be possessed by an image or event."[59] It may then seem tautological to say that Dickens's story of uncanny possession is a story of trauma *avant la lettre*. But even though Dickens's ghost stories frequently objectify states of mind, not all ghost stories are expressive primarily of trauma – *A Christmas Carol* (1843), for example, is a notable exception. In ghost stories, as in trauma, the sanctity of ordered time is violated as the past intrudes on the present. In its depiction of both the signalman's distress and the narrator's responses, this story dwells on powerlessness, heightened vigilance and a sense of impending doom, uncanny reenactment, and terror at the relived intrusion. These are all legitimate aspects of a tale of horror; they are also all thought to be characteristics of late-modern trauma. Just as Augusta de la Rue's "phantoms" emerged in the mesmerized state, so in the ghost story Dickens could give play to the phantoms or specters that intruded as hallucinations to demand that the possessed subject revisit areas of experience not fully assimilated.

The ghost story was also a way of probing unusual psychological states. As Dickens wrote to Elizabeth Gaskell in 1851, ghost stories were illustrative of "particular states of mind and processes of the imagination."[60] The possibilities in the ghost story allow Dickens in "The Signalman" to confront the disjunction in subjectivity that overwhelming experience may occasion as he dramatizes the emphatic gap between knowledge and cognition, signing and meaning, the shocking external occurrence and its internal assimilation and representation.[61] The story is Dickens's way of pondering that fateful and fatal gap in the tracks at Staplehurst, a creative way of articulating his personal experience of railway shock that seems, from the vantage point of the present, uncannily prescient of the direction and emphasis that trauma studies would take in the next century. The story suggests too the underexplored influence of the ghost story on the way trauma theory developed.

Perhaps the most compelling aspect of accident aftermath to which the story gives voice is the feeling of powerlessness in the survivor, who may not recall the disruptive event but has an overwhelming sense of impending and unavoidable doom. In Dickens's story, the narrator one evening passes a signalman's remote box, hails the signalman, and shows that he wishes to descend to the box and talk to him. The signalman tells the narrator of a specter who has been haunting him. Indeed, he takes the narrator initially to be an apparition or ghost, the very same as the one that has appeared to him on the line near his signal box a number of times. On one occasion, the specter appeared before a terrible collision; then again before the death of a young lady on the train. The signalman imagines that the apparition's reappearance precedes a further tragic event. That turns out to be the signalman's own death.[62] Dickens's story focuses obsessively on the signalman's anguish at receiving a warning in time, but finding it impossible to heed because he does not know exactly what he is being warned about.

With some justification the story could be read as a fantasy of revenge against signalmen, though in the Staplehurst disaster, strictly speaking, it was not the signalman who blundered. The foreman on the job miscalculated the time of the train's arrival; the flagman was too close to give adequate warning of the train's approach. But as Carpenter's analogy of the steam-engine suggests, there has to be some volitional agency in order for blame to be registered. If the mind functions automatically, it cannot be accountable for initiating even injurious actions, or can it? Who is to be held accountable for a crime unconsciously permitted? As blame devolves from the steam-engine, to the pointsman, whose brain is overtaxed, so it settles on the Director, responsible for the pointsman's conditions of work.

Dickens's story focuses on the equivalent of the pointsman, and the sense of responsibility that he retains despite the elements of excuse and the fact that he is the ultimate victim.

In the story, the signalman is too close to the train and does not or cannot heed the warning as the engine bears down on him. Ironically, the signalman lives in a state of heightened vigilance, yet dies because he is unable to read the precise import of the warning; he is powerless to prevent his own death on the tracks. In this story of missed signals and failed connections, the signalman's inability to understand the messages he receives from the specter suggests the mind's inability to comprehend or gain access to what it knows and fears unconsciously. Why is the signalman oblivious to the steam-whistle and the driver's cries? It could be that he is so preoccupied with his hallucinations of the specter that he is entirely abstracted from present reality. Is he functioning automatically and by rote when the train cuts him down? If we are automata, the story suggests, we have no volition and no control therefore over our fate. There is some hint, though, that the haunted man does not even want to prevent his death. He does not seem to heed the steam whistle and literally allows death to overtake him as the train comes upon him from behind and cuts him down. Dickens suggests possibly that his torture of mind and desire to free himself from the terrifying and guilt-inducing visions prompt his oblivion to the warnings. Like the young woman in Carpenter's case who could not remember anything of her near-fatal drowning, but who became agitated by the sight of running water, the signalman seems to know emotionally what is nevertheless unintelligible to ordinary conscious memory. References to the signalman's "pain of mind," "mental torture" and "unintelligible responsibility" suggest the freight carried by emotion in the absence of conscious knowledge. They suggest also that the problem raised by the signalman's sense of powerlessness has to do with his unclear status as victim or perpetrator. If he is to be an agent, then how should he act? If he is absolved of responsibility for the accidents, then is he, like the others before him, a passive victim? Is his final assertion of agency the commission of himself to his doom?

Based structurally on the principle of repetition, "The Signalman" reveals the hallmark of the unassimilated experience as unbidden repetition and return. Dickens's story seems also therefore to apprehend the repetitive cycle of trauma. The idea of unbidden return is certainly available to Victorian writers, since it is, after all, exactly what the notion of haunting captures. Even in realist texts such as *Middlemarch* and *North and South*, we encounter the idea of the unsolicited memory or dream: the images that dominate Dorothea's consciousness like magic-lantern pictures, or Mr. Thornton's almost obsessive return in his mind to the scene of his proposal to Margaret. What Dickens's story emphasizes is the accumulated and compounding distress occasioned by the repetition. Not only is the signalman compelled to witness a terrible train disaster, he is tantalized through the specter's visitations by an impossible clairvoyance. The terror compounds as the signalman is twice forewarned but is both times unable to avert death and disaster. After the first terrible accident on the line, the signalman thinks he has recovered from witnessing the carnage: "Six or seven months passed, and I had recovered from the surprise and shock."[63] At that point, the specter appears to him again and the next calamity occurs: "I ... heard terrible screams and cries. A beautiful young lady had died instantaneously in one of the compartments and was brought in here, and laid down on this floor between us" (532). Now the specter has appeared again, signaling to him of some further calamity about to occur on the line, and prompting, the signalman laments, "this cruel haunting" of him (533). Haunted not only by the past, but by a past that seems to project itself into the future, the signalman is subjected to relentless repetition and can avail himself of neither hindsight nor foresight. Indeed, the signals are crossed, so to speak, because the specter's accounts are not so much prognostications of a malleable future, but confirmations that something dreadful has happened, even though it is yet to take place. Linearity is disturbed by the fact that the specter signals the past that is paradoxically yet to come.

In the dominant interpretative paradigm of today, trauma is characterized as the inability to know the past as past – it is therefore a "disease of time" in which the events of the past continually obtrude on the present in the form of flashbacks and hallucinations.[64] Traumatic memory is the return that does not recognize itself as a return. Like the train disaster that is literally a disruption of linearity, the narrative of "The Signalman" disrupts linear sequence. In part, this sense arises from the clairvoyant specter, whose gestures enact and predict each of three train disasters before they occur. The sense of disturbed linearity or chronology arises also from the fact that the narrator seems to be taking part in something that has already happened. That is, the narrative is itself part of some uncanny repetition. When the narrator leaves the signalman's box for the first time, he has the disagreeable sensation of a train coming behind him as he walks away, a replication of the posture of the signalman just before he dies. Moreover, the fact that the narrator uses the words "For God's sake, clear the way," themselves repeated many times in the course of the story, could suggest that the narrator has just repeated his part in the replay of a past he "knows" but does not know he knows.

In support of this line of thinking, the narrator from the outset seems inexplicably drawn to approach the signalman, all the odder because initially he says he is not someone given to starting up conversations.[65] Understandably the signalman imagines that the narrator is himself a further spectral illusion, especially since the narrator hails him with the exact words that the specter has already used. After a time the signalman seems reassured that the rational, skeptical narrator is not a ghost, and confides his story to him. By persistently dismissing as "imagination" what the signalman says he has seen, by construing recurrence as coincidence, by remaining stubbornly unbelieving, the narrator refuses to witness the signalman's hallucination or spectral illusion. He refuses, in effect, to witness the trauma. But it is arguably inscribed upon him nonetheless, and he is now (as narrator) participating in the repetition by telling the story of it. When the narrator arrives at the tracks for the third time, he is struck with a "nameless horror" because he sees the "appearance of a man" in the tunnel and clearly thinks he is seeing a ghost (535). The horror that oppresses him passes when he sees that the figure is a real man. Horror gives way to fear that something is wrong. He then learns of the signalman's death. All would appear to be resolved for the rational narrator, except for the fact that the words the engine driver called out were the very ones in the narrator's thoughts. Despite the matter-of-factness of the coda, it is clear that the narrator too will be haunted by the words "For God's sake, clear the way."

It is this widening implication and involvement that warns the reader against focusing only on the signalman and seeing him as a pathological case. Graeme Tytler, for example, has diagnosed the signalman as suffering from monomania – a clinical condition in which the patient is obsessed by one dominating idea. A man with a one-track mind, the signalman is undeniably fixated. But he could equally well be diagnosed as suffering from Abercrombie's spectral illusion or Wigan's split self. John Stahl, meanwhile, has seen in the story a critique of industrialization in Dickens's representation of the alienated labor of the signalman and the stress his job entails. But rather than pathologizing the signalman as a "case of partial insanity" or substituting an alternate diagnosis stemming from stress in the workplace, I want to emphasize how the narrator and reader are drawn into the ongoing aftermath of accident, and the way the entire narrative is expressive of the logic of trauma.[66]

If the specter can be seen as an articulation of the signalman's agonized consciousness, the narrator shares characteristics of the signalman that suggest he is not just a detached interlocutor, auditor or reporter. The signalman thinks initially that the narrator is a specter; the narrator has a "monstrous thought" that the signalman is a spirit. Each finds himself in a position that makes him feel compelled to act and assume responsibility for the general safety of those on the line. When the signalman sees the apparition for a third time, he is (literally) beside himself to interpret the warning and forestall the disaster. But he cannot. Similarly the narrator feels himself compelled to act: "But what ran most in my thoughts was the consideration how ought I to act, having become the recipient of this disclosure" (534). The narrator is less worried about the uninterpretable spectral warnings than he is about the mental stability of the signalman and his job performance under present stress. He resolves to try to calm the signalman as much as possible and to return the next morning to visit with him the "wisest medical practitioner ... and to take his opinion" (535). He is also too late. The specter appears to the signalman on three occasions; the narrator descends to the signalman's box three times; the words the narrator uses are the words that the ghost has used and the train driver will use; the gesture that the signalman describes is given words by the narrator but, significantly, he does not speak these words – "For God's sake, clear the way" – before the engine driver tells the narrator that those are in fact the words he used. The narrator, the signalman, the specter and the engine driver are all bound together in a series of overlapping occurrences and repeated events and expressions, in a history that seems to have begun before the narration begins and will continue after it ends.

In "The Signalman," Dickens expresses the internal dislocations associated with the external accident. Measuring the distance between Dickens's article "Need Railway Travellers be Smashed?" and his story "The Signalman" we see – genre and overt intention notwithstanding – a shift in emphasis in Dickens's growing apprehension of railway disaster. This shift in Dickens is very much in line with what railway historian Ralph Harrington has suggested about perceptions of railway disaster in the period. Whereas the railway was associated initially with external destruction of landscape in its construction and of people in the wake of its accidents, it came later to provoke anxieties about internal disruption. Harrington also notes that the later part of the nineteenth century saw a change in the way people viewed accidents. Rather than *private* (individualized) happenings they became *public* ones, affecting or concerning the whole of society.[67] The paradox of railway shock, then, for the Victorians, was that what seemed insignificant and hidden – delayed nervous shock without physical injury – was nevertheless public in its significance. This paradox is articulated in "The Signalman," where, although the emphasis is on the internal disruption and fragmentation of the signalman's mind, there is undeniably a public dimension to the experience, both in the signalman's sense of being at once responsible yet powerless, and in the communication or transmission of the disturbance to the narrator. Just as the signalman owns the responsibility for the cryptic messages he is unable to process, so the narrator has to try and process the aftermath of the signalman's death and his implication in it. The signals amplify and irradiate.

As the editor of widely read journals, and in his novels and stories, Dickens espoused many public causes, championing the individual plight and exposing the public responsibility for what may have appeared to be merely personal or private hardship. Dickens, it is fair to say, is pre-eminently the Victorian writer who claims the public dimension of private agonies. No stranger to psychically wounding experience before the railway accident, as his continual, fictive reenactments of abandonment and childhood abuse attest, Dickens was perhaps brought through the Staplehurst accident to a sharper intimation of the nature of psychic shock and pain than ever before. He returns imaginatively to the site of the railway accident in order to master a stimulus that resists mastery. If he lost his voice in the Staplehurst accident, he found it later in articulating, in this story of ghostly clairvoyance and hindsight, the characteristics of trauma barely broached in the medical discourse of nervous shock during the 1860s.

II MYSTERIES OF CONSCIOUSNESS IN *THE MYSTERY OF EDWIN DROOD*

"Unintelligible" and "unaccountable" are key words in Dickens's last and unfinished novel, *The Mystery of Edwin Drood* (1870). In the opening scene, as Jasper wonders aloud what kinds of visions the other opium smokers are having, he assures himself that his own mutterings must be as "unintelligible" to them as theirs are to him.[68] Their words are "incoherent jargon" without "sense or sequence" (3). Much later in the novel when Jasper returns to the opium den, we learn that his "incoherence" and its "wild unmeaning gestures" are by no means unintelligible to the old woman known as Princess Puffer: "'Unintelligible!' I heard you say so, of two more than me. But don't ye be too sure always; don't be ye too sure, beauty! ... I may have learned the secret how to make ye talk, deary" (210). As yet unintelligible to the reader, Jasper's words under the influence of the opium promise to become intelligible through Princess Puffer's knowledge and manipulations.

"Surely an unaccountable sort of expedition," the narrator remarks several times of Jasper's night-time foray into the Cathedral crypt with Durdles. The purpose of drawing attention to the expedition's unaccountability is to raise questions in the reader's mind about why the choir-master wants to accompany Durdles, why he drugs Durdles, and what he does when Durdles is unconscious. Both this instance and the opening scene in the opium den have to do with alterations in consciousness, and both are clearly of great significance to the plot of the novel. The narrative attention paid to "unintelligible" and "unaccountable" teases the reader with not knowing, even as it promises that, in the fullness of closure, the reader's reward will be intelligibility and a coherent account.

As readers, we can never forget that this last novel is unfinished. Half-way through a Dickens novel, what reader can discern the terminus of all the carefully laid strands and foretell what new characters and turns of event will come in the second half? The opacity of the Dickensian plot, particularly a feature of the later novels, is compounded by the fact that *The Mystery of Edwin Drood* is specifically a novel of crime and detection, dependent on suspense and mystery. What is indissolubly perplexing in this text, concerned as it is with psychic fragmentation, is that it is itself a fragment. The reader's inability to complete the hermeneutic circle and to draw the memory of important textual details into a whole mimics the confusions of memory and lack of clarity about cause and effect, event and consequence, and chronological sequence that plague several characters in the text.

The Mystery of Edwin Drood is a haunting text among Dickens scholars because it defies processing, integration and assimilation. Unclear about the status of clues, and the end to which all is tending, the reader finds her memory, as it works in reading the narrative, less a source of information that leads to coherence and illumination than a cache of the vital information that remains frustratingly unsorted. We may indeed have significant information that would have been used later to resolve the riddles, but we do not know how to make a pattern out of what we know.

There are two questions which have governed much interpretation of the novel: what was Dickens trying to say about psychic fragmentation and can one extrapolate from all the clues present in the chapters thus far completed how the plot will unfold? It is clear that the mysteries of consciousness and memory are a significant and foregrounded concern in the novel; it is equally clear from Dickens's notes and comments to Forster, and from the clues embedded in the text as we have it, that he relished his mystery, and courted the unintelligibility of many of its elements as the novel was in process. The mystery was to be unintelligible and unaccountable until such time (closure) as the author chose to dispel it.

Among critics who consider both of these aspects of the novel, the detection aspect is mostly judged to be inferior to the explorations of consciousness; indeed, it is not an unusual gesture at the close of a discussion of this novel to argue that the mysteries of the human heart trump the question of plot.[69] Katey Dickens Collins was perhaps the first to articulate this view: "It was not ... for the intricate working of his plot alone, that my father cared to write this story ... [H]e was quite as deeply fascinated and absorbed in the study of the criminal Jasper ... but it was through ... his strange insight into the tragic secrets of the human heart, that he desired his greatest triumph to be achieved."[70] More recently, Doris Alexander claims that Dickens's subject in this novel is the "mystery of the human mind with its aberrations into criminality, with its derangements of perception and lapses of consciousness among all human beings."[71] Michael Hollington draws attention to the fact that "[d]etective novels are essentially linear fictions, their 'detective-fever' designed to infect the reader with a teleologically-oriented addiction that will drive him on compulsively towards the resolution of the mystery."[72] He continues: "It is as clear as can be that solving detective-mysteries was to be only a surface interest in *Edwin Drood*, and that it drew its deeper inspiration from meditations upon the mysteries of identity and death."[73]

But perhaps there is a false dichotomy in this assignment of depth over surface, superior over inferior elements, for solving detective-mysteries and unraveling the mysteries of consciousness and identity are here ineluctably bound together.[74] This novel asks us to credit that the mysteries of fragmented identity are like plot mysteries. In this light, the teleology of detective fiction is strangely in accord with the unraveling of psychic mysteries. Dickens is, in this sense, like Freud, who certainly understood the detective work involved in deciphering the unconscious. In his introductory lectures Freud likens his endeavor of searching for clues to unconscious repression to "a detective engaged in tracing a murder."[75] What the symbolic murder accomplishes in this sense is the formation of the unconscious and the burial of memories unbefitting the respectable self. Although Victorians construed the unconscious rather differently, the exploration of its mysteries was likewise a matter for detection. In *The Mystery of Edwin Drood*, as we shall see, the detection is directed to the "murder" of memory and knowledge as much as to the murder of Drood himself.

Unlike many commentators on the novel, I am not going to offer a solution to the question of Edwin's fate (dead or alive) and Jasper's crime (murder or attempted murder of his nephew). Rather, I want to consider how the novel engages on many levels with questions about the fragmentary self, memory and states of altered consciousness.[76] While the probable influence on Dickens of the Staplehurst disaster, discussed in the first part of this chapter, must be recognized in reading whatever he wrote after 1865, Dickens's interest in the problems of consciousness is not shaped by aftermath of railway disaster alone. It is also reflective of his previous and longstanding interest in mesmerism and trance, questions of remembering and forgetting, possessing and losing the self.[77] Moreover, his last production is in many ways a somewhat rivalrous riposte to Wilkie Collins's *The Moonstone*, whose interest in unconscious memory it shares but whose narrative method and construction Dickens was reported to have found "wearisome beyond endurance."[78]

Shock and dissociation

On the heels of the discovery that Edwin Drood has disappeared on Christmas night, Mr. Grewgious, guardian of Rosa Bud, visits John Jasper, Edwin's villainous uncle, with a further piece of news that throws Jasper into a profound state of shock. Interspersed with Grewgious's news that Edwin and Rosa have broken off their engagement, is a narrative of the effects of the intelligence on Jasper, which we see through Mr. Grewgious's eyes:

Mr. Grewgious saw a lead-colored face in the easy-chair, and on its surface dreadful starting drops or bubbles, as if of steel ... Mr. Grewgious saw a ghastly figure rise, open-mouthed, from the easy-chair, and lift its outspread hands towards its head ... Mr. Grewgious saw the ghastly figure throw back its head, clutch its hair with its hands, and turn with a writhing action from him ... Mr. Grewgious heard a terrible shriek, and saw no ghastly figure, sitting or standing; saw nothing but a heap of torn and miry clothes upon the floor. (138)

After the thrice repeated "Mr. Grewgious saw" we come to the fourth reiteration, which is a variation, for now Grewgious hears the shriek but no longer sees Jasper. As the illustration by Luke Fildes confirms, Jasper has collapsed on the floor and is fittingly described in the metonymy of "torn and miry" clothes. An earlier description of Jasper's state prepares us for this metonymic transformation: "Unkempt and disordered, bedaubed with mud that had dried upon him, and with much of his clothing torn to rags, he had but just dropped into his easy-chair, when Mr. Grewgious stood before him" (136–37). Much later Dickens returns to this evidence, recorded in Grewgious's memory, but as yet unshared with others:

> Mr. Grewgious took no pains to conceal his implacable dislike of Jasper, yet he never referred it, however distantly, to such a source [the suspicion that Jasper has murdered Edwin]. But he was a reticent as well as an eccentric man; and he made no mention of a certain evening when he warmed his hands at the Gate House fire, and looked steadily down upon a certain heap of torn and miry clothes upon the floor. (205)

The scene of shock is significant in that it draws our attention to Jasper's powerful reaction to the news of the broken engagement, more powerful by far than his response to the news of Edwin's disappearance. Unlike the news of Edwin's disappearance, about which we suspect he knows all too much, the news of the broken engagement is a genuine shock, for it means that Jasper may not have needed to murder Edwin in order to secure Rosa for himself.[79] "Discovery by the murderer of the utter needlessness of the murder for its object, was to follow hard upon commission of the deed," wrote John Forster, Dickens's friend and biographer, in his account of Dickens's last novel in *The Life of Charles Dickens* (1872–74).[80] The shock of this discovery is testimony to Jasper's knowledge of what he has done or attempted to do, and the dramatic revelation that Jasper is so shocked is a cause for suspicion, as the title of the illustration, "Mr. Grewgious has his Suspicions," suggests.

This moment of shock constitutes a turning point in the narrative, but not just because it marks Mr. Grewgious's realization that Jasper may be guilty. I would like further to argue that the shock has the effect of increasingly dissociating Jasper from the knowledge of his guilt. Having revived and explained his reaction as caused by "the shock of a piece of news of my dear boy, so entirely unexpected, and so destructive of all the castles I had built for him," Jasper declares himself hopeful that Edwin has volun-tarily disappeared (142). Thereafter few scenes feature Jasper in a major way: he declares that he has given up hope of Edwin's flight after the watch and shirt-pin are found at the Weir and devotes himself to pursuing Neville, on whom he has cast suspicion of the murder. Six months pass and we encounter him again on two significant occasions: first, when he declares his love for Rosa and attempts to make her accept him; and second, when he once again visits the London opium den. What is significant about these last two extended scenes is that he no longer gives any indication that he has knowledge of his attempted murder of Edwin. Between the time of the shock, this "overpowering disclosure," and the second visit to the opium den, Jasper seems to have lost the memory of his attempted *execution* of the crime (143). Yet he has not forgotten his *fantasies* of murdering his nephew.

In a story entitled "An Experience" that appeared in *All the Year Round* (1869) and that Dickens praised as remarkable, the hero describes his partially restored consciousness and sense of alienation after a period of delirium: "I knew all these things, but they seemed to concern some other person."[81] The story is told in two parts: in the first, the doctor/narrator successfully performs an operation on a lame child, who nevertheless dies shortly thereafter. In response to the bereft mother's curses (and the strain of professional life) he falls in a state of shock, followed by illness and delirium. In the second part, the narrator begins to gain consciousness and realizes that he must have been ill for some time. Though he harbors shadowy fears of the woman nursing him, he has no conscious memory that she is the vengeful mother of his unfortunate patient. When he is finally confronted with her plans to avenge the child's death, he does not recall all in a flash, but continues to experience a "blankness of my brain" and a sense of "benumbed" mind and body: "I have not much conscious-ness of what transacted itself in my brain, meanwhile. I think I realised nothing clearly."[82] And yet, the narrator still has a shadowy sense of something happening that he had been long expecting. He knows, but he does not know that he knows. I want to suggest that *The Mystery of Edwin Drood* has affinities with this story in that a powerful shock banishes conscious knowledge, after which the memory of the painful (guilty) past is largely occluded. What is original and unusual, however, is that Dickens bypasses the use of delirium and brain congestion, allowing the pathology of the criminal intellect to do the work of brain fever in bringing about the alienation and derangement of consciousness. Furthermore, Dickens does not use first-person narrative. In "An Experience" the reader knows all too well what the delirious doctor does not. There is horror, but no mystery.

The question of what Jasper knows, and knows consciously and consis-tently, is the fundamental mystery in this novel. Delighting in his authorial sleight of hand, and not wishing to "pay out" the plot mystery too soon, Dickens also measuredly doles out clues to the mystery of Jasper's con-sciousness and seldom attempts to narrate Jasper's thoughts or mental process. There are only a few occasions therefore in which Dickens deploys the narrative strategy of free indirect speech, a particularly useful means of conveying what is going on in other people's minds. Free indirect speech is an objectification of the others' thoughts that produces an oblique and substitutory rendering. This technique implies that one mind is responsible for the form and another for the content of the statement. Paul Hernadi refers to the strategy as a "dual perspective" but Dorrit Cohn's analysis of narrated monologue suggests a more richly ambivalent state in which content and form are not so easily divisible. In her view, narrated monologue allows a fusion of the narrative and figural personae to take place.[83] As such, narrated monologue is itself a kind of impersonation on the part of the narrator. Not only does the strategy of rendering Jasper's mind transparent work against the suspense that Dickens wishes to create, but it would also involve the narrator in imitation of and even contamination by Jasper. This realm of superimposition, in which the boundaries of the self dissolve, is therefore akin to the realm of that "unclean spirit of imitation" described in the opium den. Maintaining the separateness of Jasper as the villain means that the authorial presence is not implicated in or accountable for merging with his consciousness.[84]

By contrast, the narrator has no problem in reporting Rosa's suspicions of Jasper by means of narrated monologue. And through Rosa's confused questions about the logic of the choir-master's actions and motivation, Dickens nudges the reader with the riddle of consciousness Jasper presents:

> She ran over in her mind again, all that he had said by the sun-dial in the garden. He had persisted in treating the disappearance as murder, consistently with his whole public course since the finding of the watch and shirt-pin. *If he were afraid of the crime being traced out, would he not rather encourage the idea of a voluntary disappearance?* He had unnecessarily declared that if the ties between him and his nephew had been less strong, he might have swept "even him" away from her side. *Was that like his having really done so?* He had spoken of laying his six months' labours in the cause of a just vengeance at her feet. *Would he have done that, with that violence of passion, if they were a pretence? Would he have ranged them with his desolate heart and soul, his wasted life, his peace and his despair?* The very first sacrifice that he represented himself as making for her, was his fidelity to his dear boy after death. (Emphasis added; 176)

Rosa's thoughts here are a means of expressing the questions readers must be asking, as Jasper's behavior in zealously pursuing the murderer seems incompatible with the suspicion that he has committed the crime. So devious is he that the answers to all Rosa's questions could indeed be affirmative. But if we entertain the possibility that memory and consciousness are increasingly severed as his hypocritical and duplicitous behavior becomes a real split, these contradictions are further explicable. The passage continues with a "clue" that Jasper's criminal intellect would provide answers, did Rosa know how to construe it:

In short, the poor girl (for what could she know of the criminal intellect, which its own professed students perpetually misread, because they persist in trying to reconcile it with the average intellect of average men, instead of identifying it as a horrible wonder apart), could get by no road to any other conclusion than that he *was* a terrible man, and must be fled from. (176)

The parenthetical comment "for what could she know of the criminal intellect ... a horrible wonder apart" hints that there is a syndrome, an explanation that will reveal the logic behind the contradictions with which Rosa and the reader struggle. In this regard, the account John Forster gave of the closure Dickens envisaged is relevant:

The story, I learnt immediately afterward, was to be that of the murder of a nephew by his uncle; the originality of which was to consist in the review of the murderer's career by himself at the close, when its temptations were to be dwelt upon *as if, not he the culprit, but some other man, were the tempted.* The last chapters were to be written in the condemned cell, to which the wickedness, all elaborately elicited from him as if told to another, had brought him.[85]

While this statement has been variously interpreted by critics of the novel, I would argue that a fragmented Jasper, unable to integrate the memory of past actions, and confessing his crime as if he were not himself, is entirely consistent with the novel's preoccupation with abstracted and dissociative states.[86]

"Not quite himself"

Despite the authorial aside, in the passage detailing Rosa's thoughts, on "a horrible wonder apart," Jasper's volatile states of consciousness occur in a fictional world where even the average experience of consciousness is discontinuous and prone to interruption.[87] It is as if Dickens undertakes in this last novel to consider an entire spectrum of abstracted mental states. William Carpenter begins his account of such a spectrum with ordinary conditions such as attention and habit, which then shade into a range of "special" physiological states: memory, imagination, unconscious cerebration, reverie, dreams and somnambulism, mesmerism, delirium and insanity. Frequently, if unemphatically, *The Mystery of Edwin Drood* features moments of concentrated or divided attention, automatic behavior and absence of mind: Mr. Sapsea, "in a grandiloquent *state of absence of mind,* seems to refill his visitor's glass, which is full already; and does really refill his own, which is empty" (emphasis added; 27). Rosa is so busy thinking about Tartar's horizon-scanning blue eyes that she does not notice how she has climbed up to his garden: "This a little confused Rosebud, and may account for her *never afterwards quite knowing* how she ascended (with his help) to his garden in the air, and seemed to get into a marvellous country that came into sudden bloom like the country on the summit of the magic beanstalk" (emphasis added; 188). After learning from Princess Puffer that she talked to Edwin on the night of his disappearance, the detective Datchery falls into a state of abstraction or absent-mindedness, pausing "with the selected coins in his hand, rather as if he were falling into a *brown study* of their value, and couldn't bear to part with them." He gives them to her as if "he were *abstracting his mind* from the sacrifice" (emphasis added; 214). When prompting Jasper's confession in the opium den, Princess Puffer varies her questions to assure herself that Jasper's responses while he is under the influence of opium are "not the assent of *a mere automaton*" (emphasis added; 208).

Cases of rapt attention, abstracted meditation or automatic response provide examples of people who are, in the normal course of things, not quite themselves or "beside themselves," who lose themselves and struggle to recollect themselves.[88] As such, the novel might well be subtitled "on not being oneself." Indeed one of the strategies of the narrative is to parody the major concerns about consciousness in a minor and comic key, as in the way Mr. Sapsea's *apparent* absence of mind in refilling his glass points to Jasper's more sinister case. Raising the issue of two separate states of existence, Dickens surely mocks Collins's invocation of Dr. Elliotson in *The Moonstone* by also quoting his famous dictum, this time in a comic context in relation to Miss Twinkleton, mistress of the school that the young flower, Rosa Bud, attends:

As, in some cases of drunkenness, and in others of animal magnetism, there are two states of consciousness which never clash, but each of which pursues its separate course as though it were continuous instead of broken (thus if I hide my watch when I am drunk, I must be drunk again before I can remember where), so Miss Twinkleton has two distinct and separate phases of being. (14)

She has a romantic side of which her seminarial side pretends to be in ignorance. But even as Dickens makes fun of the notion of separate spheres, implying that it applies to selves, and showing the self-serving split in Miss Twinkleton, so in the rest of the novel he explores this notion of alternating states of existence more seriously and critically.

No one in the novel has a firm grasp on the first-person pronoun and indeed several characters refer to themselves in the impersonal third.[89] Of Durdles, the stonemason, the narrator tells us "[h]e often speaks of himself in the third person; perhaps being a little misty as to his own identity when he narrates" (29). Mr. Grewgious, catching sight of his face in the looking-glass addresses it in the second person as if it were someone else: "A likely some one, *you*, to come into anybody's thoughts in such an aspect ...There, there, there! Get to bed, poor man, and cease to jabber!" (97). Jasper is only the most obvious example of someone who is often "not himself." When Jasper returns to Cloisterham from the London opium den of the famous opening scene, Mr. Tope reports that: "Mr Jasper's breathing was so remarkably short ... which was perhaps the cause of his having a kind of fit on him after a little. His memory grew DAZED." He continues: "However, a little time and water brought him out of his DAZE." In response to this, the Dean asks "And Mr Jasper has gone home quite himself, has he?" (4). The play on the common expression "not himself" considered in relation to Forster's remarks about the novel suggests Dickens's interest in the slippage of a coherent sense of self with an integrated and unitary mode of memory. Furthermore, Jasper seems not to "mind it particularly, himself" – that is, he is unaware that or how he has slipped from ordinary consciousness into this other state.

If Jasper sometimes appears dazed, with a "dimness and giddiness" come upon him, he is all attention whenever he is looking at his nephew Edwin. It is as if Jasper's concentrated attention is a form of self-possession or mesmeric trance:

Mr. Jasper stands still, and looks on intently at the young fellow, divesting himself of his outer coat, hat, gloves, and so forth. Once for all, a look of intentness and intensity – a look of hungry, exacting, watchful, and yet devoted affection – is always, now and ever afterwards, on the Jasper face whenever the Jasper face is addressed in this direction. And whenever it is so addressed, it is never, on this occasion or on any other, dividedly addressed; it is always concentrated. (6–7)

Regarding the sleeping Edwin, Jasper stands with "his unlighted pipe in his hand, for some time, with a fixed and deep attention," after which he lights the pipe and delivers himself to "the Spectres it invokes at midnight" (36). Dickens always describes his external appearance so as to signal altered consciousness: "Mr. Jasper's steadiness of face and figure becomes so marvellous that his breathing seems to have stopped" (11); he appears "as if in a kind of fascination attendant on his strong interest" in the young man; he often has white lips, and a glare that is perplexing (12). Above all, a film comes over his eyes, which makes him appear as if in a trance. In this he reminds us of the filmy-eyed Obenreizer in *No Thoroughfare* (1867), written collaboratively with Collins just prior to this last novel:

But the great Obenreizer peculiarity was, that a certain nameless film would come over his eyes – apparently by the action of his own will – which would impenetrably veil, not only from those tellers of tales, but from his face at large, every expression save one of attention. It by no means followed that his attention should be wholly given to the person with whom he spoke, or even wholly bestowed on present sounds and objects. Rather, it was a comprehensive watchfulness of everything he had in his own mind, and everything that he knew to be, or suspected to be, in the minds of other men.[90]

In *Edwin Drood*, both Jasper and Princess Puffer have "a curious film" which passes over their eyes and which allows for an identificatory moment linking them in Edwin's perception. The film is likewise a shorthand for an altered state of consciousness, frequently but not always associated with opium.[91] A "film" also comes over Rosa's eyes "as though he had turned her faint," when Jasper confesses his mad love to her (171). Rosa feels Jasper "haunts [her] thoughts, like a dreadful ghost" (53) and complains of his mesmeric powers which are also linked to an abstracted gaze: "Even when a glaze comes over them [his eyes] and he seems to wander away into a frightful sort of dream in which he threatens most, he obliges me to know it, and to know that he is sitting close at my side, more terrible to me than ever" (53). If Jasper wanders away into a dream-like state, Rosa, though mesmerized, is never oblivious to her captivation: "Rosa no sooner came to herself than the whole of the late interview was before her. It even seemed as if it had pursued her into her insensibility, and she had not had a moment's unconsciousness of it" (175). As these examples show, Dickens keeps unsettled the question of unconscious or dissociated knowledge.

Not only are many characters subject to lapses of consciousness, but on several occasions people are "not themselves," either because their consciousness has been tampered with through intoxication (Durdles, Edwin and Neville) or because they may be acting under the influence of another's mesmeric power.[92] Rosa's complaint about Jasper is an obvious example. In Chapter 16, Mr. Crisparkle finds himself unaccountably taking a walk to the Weir. Since it is a frequent haunt, there is nothing remarkable in his footsteps wending that way without his conscious direction. Finding himself there, he asks himself why he came there and how he came there, and as he stands looking at the Weir he has a "strange idea that something unusual hung about the place" (145). The reader may wonder whether this strange idea has been implanted while Crisparkle was in a kind of hypnotic trance and whether he is now following some post-hypnotic suggestion. This scene closely follows the one in which Jasper declares himself sanguine about Edwin's absence and promises to give up his suspicion of Neville so long as "no trace of his dear boy were found" (144). It is entirely possible that Jasper may have engineered Crisparkle's discovery of the watch and shirt-pin in the Weir.

But Dickens also allows for the more innocuous possibility that Crisparkle – whose home, Minor Canon Corner, produces a "serenely romantic state of the mind" (38) and who is known to fall into "reveries" and musings – is merely pre-occupied, and arrives at the Weir simply by repeating habitual actions unconsciously. His sense of wonder at finding himself there is increased by the allusion to Milton, which emphasizes fantasies and memory:

> What might this be? A thousand fantasies
> Begin to throng into my memory
> Of calling shapes, and beckning shadows dire
> And airy tongues, that syllable men's names
> On Sands and Shoars and desert Wildernesses.[93]

Whether the will of another has directed him there or he has gone by his own unconscious motivation, Dickens clearly signals that a shift in ordinary consciousness has taken place.

Special communicative powers of mind are associated with the Landless twins: Neville and Helena appear to communicate by means of thought transfer, or what would later in the century be referred to as "telepathic" powers. Even in the absence of verbal communication, she is able to know exactly what he thinks. Neville tells Crisparkle:

You don't know, sir, yet, what a complete understanding can exist between my sister and me, though no spoken word – perhaps hardly as much as a look – may have passed between us. She not only feels as I have described, but she very well knows that I am taking this opportunity of speaking to you, both for her and for myself. (48)

The idea of consciousness as mixed and discontinuous is further underscored by images suggesting a psychology of layers or levels of the mind in which motivation, memory and intention may not be unified – Edwin recalls how Rosa has looked at him curiously when they parted: "Did it mean that she saw below the surface of his thoughts and down into their twilight depths?" (125). Dickens draws attention to the clarity and soundness of mind and body in Crisparkle, as opposed to Jasper. The latter refers to this himself when he says "You are always training yourself to be, in mind and body, as clear as crystal, and you always are, and never change; whereas I am a muddy solitary, moping weed" (130). Rosa's turbulent thoughts are described as a "stormtost" sea: "Rosa's mind throughout the last six months had been stormily confused. A half-formed, wholly unexpressed suspicion tossed in it, now heaving itself up, and now sinking into the deep; now gaining palpability, and now losing it" (175–76).

In accordance with the novel's interest in possession and haunted states of mind, references to phantoms, phantasmagoria, haunting and ghosts abound. Jasper "delivers himself to the Spectres [his pipe] invokes at midnight" (36). Jasper's swoon leaves him prostrate, a "ghastly figure" (138). In lighter vein, Dickens treats "spirits" as a pun. When Jasper and Durdles are about to set out for the crypt, Durdles says "I am ready, Mister Jarsper. Let the old 'uns come out if they dare, when we go among their tombs. My spirits is ready for 'em." And Jasper returns, "Do you mean animal spirits, or ardent?" (103). Durdles is perennially prowling around the graves and ruins "like a Ghoule" (103). Ghosts feature in the narrative in the form of folklore or local superstition, as in the story of a mysterious lady, with a child in her arms and a rope dangling from her neck, seen flitting about in the crypt "by sundry witnesses as intangible as herself" (105). Characteristically, Dickens teases the reader with what is fanciful and what may turn out to be real and important. Just as we suspect the story of the noosed woman may have some bearing on the narrative, so we can credit the significance of the "ghost of one terrific shriek," which Durdles heard last Christmas Eve, and which was "followed by the ghost of a howl of a dog ... such as a dog gives when a person's dead" (106).[94]

Dickens also plays punningly on ideas about nightmare and dream when Mr. Grewgious, after visiting Rosa at school, asks if one young lady "under a cloud" might be let off her punishment. Miss Twinkleton responds:

"O you gentlemen, you gentlemen! Fie for shame, that you are so hard upon us poor maligned disciplinarians of our sex, for your sakes! But as Miss Ferdinand is at present weighed down by an incubus" – Miss Twinkleton might have said a pen-and-ink-ubus of writing out Monsieur La Fontaine – "go to her, Rosa my dear, and tell her the penalty is remitted, in deference to the intercession of your guardian, Mr. Grewgious." (73)

The drugged Durdles, on his midnight expedition with John Jasper to the vault, is described as dreaming: "It is not much of a dream, considering the vast extent of the domains of dreamland, and their wonderful productions; it is only remarkable for being unusually restless and unusually real" (108). The narrator uses Durdles' confused state of consciousness to describe how Jasper takes the keys from him. In this instance the narrator tells us what is really happening while Durdles thinks he is dreaming. So throughout the novel Dickens blurs the clear boundary between sleeping and waking, trance and ordinary consciousness. Jasper is described as lying on the couch "in a delirious state between sleeping and waking" when Crisparkle walks in. The narrator tells us that Crisparkle had cause later to remember how Jasper sprang up in a delirious state, crying, "What is the matter, Who did it?" (84). Jasper then explains his response by attributing it to an indigestive after-dinner sleep, a common explanation for bad dreams.

Remembering The Moonstone

The boundary between sleeping and waking is blurred in the novel because Dickens deliberately engages the question of levels of consciousness en route to exploring in Jasper what may be known yet inaccessible to ordinary consciousness. If, as in *The Moonstone*, the detection is inward and the mysteries are psychic, then just as Franklin Blake unknowingly pursues himself when he pursues the thief of the diamond, so Jasper pursues himself in pursuing the murderer of Edwin. But whereas the reenactment of the opium scene ultimately delivers Blake to himself – integrates him – Jasper's habitual slippage from one state of consciousness to another does not suggest such clear demarcations of memory as Dr. Elliotson proposed: "As, in some cases of drunkenness, and in others of animal magnetism, there are two states of consciousness which never clash, but each of which pursues its separate course as though it were continuous instead of broken" (14). From the outset, Dickens is exploring a more mixed condition of consciousness. The opening scene – an opium-induced vision – introduces Jasper to us as one whose "consciousness has fantastically … pieced itself together" (1) as he comes down from his Eastern fantasy to recognize the dingy surroundings of the opium den. He knows and remembers what his visions are and what he has experienced during his opium trance.

The crucial point here is that Jasper does not start out a double self with two separate phases of existence – the respectable choir-master, within whom lurks an unknown, dark, murderous alter ego. Critics of the novel who posit a split self for Jasper work on the assumption that, in one state of consciousness, he is Edwin's loving and "moddly coddlying" uncle, while in another, induced by opium, he is Edwin's murderous rival. The division between good-uncle / bad-uncle states is far too categoric for the shifting states of mind that characterize Jasper.[95] We could just as well ascribe his behavior to a studied and habitual duplicity, whereby he performs as the benign uncle but all the while harbors perfectly conscious feral fantasies of expunging his nephew.[96] Furthermore, even when he seems to have left his opium-induced state, he is well aware of his murderous "visions" and knows that they need to be concealed. While he wishes them to remain intelligible, they are something approaching a point of pride. Hence Jasper disparages the opium visions that the old woman or her other clients might have: "What visions can *she* have? ... What can she rise to, under any quantity of opium ..." (2).

From all we see of Jasper, therefore, he seems to be quite conscious of his dark desires. He has a double life, to be sure, but, as the early chapters reveal, he is very well aware of it and knows that he is obsessed, seething and angry. Though a respected choir-master, Jasper reveals himself to be frustrated by his stultifying life in the backwater of Cloisterham, to and from which no railway service is planned. In an outburst about his boredom with his job as choir-master, Jasper rages that, like the wretched monk who took to carving demons out of the stalls and seats and desks, he will have to take to carving them out of his heart (10). This suggests the inward, self-destructive turn of outwardly vented frustration, and is construed by Jasper as a form of self-control over anarchic and murderous tendencies. If Jasper were simply two personalities – one, a loving and tender uncle, the other, a plotting and vicious murderer – Dickens would hardly take pains to show that Jasper knows of his rage and anger. The very reason that he goes to the opium den is to still a "pain" – the opium allows him to revel in the fantasy of murder, which is satisfying because it feels like a reality.

Prior to Edwin's disappearance, Jasper seems frequently to act with malice aforethought, quite aware of his sinister and deliberate plans. In order to set Edwin and Neville against each other, Jasper has spiked their drinks, or so the narrator strongly hints as Jasper prepares them a glass of mulled wine that seemed to "require much mixing and compounding" (59). When Jasper goads Neville with the image of Edwin's easy prospects – a life of stirring adventure, a life of domestic ease and love – he recapitulates the discussion he had earlier with Edwin in which he raged against the monotony of his own life. The young men become flushed and argumentative, their speech thick and indistinct. That Jasper has orchestrated the friction is beyond doubt. In addition, we know that he certainly drugs Durdles so that he can take his key in the crypt. These instances suggest that we never see Jasper but that he is consciously plotting and planning the murder of Edwin. In support of this view, Dickens's notes clearly indicate intention and planning on Jasper's part – Jasper lays his ground, fomenting the quarrel: smoothing the way, that is, for Jasper's plan. At least in the scenes before the attempted murder, Jasper never appears in a state that seems unaware of his murderous plans. By the time we see him wooing Rosa, he seems either more duplicitous than ever, or truly estranged from memory of his murderous attempt on Edwin's life.

The trajectory here is thus the opposite of that in *The Moonstone*. Jasper starts out knowing his dark plot but becomes dissociated from knowledge of it; he will thus never come to the same startling conclusion as Franklin Blake – that he himself is the unwitting guilty party he has been pursuing. The point is that Jasper develops a divided consciousness as a *result* of the crime, not that he commits the crime in or because of a state of dual consciousness.

The second opium-den scene offers support for this view. Here Jasper seems far less sure of the line between fantasy and reality, and the distinction between what he has done and what he has only fantasized doing. Both the reader and John Jasper are perplexed about the line between what is remembered and what is imagined, seen and only envisioned. In this scene there are repeated contrasts between the vision and reality: "it was *really* done," "it was *really* made," "it comes to be *real* at last," "that must be *real*" (208–10). As we know, Jasper has fantasized for some time the killing of his nephew, has done it over and over, countless times in his fancy. Under the influence of opium, he seems to know that he did really do it. Before he succumbs entirely to the trance state, he asks if there were something on one's mind that one had not "quite determined to do," would one fantasize about it under the influence of the opium? But then, falling deeper into the visions that the opium induces, he says: "I did it so often, and through such expanses of time, that when it was really done, it seemed not worth the doing, it was done so soon" (208).[97] Jasper suddenly seems to be recalling the real event or seeing a different vision from the usual. This one is "'the poorest of all. No struggle, no consciousness of peril, no entreaty – and yet I never saw that before.' With a start … 'Look at it! Look what a poor, mean, miserable thing it is! *That* must be real. It's over!'" (210). What this scene inscribes is Jasper's confusion in memory. The opium visions reveal a blurred line between reality relived (that is, vivid memory) and fantasy revisited. Jasper is seeing something that does not match his past fantasies and may therefore be a flashback – an accurate record – of the real that is nevertheless unavailable to ordinary conscious memory. In the passage just quoted, the referents to the important little words "that" and "it" are crucial and unidentifiable. Whether referring to the vision or the victim, "it" is a poor second to its prior luxuriant fantasies. What Jasper doesn't know when he visits Princess Puffer on this occasion is whether his opium trance reveals a poor fantasy or a transcription of reality, no longer available to him as an integrated memory.

Like Doctor Candy's disjointed and delirious confession revealing his drugging of Franklin Blake, the words are intelligible only to the prepared listener.[98] In *The Moonstone*, this is someone with both medical knowledge and personal experience of altered states of mind – the enigmatic Ezra

Jennings; in *Edwin Drood*, we can be fairly sure that Princess Puffer, an addict herself and dispenser of a professional pipe, finds his words intelligible. If the vision of the paltry murder is a memory, it will no doubt provide an explanation of what Jasper has done and to whom.

I want to return to the question of accountability with which I began. If Durdles' expedition is "unaccountable" in the sense that there are insufficient reasons and causes to explain it, there is a further meaning of "accountable" which becomes important in the novel: accountability as responsibility. Thus Neville defends himself to Edwin after he has brought up the subject of Edwin's engagement: "I am not accountable for Mr. Crisparkle's mentioning the matter to me, quite openly" (55). The question in *Edwin Drood* is whether, when the plot becomes accountable (explained and coherent), Jasper will also be accountable (responsible). To the extent that the novel broaches issues of dissociation and fragmentation, it also raises the question of criminal responsibility and accountability which, as Joel Eigen has observed, would come to be hotly debated in cases of multiple personality. In this last Dickensian foray into crime and punishment, I would argue, Dickens is particularly interested in the aftermath of crime and the way the mind, riven by guilt (and, in Jasper's case, shock that the murder was unnecessary), dissociates itself from responsibility. "Alibi" means literally "in another place"; Jasper's alibi will doubtless not hold, which is why he will find himself in the condemned cell. What will hold, however, is the alibi of discontinuousness, from whose elsewhere he does not return and which takes him mentally to a place other than the confrontation of his own responsibility. Hypocrisy and what Dickens calls in *Great Expectations* "self-swindling" easily become habitual. In Pip's case, a brain fever produces delirium but ultimately restores him to himself and allows him to settle his account. The more frenzied and intense such states of hypocritical pretense become, Dickens seems to argue, the more discontinuous and truly fragmenting they may end up being.

CHAPTER 4

Overwhelming emotion and psychic shock in George Eliot's The Lifted Veil and Daniel Deronda

I "FINELY ORGANISED FOR PAIN": THE HORROR OF AMPLIFIED EMOTION IN THE LIFTED VEIL

There is much pain that is quite noiseless; and vibrations that make human agonies are often a mere whisper in the roar of hurrying existence.
George Eliot, Felix Holt, the Radical

[N]o living being can penetrate the consciousness of another.
Alexander Bain, The Emotions and the Will (1859, 49–50)

The intricate relationship of emotion to thought, memory and judgment – indeed all processes of cognition – is the subject of much of George Eliot's fiction as well as being part of its avowed practical project. Following her agnosticism and her belief in human community and fellow-feeling as the well-spring of moral values, her manifesto as a fictional artist is to arouse and educate emotions, particularly the capacity to feel sympathy, in her readers. The primacy of affective life is so powerfully asserted in her fiction that it is not entirely surprising to find George Eliot discussed in the company of Spinoza and Darwin in a recent academic textbook on the emotions.[1] Lydgate's project as a scientist is to get to the core physiology of emotion: "to pierce the obscurity of those minute processes which prepare human misery and joy, those invisible thoroughfares which are the first lurking-places of anguish, mania, and crime, that delicate poise and tran-sition that determine the growth of happy or unhappy consciousness."[2] The Finale of Middlemarch (1872) reflects on Dorothea's diffusive influence, regretting her anonymity but offering the consolation that there was no life "possible to Dorothea which was not filled with emotion." The same could be said for any character in George Eliot's fiction that makes its painful way with any degree of success. Affective life is generally represented as a good – something to be nourished and respected. It is understood as connection and manifested as love, compassion and sympathy. Only in a few instances does George Eliot explore at length the implications of unmitigated negative emotions and their effects on consciousness. *The Lifted Veil* is the most sustained and prolonged instance.

Once considered to be an aberration in the George Eliot oeuvre and described by the author herself as a "jeu de melancholie," *The Lifted Veil* articulates, albeit in an inverse way, George Eliot's engagement with problems of consciousness and the sympathy that should arise from knowing what transpires in other minds. George Henry Lewes was reported to have said that the moral of the tale is plain enough: "[I]t is only an exaggeration of what happens – the one-sided knowing of things in relation to the self – not whole knowledge because 'tout comprehendre [*sic*] est tout pardoner.'"[3] Lewes's statement has been influential in subsequent criticism of the novella; not only was he George Eliot's close confidant and spouse, but his physiological research is a crucial context for understanding the novella. His comments have been the spur for discussions of Latimer's egotism, and the importance of sympathy and fellow-feeling, those two great keywords in the terrain of George Eliot's fiction. Some fourteen years after the novella was first published, George Eliot added an epigraph cementing the importance attached to knowledge in the service of "human fellowship." I rehearse these two factors as contributing to the common critical assumption that, when George Eliot is talking about feeling and emotion, she is primarily interested in sympathy. I want, however, to focus more broadly on a wide array of emotional response – particularly painful and negative emotions – in order to explore George Eliot's developing understanding of the inextricability of thought and feeling, or, to put it another way, the thought-like qualities of emotion and its behavior under overwhelming circumstances.

The Lifted Veil explores the way in which we process emotion and how emotions both reveal and influence our cognitive schemes – questions that are of significance to this study since they are closely related to the idea of affect regulation and therefore to some twentieth-century conceptions of trauma. As I have outlined in previous chapters, current ideas about trauma center on the too-powerful effect of certain kinds of negative emotional experience. In some theories of trauma, overpowering emotion affects cognition in that it interrupts the assimilation and integration of the experience as part of the subject's conscious memory. The inability to regulate powerful and unbidden emotional responses triggered by association with the cataclysmic event disables the trauma sufferer.

The Lifted Veil is a narrative about excessive exposure and the vulnerable subject's inability to regulate stimuli and response. Ideas about the

processing of overwhelming feelings, their unbidden and intrusive manifestation, and the withdrawal or dissociation they occasion are central to this
story, as they are to contemporary trauma theory. The crucial difference is
that Latimer experiences the *other's* thoughts and emotions, rather than his
own, as the unregulated intrusion. Trauma is a concept about the inadequacy of self-protection and defense. The distancing or regulating mechanisms of memory, narrative and other forms of mediation render ordinary
experience assimilable. Without the ability to regulate what comes inside,
the subject is unable to process experience in the ordinary way. In this sense,
the protective insulation or imperviousness of the self is the veil. Its lifting
allows a long, hard look at the horror and shock of heightened and unwilling
access to the minds of others. To be "better able to *imagine* and to *feel* the
pains and the joys of those who differ from themselves" may be the corner-
stone of George Eliot's belief in the sympathetic identification encouraged
by aesthetic experience; but what if heightened access turns out to be
painful and damaging?[4] In *Daniel Deronda* (1876), George Eliot writes
that "[n]o chemical process shows a more wonderful activity than the
transforming influence of the thoughts we imagine to be going on in
another."[5] If the effect of such fantasies is so powerful and (following the
idea of a chemical process) transformative, what, *The Lifted Veil* asks,
would be the transforming influence of *knowing* rather than imagining?
And what if such knowing were experienced as an inundation that
rendered the self and its borders precarious? Why would withdrawal
rather than outreach not be the response of the subject, vulnerable to
the incessant burden of others' thoughts and feelings? What, to invoke
Lydgate's quest, are the minute processes that prepare misery or joy,
happy or unhappy consciousness, sympathetic identification or self-
protective retreat? The text articulates the puzzle of poise – the necessity
of a separate self, reasonably insulated from the outside, and, at the same
time, an inner world healthy enough to accommodate the other without
a sense of being besieged.

Emotional transactions

Beryl Gray refers in her landmark essay "Pseudoscience and George Eliot's
'The Lifted Veil'" to Latimer as being "cursed with the disease of involun-
tary thought-reading."[6] But almost every time George Eliot refers to
Latimer's powers of superadded consciousness, she writes of his ability to
read *emotions* or *feelings* along with thoughts and ideas. More recently in
"Blood, Bodies and *The Lifted Veil*," Kate Flint has noted that "the workings

of the body are inseparably bound in with the emotions," an observation that rightly serves to locate George Eliot in the context of the new physiological psychology, and to underscore Flint's focus on the importance of the body in the novella.[7] But how George Eliot conceives of emotions is itself a complex question, as I have begun to suggest in Chapter 1. How does emotional experience shape, augment or impede cognition?[8] To put it in terms of Martha Nussbaum's recent inquiry into the cognitive nature of emotions, "What is the intelligence of emotions in this novella?"[9]

This question has a legacy in the physiological psychology of the mid nineteenth century. At the time George Eliot was writing *The Lifted Veil*, there was considerable debate about the nature of emotions – their relations to the body, and their distinction from the will and the intellect. The novella was published in the same year as Alexander Bain's *The Emotions and the Will*, the companion volume to his earlier *The Senses and the Intellect* (1855). Herbert Spencer had recently published the monumental *Principles of Psychology* (1855), which, George Eliot wrote, "gave a new impulse to psychology," and George Henry Lewes, who would come to be regarded with growing respect in scientific communities despite his essentially amateur status, was developing his ideas about physiology and psychology in *The Physiology of Common Life* (1859–60).[10] Placing George Eliot's story in the context of Victorian and subsequent emotion theory, I begin by exploring Latimer's narrative as an affective memoir.

If we think of Latimer's account of himself as engaged in debates about the nature of emotion, it leaps into life as a memoir of his constrained and increasingly attenuated emotional life. Addressed to strangers rather than loved ones, it immediately invokes an emotional appraisal of his place in the world as unloved and unremembered, indeed injured: "I have no near relatives who will make up, by weeping over my grave, for the wounds they inflicted on me when I was among them."[11] Although the narrative that ensues looks like an autobiographical account of the facts of Latimer's childhood and education, it is emphatically a careful canvassing of issues that are germane to nineteenth-century discussions of the role of emotion and passions in forming and constituting the self. That is, the terms in which Latimer recounts his autobiography are primarily affective: a childhood that "seems happier ... than it really was" suggests the importance of feeling and emotional experience in structuring his recollections:

I had a tender mother: even now, after the dreary lapse of long years, a slight trace of sensation accompanies the remembrance of her caress as she held me on her knee – her arms round my little body, her cheek pressed on mine. I had a complaint of the eyes that made me blind for a little while, and she kept me on her knee from morning till night. That unequalled love soon vanished out of my life, and even to my childish consciousness it was as if that life had become more chill. I rode my little white pony with the groom by my side as before, but there were no loving eyes looking at me as I mounted, no glad arms opened to me when I came back. Perhaps I missed my mother's love more than most children of seven or eight would have done, to whom the other pleasures of life remained as before; for I was certainly a very sensitive child. (4–5)

What is immediately noteworthy in this passage is the way in which, despite its unemotional tone and matter-of-fact narration, Latimer's memories are focused on emotion and feeling: the sensation of his mother's caress; the loss of her unequaled love; the fact that the same activity – riding his pony as before – feels different now that his mother is gone. As if to counter the idea that young children don't register such loss, he says that *even* his "childish consciousness" experiences the chill of her departure. Latimer's narrative communicates this great loss dispassionately, from which we may judge its devastating effects – a progressive recoil and distancing from any contact that provokes feelings. It is worth remembering that, at the time of writing the novella, George Eliot was also composing the opening scenes of *The Mill on the Floss*, whose omniscient narrator, in the opening paragraphs, has a memorable, personalized and reminiscential moment suffused with the emotional remembrance of things past. This moment serves to usher in the novel's emphasis on the formative power of bonds created by early childhood experiences. Latimer's formative experiences have resulted in a warped and twisted emotional growth: his nature, as he emphasizes, has been formed in an "uncongenial medium, which could never foster it into happy, healthy development" (7). Unsafe, unloved and defensive, the child Latimer is father of the man.

In his telescoped account of childhood, Latimer is at pains to show what a "sensitive" child he was, "affected" by loud noises, which provoked emotional responses evident in his sobbing and trembling. Latimer, it seems, was always especially accessible and susceptible. In contrast, his unyielding, unemotional father is "one of those people who are always like themselves from day to day," a stranger to the moods, fluctuations and fraught responsiveness of his younger, unfavored son (5). While the narrative of the phrenologically inclined Mr. Letherall has provoked critical discussion about the status of phrenology in the text, and George Eliot's changing attitudes towards Combe's ideas, the schoolmaster is expressly important in Latimer's account as the object of the child's first vehement emotion – hatred.

As a young man he is relatively happy in Geneva but only because he is able to seclude himself from painful human contacts. Alone, he "finds no vent but in silent tears on the sunny bank, when the noonday light sparkles on the water, or in an inward shudder at the sound of harsh human tones, the sight of a cold human eye – this dumb passion brings with it a fatal solitude of soul in the society of one's fellow-men" (7). He thus feels least solitary when surrounded by the mountains and lakes, which provide "a cherishing love such as no human face had shed on me since my mother's love had vanished out of my life" (7). Given this disposition, Latimer explains, it is understandable that he formed no close contacts, the exception being a similarly shunned youth, Meunier, orphaned, poor, ugly and derided, who will become an important player later in the tale. The bond was not intellectual, Latimer specifies; he timidly approached Meunier out of "sympathetic resentment" and comradeship arose from "community of feeling" (8).

Having carefully set up a narrator whose capacity for relationship and healthy emotional exchange has been warped by his early years, George Eliot then imagines what it would mean to foist on him (rather than merely grant him access to) the consciousness of others. Drawing on the well-established view that a serious illness could bring about remarkable, even miraculous, changes in consciousness, George Eliot has Latimer undergo his first clairvoyant experience after a long convalescence. Like the young woman in Coleridge's example, whose illness brought to consciousness her hidden and unconscious memory of foreign tongues, Latimer too experiences a marvelous and inexplicable shift in powers of mind. In George Eliot's conception, he does not, however, recover knowledge that he has unknowingly stored in the recesses of the unconscious mind, but is able to see a place he has never seen before. This new-found clairvoyance seems also to reverberate in some way with the fact of his temporary period of blindness as a young child. It is as if this "second sight" (as clairvoyance is often termed) relates to the earlier episode as yet another disturbance of vision. Whereas the first was associated with deprivation, this is a superadded faculty. More tellingly, the blindness was compensated for and remembered in terms of enhanced maternal love; the advent of insight is thus, in the logic of his emotions, linked to Latimer's increasing alienation and withdrawal from others.

George Eliot had recently drawn on the idea of clairvoyance in describing the novelist's craft in her first major novel, *Adam Bede* (1859). Just as the drop of ink on the palm of a young innocent child was supposed to be able to reveal to Indian seers places not present, so the drop of ink at the end of the novelist's pen will conjure similar far-flung representations. Invoking clairvoyance again in *The Lifted Veil*, George Eliot is not so much investigating the practice and validity of mesmerism, as several critics have suggested, or gesturing to the visionary realism of the novelist, but using this much-discussed (if little understood) phenomenon as a technology to investigate what kinds of knowledge matter.[12]

George Eliot invokes several current explanations for aberrations in consciousness in order to eliminate them as adequate accounts for Latimer's condition. Latimer immediately imagines that his precise visualization of Prague is the advent of poetic creativity, an association that speaks to a well-established discourse linking the imagination, creativity and unconscious mental process. Attempts to explain unconscious processes were, since the eighteenth century, closely allied to discussions of poetic or literary imagination. When E. S. Dallas described the action of the imagination in *The Gay Science*, he drew on the notion of the "hidden soul" and the idea of the fruitful traffic between conscious and unconscious realms. What Latimer finds, however, is that creativity has nothing to do with what he perceives, since he cannot repeat the experience or exercise his will to summon other similar experiences. He has not found his "hidden soul," or, as he calls it, the "flash of strange light" – his visionary, poetic power – that he awaits with "palpitating eagerness" (11). The scene in Prague will function later as a validation of his powers, proving that what he sees is real rather than imagined. But more importantly, in terms of my focus, it serves the narrative as a trigger for emotional response. He is joyful and eager when he understands the experience to be evidence of his poetic creativity, hopeful about his future prowess and career, as if the stocks in a rather lowly self-estimation are suddenly on the rise.

Latimer's next experience of extraordinary consciousness is a prevision of his father with a young woman, Bertha Grant, whom he will soon meet. George Eliot moves from a consideration of poetic genius to an alternative common explanation of heightened consciousness – diseased mental functioning. "Might it not rather be ... a sort of intermittent delirium, concentrating my energy of brain into moments of unhealthy activity, and leaving my saner hours all the more barren?" (12). Once again, Latimer's attempt to account for his powers recapitulates contemporary debates about the nature of aberrant states of consciousness.

In what seems to be a very deliberate ironic twist, George Eliot decrees that her protagonist, who shuns human society and is least unhappy when solitary, should be sentenced to involuntary access to the ongoing "mental processes" of those around him. He cannot filter or block the "vagrant, frivolous ideas and emotions of some uninteresting acquaintance ... [which] would force themselves on my consciousness" (13). And it is precisely because of Latimer's distaste for interaction, his aversion and sensitivity, that he experiences their interiority as irksome. Latimer recoils in horror from what he experiences as a "fermenting heap," the "naked skinless complication" of others' thoughts and emotions. As she will articulate it elsewhere (the roar that lies on the other side of silence), George Eliot imagines this heightened attunement to others as potentially shocking and painful. To endure other people's stream of consciousness (a phrase first used by Lewes) is not a boon of sensitivity but an impossible burden.[13] In general, George Eliot's fiction seeks to amplify experience – to turn up the volume on what is usually unheard – so that we feel more compassion and responsibility for the noiseless suffering of others. But how high should that volume be, and what are the conditions in which compassion might be engendered? Turning up the volume alone is not enough.

Latimer is instructively unusual because he allows George Eliot to show that all his emotional responses and investments relate to a particular set of values and self-perceptions. Shrinking from interaction, nervous and ill-disposed, Latimer of course finds it especially annoying to have the uninteresting stream of consciousness of an acquaintance impinging on his thoughts. And since his relationship with his father and brother is especially strained and unrewarding, it is an "intense pain and grief" to have the "souls" of those closest to him bared, as if under "microscopic vision" (14). Again, the narrative gives prominence to Latimer's emotional responses to his powers – a spectrum that ranges from annoyance to grief and pain. George Eliot's characterization of fraternal rivalry is especially keen. To see into his brother's soul is to find cause for hatred arising from already well-established envy and antipathy:

I am not sure that my disposition was good enough for me to have been quite free from *envy* towards him, even if our desires had not clashed, and if I had been in the healthy human condition which admits of generous confidence and charitable construction. There must always have been an *antipathy* between our natures. As it was, he became in a few weeks an object of *intense hatred* to me; and when he entered the room, still more when he spoke, it was as if a sensation of grating metal had set my teeth on edge. My diseased consciousness was more intensely and continually occupied with his *thoughts and emotions*, than with those of any other person who came in my way. I was perpetually *exasperated* with the petty promptings of his conceit and his love of patronage, with his self-complacent belief in Bertha Grant's passion for him, with his half-pitying contempt for me – seen not in the ordinary indications of intonation and phrase and slight action, which an acute and suspicious mind is on the watch for, but in all their naked skinless complication. (Emphasis added; 14–15)

My epigraph from Bain's *The Emotions and the Will* – "no living being can penetrate the consciousness of another" – suggests that we are obliged to work with outward manifestations of emotion. As Bain explains, "If there be any peculiar shade, tone or colouring of emotion that has no outward sign or efficacy, such peculiarity is inscrutable to the inquirer. It is enough for us to lay hold of the outward manifestations, and to recognise all the distinctions that they bring to light."[14] As the experimental exception, Latimer is ironically unable to resist penetrating the consciousness of others.

But what he sees is not, contrary to his insistence, the naked truth. Time and again, the narrative reveals that whatever knowledge Latimer's special powers provide is inflected by his habitual emotional landscape. His knowledge of the other is profoundly shaped by the way he is oriented towards the world and those around him. We experience the world through an emotional lens; even when that lens is powerful and microscopic, as in the case of Latimer's special consciousness, it is still inextricably colored by our own emotional make-up. Whereas someone else might interpret the stuff of his brother's thoughts and feelings more generously, recognizing in another's fallibilities his own shortcomings as an erring, struggling human being, Latimer himself admits that his condition makes charitable construction impossible. But the fact that he is an unusual case underlines rather than diminishes the force of George Eliot's implicit conclusion here: emotions change the equation; they operate so as to shape and appraise what we take to be "measured fact" or unadorned information. Emotions are important, because, as Martha Nussbaum asserts, "they reveal the world to the creature, the creature's deepest goals to itself, and all of this to the astute observer."[15] Nussbaum draws here on the work of psychologist Richard Lazarus, who suggests that emotions are a form of intense attention, engagement and appraisal:

From an emotional reaction we can learn much about what a person has at stake in the encounter with the environment or in life in general, how that person interprets self and world, and how harms, threats and challenges are coped with. No other concept in psychology is as richly revealing of the way an individual relates to life and to ... the specifics of the physical and social environment.[16]

The concept of *eudaimonia* is relevant in this regard. An ancient Greek term signifying all that is concerned with what allows a person to flourish, "*eudaimonia* is taken to be inclusive of all to which the agent ascribes intrinsic value."[17] In *Upheavals of Thought: The Intelligence of Emotions* (2001), Martha Nussbaum argues that emotions are eudaimonistic in that they

> embody the person's own commitment to the object as part of her scheme of ends. This is why, in the negative cases, they are felt as tearing the self apart: because they have to do with me and my own, my plans and goals, what is important in my own conception (or more inchoate sense) of what it is for me to live well.[18]

Nussbaum argues persuasively for a cognitive–evaluative understanding of emotion. By "cognitive" she means simply "concerned with receiving and processing information," not necessarily "the presence of elaborate calcu-lation, of computation, or even of reflexive self-awareness."[19] Emotions contain assessments of well-being, flourishing and value. Indeed, they have attributes that make them "look very much like thoughts, after all" – attributes such as "their aboutness, their intentionality, their basis in beliefs, their connection with evaluation."[20]

According to Thomas Dixon's explanation of the Victorian physiology of emotions, which I outlined in Chapter 1, all of Bain, Spencer and Darwin produced physiological and non-cognitive theories of the emotions:

> Spencer adopted a model of the mind very similar to Brown's, in which mental states were divided into cognitions on the one hand and non-cognitive "feelings" on the other. The feelings were then divided into sensations and emotions. Emotions for Spencer, as for Brown, Chalmers and Bain, were, simply by definition, non-cognitive feelings. For Spencer, Bain and Darwin these emotions were virtually constituted by the bodily agitations and nervous activities associated with them.[21]

A closer reading of Bain's *The Emotions and the Will* shows, however, that he pays attention to what he calls the mental side of feelings and emotions, even though these are dependent on the body. And Spencer begins his discussion in a chapter entitled "The Feelings" by admitting at once that "intellectual processes cannot be separated from epi-peripheral feelings, real or ideal; since invariably, these are either the immediate terms, or the ultimate components of the terms, between which relations are established in every cognition." He repeatedly owns that "no kind of feeling, sensational or emotional, can be wholly freed from the intellectual element" and that, though psychical intellectual states may appear to be dissociated from emotional states, such states can be shown to be both emotive and cognitive. Cognition and emotion, he avers, are "inextricably entangled"; "no emotion can be *absolutely* free from cognition."[22] While certainly endeavoring to draw attention to the bodily or physiological nature of emotions, neither Bain nor Spencer sought to deny or rule out their cognitive component.

A more thoroughly integrated view of mental process is to be found in George Henry Lewes's *The Physiology of Common Life*, which repeatedly emphasizes the interconnectedness of all centers of the body and mind. Lewes's vision of the mind–body entity is like George Eliot's vision of the social body. Every part is connected and exerts an influence on all others:

It is a consequence of the wonderful complexity of our organism, in which each part plays on another, that remote and unsuspected influences produce important results. Mental agitation will suddenly arrest or increase the secretions; imperfect, or too abundant, secretion will depress, or confuse the mind. An idea will agitate the heart, and disturb the liver; a languid liver will disturb the serenity of the mind; a worm in the intestine will produce melancholy, and even madness. – So indissolubly is our mental life bound up with our bodily life.[23]

Lewes defines emotion as "the form of cerebral sensibility which is determined by connections with the ganglia of visceral sensation." It is not for nothing that the ancients "believed that the heart, the liver, and the spleen were seats of the passions; popular language still preserves this notion ... Both the ancient and the modern doctrine are reconciled in the view I have put forth, which makes the viscera the main source of emotions, just as the organs of sense are the main source of ideas."[24] The system just articulated would seem to render emotion corporeal and physical, but from Lewes's perspective every mental process begins in sensation. The sensations of sense derived from special organs link us to the external world. Emotions, by contrast, bring us knowledge of what is going on inside us.

Reason has often been considered impersonal, but no one has ever considered Emotion to be so. The intellectual operations always imply an externality; even when we are speculating about our own feelings or mental operations, we always view them as if *apart* from ourselves. The Emotions have a deeper root in personality. Every man, unless he be a subtle psychologist, believes that the redness is in the rose, the sweetness in the apple, and the loudness in the thunder. But no man, not even the psychologist, believes that love, or hate, the fear or reverence, the desire or disgust, which moves him, belongs to the object which excites the feeling.[25]

In light of this distinction, *The Lifted Veil* operates tantalizingly to make us think about the status of Latimer's heightened knowledge. While the access to other minds suggests that the knowledge is objective – the loudness is in the thunder – Latimer's emotional responses cannot be separated out from the "truth" of what he learns. Moved by hate, desire, disgust and envy, Latimer's feelings belong to him and not to the "objects" that excite them; that is, the kind of knowledge that emotions convey is knowledge of our own evaluative responses and processes. Latimer's reactions to his brother, his father and Bertha are therefore revelations not so much about them as about himself and his emotional orientation to the world around him. This is the "one-sided knowing" to which Lewes refers in his comments on the moral of the tale. Further, George Eliot shows that how we feel about things at any given moment is significantly inflected by prior experience. Emotions incorporate history. Whereas Darwin, Spencer and later William James were interested in emotion as an expression of inherited habits – the history of the human race – George Eliot is more immediately interested in this story in individual and personal history and its shaping of emotional geography.

As if to solidify the importance of the emotional component in thought, George Eliot allows a control situation for her experiment. The notable and singular exception to Latimer's reluctant penetration of the inner world of others is Bertha. Only in her case is he free to project his desires on to her and imagine that the emotions he feels are correspondingly felt by her: "[A] young enthusiast is unable to imagine the total negation in another mind of the emotions which are stirring his own" (15). As reluctant as we are to take in the feelings of others, so we are eager to imagine our own emotions matched and met in the other. In this regard George Eliot demonstrates the relational, interactive and indeed phantasmatic aspects of human emotion: "The most independent people feel the effect of a man's silence in heightening their value for his opinion" (15). Only in Bertha's case is Latimer compelled to read (and misread) the "outward signs," waiting before the "closed secret" of her face "as if it were the shrine of the doubtfully benignant deity who ruled his destiny" (15). George Eliot thus sets up a system in which transmission and reception of two kinds can be contrasted. On the one hand, we have excess or overload – the inadvertent transmission and unwilling reception of the whole "fermenting heap" – the conscious and unconscious thoughts and feelings of others. On the other, she constructs a scenario of dearth or scarcity – the eager and anxious detection and decoding of slight and semiotically unstable signals. In the case of Bertha, a "mysterious seclusion of soul" renders Latimer's youthful delusions about her feelings possible. In relation to Bertha alone, he is compelled to proceed on less than full disclosure of interiority, forced to imagine because he cannot really know, an act of dubious faith signaled by the phrase "I believe she must inwardly …" (16).

It is not just Bertha's opacity that makes her a site for Latimer's projections and delusions. There is also an interesting concession to other forces known to cheat "psychological prediction," namely, desire and physical attraction. George Eliot allows here that how we interpret the usual signs transmitted by others about their inner feelings is inevitably distorted by our own feelings, particularly the force of physical desire. These interferences with reasoned interpretation are termed "fascinations." To be fascinated, in the language of mid-century discourses of consciousness, is to be entranced, mesmerized, put into an altered state of consciousness. Hence critics have concluded that Bertha does actually mesmerize Latimer. But Latimer's fascination for Bertha, which works like a spell over his consciousness, is quite understandable without having to make her a deliberate mesmerist.[26] The fascinating force is less Bertha than Latimer's own emotional state which does the work of entrancing him and putting him into an altered state of consciousness.

When Bertha's mind is for the first time revealed to Latimer, George Eliot constructs a moment of face-off between the two modes of knowing that have been contrasted: knowledge of "measured fact" and emotionally driven appraisal and interpretation. Shifting the use of the term "double consciousness" from signifying alternating states of mind, George Eliot uses it to mean *dual* consciousness, not alternating but parallel: "Are you unable to imagine this double consciousness at work within me, flowing on like two parallel streams that never mingle their waters and blend into a common hue?" In the war between "insight" and "passion," the latter may triumph, which is to say that emotion-based evaluation may have more sway even in the face of fairly certain facts. Ideas, as George Eliot, often points out, are a poor match for the "might of impulse" (21). And so, despite his knowledge of Bertha's evil, Latimer still chooses to pursue and win her. When Latimer finally challenges Bertha on her feelings for his brother, the shadow of his vision of her heartlessness provides a chill of horror in sharp distinction from the "warm-breathing presence" that a moment later possesses him again, like a "returning syren melody which had been overpowered for an instant by the roar of threatening waves" (26). His "superadded consciousness" notwithstanding, it is from "the subtlest web of scarcely perceptible signs" that Latimer weaves fanciful delusions (29). Emotions function like consciousness-altering drugs. As he says, "[a] half-repressed word, a moment's unexpected silence, even an easy fit of petulance on our account, will serve us as *hashish* for a long while" (29).

Heightened or special knowledge avails us nothing, George Eliot seems to be suggesting, if it is out of synchrony with our emotional needs. Latimer tries to convince himself that if he could have foreseen the fate of his brother, if he had had a different image of Bertha, perhaps then his rivalry and competition would have been tempered: "We try to believe … that the egoism within us would have easily been melted, and that it was only the narrowness of our knowledge which hemmed in our generosity, our awe, our human piety, and hindered them from submerging our hard indifference to the sensations and emotions of our fellow" (21–22). It is emphatically not, therefore, a question of the extent or narrowness of knowledge, for one can have full knowledge of the future and still choose a present course in defiance of it. The narrative underlines that it is a question of our own emotional orientation, which will make one thing or another of that knowledge.

Latimer's spite, triumph and rivalry are recognized subsequently as an "egoism," which is dislodged somewhat by his brother's death. There is one small step for Latimer out of his habitual emotional landscape of irritation, envy, pain and annoyance. At the point of his brother's death, a new experience comes to him – the feeling of compassion for and connection to his desolated and disappointed father. Previously, perceptions of paternal inner life have been a source of affliction to Latimer, serving only to reinforce his sense of the incompatibility of their natures; "But now, as I went up to him, and stood beside him in sad silence, I felt the presence of a new element that blended us as we had never been blent before" (27). Latimer describes this access of softened feeling as an involuntary experience: "As I saw into the desolation of my father's heart, I felt a movement of deep pity towards him, which was the beginning of a new affection" (28). Although he does not try to account for this change, it is perhaps prompted by Latimer's own suffering and disappointment. Failing imagination and the education of feeling so that identification becomes a habit, it is personal suffering alone that provides a basis for connection. Where his father was previously only unlike him, they are now alike in their desolation. But as this new affection occurs only in his father's last days, it does not establish itself as a strong element in Latimer's emotional cosmology. Rather, similar small movements towards sympathetic identification are later a cue for decamping. Latimer subsequently recounts that whenever he felt his heart going out towards others who were becoming familiar, he recoiled for fear that his power of insight would return. We see him arrested, therefore, in emotional development, resisting connection to others as it will make him painfully vulnerable to their clamoring interiority. But this painful accessibility is what relationship always is, George Eliot insists, here and elsewhere.

When finally Bertha's shrouded self is ongoingly revealed to Latimer, the last possibility of doubt, mystery and expectation is banished. Up to this point, apart from that early (disregarded) moment in which her inner world was revealed, he has "read her thoughts only through the language of her lips and demeanour" (31). As with other revelations regarding Bertha, he feels a "cold tremulousness" (32) akin to the painful sensation of a "sharp," "cutting" wind which he felt in his first vision of her (11), or the sensation of being poisoned in the vision prompted by the portrait of Lucrezia Borgia. The revelation of her interiority removes Latimer from her power as he now wants nothing from her and she can affect him in no other way than to produce a "chill shudder of repulsion" (32). Latimer cannot move beyond these alternatives: the rule of desire and impulse that disregards insight, or the withdrawal and death of desire and affect in the face of knowledge. What is missing is the hard-won affective bond, the struggle for intimacy and connection despite the revelation of wounding and unpalatable knowledge.

As Latimer shrinks from the shock of contact, so he defends himself from painful affect and indeed loses the power of insight:

[F]or the last year or more a modification had been going forward in my mental condition, and was growing more and more marked. My insight into the minds of those around me was becoming dimmer and more fitful, and the ideas that crowded my double consciousness became less and less dependent on any personal contact. All that was personal in me seemed to be suffering a gradual death, so that I was losing the organ through which the personal agitations and projects of others could affect me. (35)

In its place, his mind travels clairvoyantly to far-flung places:

It was as if the relation between me and my fellow-men was more and more deadened, and my relation to what we call the inanimate was quickened into new life. The more I lived apart from society, and in proportion as my wretchedness subsided from the violent throb of agonized passion into the dullness of habitual pain, the more frequent and vivid became such visions … (36)

As the capacity for affect diminishes, it is replaced by a sense of a pitiless, unknown presence. Without affect, problematic and painful as it may sometimes be, neither human community nor the external world offers any possibility of accommodation.

Science and the "unknowable"

Latimer was educated to offset his perceived deficiencies, which meant being forced to learn what did not interest him: "I was hungry for human deeds and human emotions," he explains, "so I was to be plentifully crammed with the mechanical powers, the elementary bodies, and the phenomena of electricity and magnetism" (6). No doubt, he continues, "[a] better-constituted boy would certainly have ... found the phenomena of electricity and magnetism as fascinating as I was, every Thursday, assured they were" (6). While the passage seems at face value an energetic indictment of schooling that makes the least of a child's talents and interests – think of Tom Tulliver, who will be humiliated by the classics and geometry at the hands of Mr. Stelling – I want to pause over George Eliot's repeated reference to "electricity and magnetism." As we have seen, physiological psychology was engaged in exploring how such scientific phenomena could explain the workings of nerves, consciousness, emotions and mind. Magnetism was of course closely associated with theories of mesmerism, also known as animal magnetism. Electricity (or something like it) was increasingly understood as the technology by which nerves transmitted messages, and the idea of the body as a battery that could be charged or depleted gained dominance during the century.[27]

The invisible force of electricity, apparently an immaterial phenomenon, spurred the cultural imagination of communication and transmission (as in the telegraph) that collapsed time and space. The new technologies of invisible and instantaneous transmission fed explanations of the ways in which, within the mind, impulses and messages might be transmitted, as well as theories of how minds might communicate with each other. In 1882, Frederick Myers would introduce the term "telepathy" to name the process he fervently hoped to find scientifically provable: the transmission from one mind to another of impressions conveyed independently of ordinary organs of sense.[28] But well before the term "telepathy" was coined, technologies such as telegraphy revolutionized the transmission of messages from one mind to another by electrical signal and seemed to presage even more miraculous means of communication.

If mental physiologists were interested in phenomena such as electricity and magnetism and the technologies to which they gave rise, how valid is Latimer's opposition in his narrative between human deeds and emotions, on the one hand, and scientific phenomena, on the other? Remote and opposed as it seems, the study of magnetism and electricity turns out to have bearing on the way human emotion works.

There is therefore some irony in the facts that Meunier's great interest has been the "psychological relations of disease" and that Latimer wishes to avail himself of the opportunity to tell him the "secrets of [his] lot" in the hope that he might receive some "comprehension and sympathy" in his "large and susceptible mind" (38). That Latimer hopes for understanding of "human deeds and human emotions" (6) from a famous scientist suggests a larger scope for science in its application to human problems than Latimer originally allowed. Meunier's own suffering, perhaps, has led him to pursue the relationship between body and mind, feeling and thought, in a way that Latimer, thinking oppositionally, could not have imagined.

The contentious revivification scene continues this focus on the possibility of scientific explanation of human problems. Indeed, it thoroughly undermines the contrast between human deeds and emotions, on the one hand, and scientific learning, on the other.[29] In this regard, it reverberates with the final chapter of Lewes's *The Physiology of Common Life*, which is entitled "Life and Death." Lewes here dispels any notion of a vital force or principle separate from the body itself. "Can we suppose the existence of some vital centre from which all vital actions issue?" No, says Lewes. Only if vital force "merely indicates the dynamical condition of the organism" is the phrase unobjectionable.[30] Just as in the case of the locomotive we cannot imagine a "moving principle driving the engine, irrespective of coal burned and water expended," so we must favor the physiological over the metaphysiological conception.[31] Mrs. Archer's revival banishes the idea that a soul or Vital Principle is independent of the body as a system. She is like the watch that has stopped (another analogy used by Lewes and others) and is for a short time rewound; it simply begins ticking again when its parts are reactivated and continues its action at the moment it ceased to move.

But, Lewes is clear to point out, studying and understanding the physiology of life in no way diminishes the fact that "Life," as a revelation of the "Unknowable," is still a great and impenetrable mystery.[32] We may understand life as the dynamic condition of the organism and yet recognize that "the mystery which underlies all Existence cannot be unveiled by us."[33] The lifting of the veil between one mind and another, or even between the states of the organism we call "life" or "death" is not the unveiling of the mystery to which Lewes is referring. That mystery is what underlies the processes of life. It is as George Eliot wrote to Barbara Bodichon in a much-quoted letter of December 1859 after the publication of Darwin's *The Origin of Species*: "So the world gets on step by step towards brave clearness and honesty! But to me the Development theory and all other explanations of processes by which things came to be, produce a feeble impression compared with the mystery that lies under the processes."[34] The fact that Mrs. Archer is revived means that the body is briefly restored to a dynamic condition before decay has set in. It does not solve the mystery of what lies under the process of "Life," which remains "Unknowable." It therefore returns Meunier to the fact that life is much more than a "scientific problem" (42). Critics have discussed this scene as evidence of the novel's caveat against human overreaching and taboo knowledge, but I would suggest that George Eliot includes it to underline that, even if we know for a fact that our bodies and minds are corporeal, we have not explained the "Unknowable" and we need not recoil in horror as if the mystery were dispelled.[35]

For Latimer, however, the scene is of a piece with what he has learned – to see and hear beyond the ordinary boundaries of the senses, to know beyond the ordinary capacity of the mind, is to uncover the horror of others: "As for me, this scene seemed of one texture with the rest of my existence: horror was my familiar, and this new revelation was only like an old pain recurring with new circumstances" (42).

Sound and shock

Latimer describes himself as a wounded creature, "a being finely organised for pain," suffering from an "old pain," a "habitual pain." These are references to specifically mental or psychic anguish. On several occasions, George Eliot writes about psychic pain as noiseless and silent. The association of pain and noise occurs throughout *The Lifted Veil*, giving rise to a cluster of metaphors that, I would argue, go beyond the figurative. While several critics have drawn attention to metaphors of visuality in the novella, rightly prompted by the image of the lifted veil itself and a "microscopic vision" that renders the hidden visible, George Eliot also frequently deploys metaphors of sound to represent Latimer's extraordinary attunement.[36] The participation of Latimer's "abnormal" consciousness in the minds of others is experienced as the din of an "importunate, ill-played musical instrument" or the "loud activity of an imprisoned insect" (13); it is "a ringing in the ears [that cannot] be got rid of" (18) or a "preternaturally heightened sense of hearing" that makes "audible to one a roar of sound where others find perfect stillness" (18).[37] Latimer can indeed hear the roar that lies on the other side of silence, as George Eliot would later famously formulate this audible insight in *Middlemarch*. The cessation at times of such noise pollution is "like the relief such as silence brings to wearied nerves" (13).

While the technology of the telegraph was already well established, it would be another few decades before the advent of the telephone, the transmission of recorded sound over long distances. Most research on the Victorian acoustic world focuses on the last quarter of the century, in which inventions in electronic communication by Edison and Bell made possible the telephone, phonograph and wireless.[38] But already in the

1850s inventions such as that of the phonoautograph were stimulating the cultural imagination of what it might mean to create a picture of sound and possibly record voices for posterity. Well before the invention of the microphone, the idea of acoustic amplification, analogous to the visual magnification of the microscope, was registered as a technological possibility.

Attentive to new inventions in sound technology, George Eliot was already, and would continue to be, fascinated with the idea of turning up the volume on apparently silent, interior processes.[39] In the author's introduction to *Felix Holt*, she writes that

There is much pain that is quite noiseless; and vibrations that make human agonies are often a mere whisper in the roar of hurrying existence. There are glances of hatred that stab and raise no cry of murder; robberies that leave man or woman for ever beggared of peace and joy – yet kept secret by the sufferer, committed to no sound except that of low moans in the night, seen in no writing except that made on the face by the slow months of suppressed anguish and early morning tears. Many an inherited sorrow that has marred a life has been breathed into no human ear.[40]

And in *Impressions of Theophrastus Such* (1879), she writes about the "microphone which detects the cadence of the fly's foot on the ceiling and may be expected presently to discriminate the noises of our various follies as they soliloquise or converse in our brains."[41]

Furthermore, both Lewes and Spencer draw on the perception of sound in their theorizations of consciousness. When Spencer theorizes that subjective feeling is composed of "rapidly recurring mental shocks" which correspond with the objective cause – "the rapidly-recurring shocks of molecular change" – his explanation draws on the "typical case of musical sound" to illustrate his argument:

We have a single aërial wave, a single movement of the drum of the ear, a single impact on the expansion of the auditory nerve, a single wave propagated to the auditory centre, and a single shock of feeling known as a crack or a report; and then, when there is externally generated a succession of such aërial waves, each working its individual physical effect on the auditory structures, and its individual psychical effect as a kind of shock, we see that if the recurrent physical effects exceed a certain speed, the recurrent psychical effects are consolidated into a sensation of tone. So that here the nerve pulses and the pulses of feeling clearly answer to one another; and it can scarcely be doubted that they do so throughout.[42]

As he later summarizes in his chapter on the composition of mind, "the method of composition remains the same throughout the entire fabric of Mind, from the formation of its simplest feelings up to the formation of those immense and complex aggregates of feelings which characterize its highest developments."[43] If the basic unit of consciousness is a shock registered in response to an external stimulus of change, then consciousness itself, *could we but monitor it*, works like the transmission of sound to the ear. Although Lewes doesn't use the language of shock as does Spencer, he refers to "thrill" and "irradiated disturbance" and incessant stimulation to describe the effect of stimuli on consciousness.[44] A sound, for example,

sends a thrill which excites emotion, causes the heart to beat faster, the muscles to quiver, the skin-glands to pour forth their secretion; yet this same sound heard by another man, or the same man under other conditions, physical or historical, merely sends a faint thrill, just vivid enough to detach itself as a sensation … so faint and fugitive as to pass away unconsciously.[45]

The amplification of consciousness, which is the crux of *The Lifted Veil*, is therefore readily expressed in auditory images.[46]

George Eliot writes that the artist's role is to develop a "higher sensibility as a medium, a delicate acoustic or optical instrument, bringing home to our coarser senses what would otherwise be unperceived by us."[47] Her oft-quoted manifesto resonates in this context: Art is a means of "amplifying experience and extending our contact with our fellow-men beyond the bounds of our personal lot."[48] *The Lifted Veil* reminds us of how dependent this amplification is on the artist who must make more subtle our "coarser senses." What is absent from Latimer's narrative is the wise and wide-ranging narrator of the novels, who will lift the experience out of the local and personal and articulate its broader import. At times, we catch the cadences of this narratorial voice, a voice that seems to jar with Latimer's limited self-knowledge and narrow emotional investments:

My self-consciousness was heightened to that pitch of intensity *in which our own emotions take the form of a drama which urges itself imperatively on our contemplation, and we begin to weep, less under the sense of our suffering than at the thought of it.* I felt a sort of pitying anguish over the pathos of my own lot: the lot of a being finely organised for pain … (Emphasis added; 24)

Emphasizing the power of emotion, George Eliot wrote to Charles Bray in 1859,

If Art does not enlarge men's sympathies, it does nothing morally. I have had heart-cutting experience that opinions are a poor cement between human souls; and the only effect I ardently long to produce by my writings is, that those who read them should be better able to *imagine* and to *feel* the pains and the joys of those who differ from themselves in everything but the broad fact of being struggling erring human creatures.[49]

The crucial question, as Latimer's negative example shows, is how to harness emotional capacity so that it becomes sympathy, compassion and fellow-feeling, rather than annoyance, hatred, jealousy or self-deluding desire. What confounds us as readers is that this work does not lift the veil on how to do so. Should Latimer be better equipped to feel the pains and joys of others with his heightened capacities? Or would we all retreat in horror from the pain and shock of such overwhelming encounters with the other? George Eliot's next interposing fiction, *Silas Marner*, goes much further to explore how the self, having retreated in pain from bruising contact with the outside world, is reconstituted through affect. But in her psycho-gothic "jeu de melancolie," she allows herself to stare fixedly into the conditions under which sympathetic imagination and feeling do not and perhaps cannot grow. Sympathy is related, it would seem, to the ability to regulate affect. In contemplating the onslaught of external stimuli and how excessive information is processed in a particular emotional environment, the novella draws attention to the psychic process of defense, the management of vulnerability and pain.

Furthermore, the question of regulation plays out interestingly in relation to novelistic form. One of the great pleasures of reading, Alan Palmer rightly observes in *Fictional Minds*, is the untrammeled access it offers to the minds of others. Under no other circumstances are minds rendered transparent so that we can partake of Latimer's "gift" – the ability to know the "thoughts and feelings going on in another." What seems natural in the world of the novel – knowing precisely what other people think and feel – is really very odd. George Poulet notes: "Because of the strange invasion of my person by the thoughts of another, I am a self who is granted the experience of thinking thoughts foreign to him. I am the subject of thoughts other than my own. My consciousness behaves as though it were the consciousness of another."[50] We do not experience reading as a "strange invasion" because the pleasure of inhabiting the other's mind is dependent on regulation and safety. We can sympathize and identify because we know we are not *really* being taken over by the thoughts and feelings of others. When this make-believe becomes a reality, as *The Lifted Veil* imagines it, pleasure becomes shock and pain. Having trapped her readers in Latimer's first-person account, George Eliot leaves us to weigh up the extent to which his uncongenial emotional climate and morbidity make his powers horrendous, or whether anyone subject to the clamorous invasion of his or her interiority would respond with aversion and recoil.

II TERROR, CLAIRVOYANCE AND THE GENEALOGY
OF PSYCHIC SHOCK IN *DANIEL DERONDA*

In the penultimate book of *Daniel Deronda*, Gwendolen Harleth appears in a state of physical and mental shock after the drowning of her detested husband. Exposed to an increasingly popularized discourse of trauma and dissociative disorders, today's readers would have little trouble in identifying and labeling Gwendolen as a traumatized subject, suffering from a variety of typical symptoms in the aftermath of her terrible experience.[51] She is fixated on the "dead face" of Grandcourt in the water, hallucinating it everywhere. Later, she complains that she "can't sleep much" and that "[t]hings repeat themselves in me so. They come back – they will all come back" (659). Disoriented in the present, she seems to return repeatedly to the past, the line between her interior world and the external world growing increasingly tenuous: "She unconsciously left intervals in her retrospect, not clearly distinguishing between what she said and what she had only an inward vision of" (594). In her conversation with Daniel Deronda, she is described as being silent for a moment or two, "as if her memory had lost itself in a web where each mesh drew all the rest" (592). Deronda wonders whether she "[w]as she seeing the whole event – her own acts included – through an exaggerating medium of excitement and horror" (591). She goes on with that "fitful wandering confession where the sameness of experience seems to *nullify the sense of time or of order in events*" (emphasis added; 592). Later, she appears as "one who had visited the spirit-world and was full to the lips of an unutterable experience that threw a strange unreality over all the talk she was hearing of her own and the world's business" (652). The narrator comments that "poor *Gwendolen's memory had been stunned*, and all outside the lava-lit track of her troubled conscience, and her effort to get deliverance from it, lay for her in dim forgetfulness" (emphasis added; 661). In response to a cataclysmic experience, Gwendolen suffers from nightmares, dysfunctions of memory, and a sense of the dislocation of time – textbook symptoms of trauma or PTSD. Yet when George Eliot was writing *Daniel Deronda* in 1876, the concept of trauma as a medical syndrome was barely on the horizon. In its definition of "trauma," the *Oxford English Dictionary* notes the first usage of the term "traumata" in conjunction with psychic injury as occurring in 1894, some eighteen years after the publication of George Eliot's last novel.[52]

Exploring George Eliot's representation of psychic shock, this section complicates the assumption that trauma is an ahistorical or transhistorical experience, which, even if unnamed, was similarly experienced in the past.

Rather, I wish to tease out the discursive strands which George Eliot drew together in her representation of Gwendolen's troubled consciousness, not just in the drowning episode, but at other key points in the novel, and to place her representation in the context of an emergent cultural and scientific discourse of psychic wounding and its effects on memory and emotion, a discourse that arguably helped to produce the way we understand trauma today. In order to explore what specifically Victorian assumptions about mind lie behind the representation of Gwendolen's psychic anguish, I will focus initially on psychological accounts of the effect of terror on memory and on George Henry Lewes's theories of unconscious mental processes. I will argue that attention to emotion, the unconscious and shock provides further purchase on questions that remain problematic in criticism of the novel – the meaning of Gwendolen's native terror and superstition, her apparent clairvoyance about the drowning accident, her relationship to other prefigurations that occur in the novel (Mordecai's recognition of Daniel), and the question of her status as a guilty rather than innocent bystander in Grandcourt's death. I will suggest too that Romantic conceptions of the sublime and the literary conventions and language of mid-nineteenth-century gothic fiction enable George Eliot's mediation of Gwendolen's haunted consciousness. Finally, I explore how the encounter George Eliot stages between the world and the subject sheds light on important differences between nineteenth- and twentieth-century conceptions of psychic wounding.

Memory and unconscious processes

It is noteworthy that George Eliot refers to Gwendolen's disoriented and stunned memory in the aftermath of the drowning accident. I have suggested in the previous chapter that Victorian psycho-medical theories of overwhelming emotion and psychic shock did not emphasize the disturbance of memory as a primary symptom. That said, however, loose connections between terror and memory disturbance are noted in medical case histories as early as the 1830s. Writing about a young woman, Mary Parker, who had two distinct selves, one of which had no knowledge or memory of the other, T. O. Ward noted the disjunction in memory between one state of consciousness and another.

Double consciousness is now established, for while delirious, she has little or no recollection of persons she has seen, or events which have occurred during the state of sanity, nor does she complain of any bodily pain or suffering. In the opposite state, on the contrary, she is extremely depressed, incompetent to any exertion, complains of pain in her head, side, and stomach, and is equally forgetful of all that has passed during the delirium.[53]

Ward draws attention to the relationship between such cases as Mary Parker's and conditions of hysteria and delirium occasioned by typhus. He also goes on to ponder their similarity to altered states induced by mesmerism, somnambulism and even drunkenness, speculating about what could cause conditions of double consciousness in male as well as female patients: "[t]he cases of double consciousness, hitherto published, have mostly occurred in young females in whom the uterine functions were disturbed, or, if in the male sex, where the *nervous system had been weakened by excesses, terror, or other cerebral excitement*" (emphasis added).[54] While Ward does indeed countenance the idea that shock or terror may produce disturbances in "the Sensorium," he is focusing less on describing what may happen to memory in the face of overwhelming experience than looking for a way to include male subjects in his understanding of double consciousness. Females suffer the condition by virtue of their unstable uterine economies; males have to be rendered unstable from without. The question of memory in such cases of double consciousness was greatly intriguing to the Victorians, but until much later in the century the connections among terror and shock, dissociation and amnesia were made only indirectly.

The relationship between memory and the emotions of fear and terror is touched on in several mid-nineteenth-century texts in physiological psychology. In *The Emotions and the Will* (1859), Alexander Bain suggests that powerful emotion can either indelibly stamp on memory the events with which it is associated or destroy memory altogether. A section on the "intellectual influence of feelings" draws attention to the "intellectual efficacy" of powerful emotions: "By the power of mere excitement a painful incident will seize the attention and imprint itself on the memory."[55] But he also acknowledges that strong feelings can "play the part of rebels or innovators against the canons of the past" and are "like destroying Vandals, who efface and consume the records of what has been."[56] While such statements seem to anticipate Freud's assertion that shock or fright of an overwhelming nature may cause the subject to dissociate from the knowledge of the overwhelming experience, Bain does not develop the idea of strong emotion as a cause for disruptions or inaccessible storage of memory. He is suggesting more conventionally that strong emotion interferes with rational, intellectual process. "Our feelings pervert our convictions by smiting us with intellectual blindness," he avers, and we may suffer "deep-seated intellectual corruption due to the ascendancy of the feelings."[57]

The chapter on dread, terror and fear in *The Emotions and the Will* characterizes these largely as states of anxious anticipation of, or uncertainty about, the future, and holds that knowledge usually dispels fear. If undispelled, cumulative fear and dread themselves may weaken the system:

The question may be raised, how far mere *intensity* of sensation, viewed by itself, induces the condition of dread. The nervous disturbance, due to a violent shock, would seem to be something akin to fear. As a weakening influence, it would pave the way for the state of fright; so that any suggestion of danger would find the system an easier prey.[58]

In terms of the effect of fear on memory, he notes that past fear can make "a more indelible stamp than even an acute bodily infliction."[59] The power of associative memory is treated more fully in his earlier work, *The Senses and the Intellect* (1855), where he explains that "the passion of terror is connected with the things that have roused the feeling in the course of each one's experience," and the reappearance of such things, even loosely connected in images in the mind to the initial scene of terror – such as "the approach of a hurried messenger with distracted countenance" – can cause the initial experience of terror to be revisited.[60]

Although, as we have seen, many Victorian psycho-physiologists were reluctant to grant agency to unconscious mental process, they did not wish to relegate unconscious processes to the realm of reflex or automatic action. Among those who argued eloquently for the importance of unconscious mental process was George Henry Lewes, whose views on consciousness and unconsciousness are of particular significance in understanding George Eliot's representation of psychic shock and pain in her last novel.

Lewes had long disputed the idea that all conscious behavior was mental, and all unconscious physical. That is, he understood "unconscious" as a term to be applied to far more than reflex action. Broadly characterized, Lewes's work in physiological psychology brought the unconscious and the bodily into the conception of mind. James Sully, himself a respected authority on the mind, drew attention to Lewes's distinctive emphasis on "the organic oneness, the interpenetration of the neural and the psychical."[61] In *The Physiology of Common Life*, Lewes laid out an integrated and holistic approach to the mind: "I do not agree in this opinion respecting the Brain as 'the organ' of the mind. One of the principal conclusions to which fact and argument will direct us in these pages will be, that the Brain is only *one* organ of the Mind, and not by any means the exclusive centre of Consciousness."[62] "Mind," in Lewes's view, does not designate intellectual operations only. It includes "all Sensation, all Volition, and all Thought: it means the whole psychical Life; and this psychical Life has no one special centre, any more than the physical Life has one special centre: it belongs to the whole, and animates the whole."[63]

Lewes takes the position that we do indeed "have many sensations, which are not perceived at all, of which we are said to be wholly 'unconscious.'"[64] It is not therefore correct to say that unless a sensation is perceived it does not exist.[65] Sensations that are unperceived are not necessarily lost: "they were not altered in character because their subsequent effects were not manifest in Thought; they were not without their influence in adding to the sum of general Consciousness."[66] Part of the problem, Lewes realizes, lies in terminology. The term "consciousness," for example, is prone to misconception. Those who argue that, unless it is perceived, no sensation can exist, are soon led to "glaring contradictions" in trying to write about "unfelt feelings" and "unconscious consciousness."[67] As Lewes admits later in *The Physical Basis of Mind* (1877), however, the term "Consciousness" is too widespread to be changed; we should therefore specify a general and special use of it: "The general usage identifies it with Sensibility, in its subject aspect as Sentience, including all psychical states, both those classed under Sensation, and those under Thought."[68] In the "special usage it is distinguished ... by a peculiar reflected feeling of Attention, whereby we not only *have* a sensation, but also *feel* that we have it; we not only think, but are conscious of what we are thinking."[69] Working with the general usage, Lewes thus proposes to think of consciousness and unconsciousness not as oppositions, the first as a mental and the second as a physical process, but as points on a spectrum of what he calls "Sentience," which is defined as "the activity of the nervous system viewed subjectively."[70] The metaphor of darkness and light allows Lewes to explain that the relationship between consciousness and unconsciousness is only apparently that of opposites:

Just as Darkness is a positive optical sensation very different from mere privation – just as it replaces the sensation of Light, blends with it, struggles with it, and in all respects differs from the *absence* of all optical sensibility in the skin; so Unconsciousness struggles with, blends with, and replaces Consciousness in the organism, and is a positive state of the sentient organism, not to be confounded with a mere negation of Sentience; above all, not to be relegated to merely mechanical processes.[71]

Instead of viewing the "Thinking Principle" as an "antecedent," he regarded it as "a resultant, not an entity but a convergence of manifold activities."[72] "Consciousness," he argued, in the final, posthumous volume of *Problems of Life and Mind*, "is not an agent but a symptom."[73]

For the novelist similarly interested in unconscious processes, Lewes's conception of consciousness as a sum, product, symptom and result opens up for scrutiny the way the mind–body works on many levels and allows exploration of a range of emotions and sensations whose effects are important but not necessarily "manifest in Thought."[74] The idea of consciousness as the "confluence of many streams of sensation," and as a blending or struggling with unconsciousness, means that the conscious self is at all times susceptible to the influence of the unconscious.[75] In a perceptive essay on George Eliot's novelistic anatomy of consciousness in the context of Lewes's vivisection experiments, Richard Menke observes that "physiologists ... could administer electric shocks but not emotional ones; Eliot appropriates the framework of Victorian physiology to go where science itself could not, to develop her own novelistic techniques for the close analysis of imaginary minds and bodies."[76] Drawing on the idea of the novelist as an experimenter in the effects of emotional shock, I turn now to George Eliot's exploration of Gwendolen's "whole Psychical Life."

Dread, terror and clairvoyance

Gwendolen's agonized state of mind after Grandcourt's drowning and the symptoms of memory dysfunction and disorientation she experiences are an accumulation of past experience as well as present terror: that is, it is not the drowning alone, shocking as it may be, that produces Gwendolen's sub-sequent symptoms. The horror of witnessing the death (and her possibly guilty omission in preventing it) is compounded by the fact that it is a culmination of much fear and dread, the convergence of her secret wishes for his death and the images of the face and fleeing figure that terrify her early in the novel. The overwhelming experience is therefore linked to, and prepared for by, a range of earlier responses. Although anyone witness-ing a drowning accident might develop symptoms of shock, Gwendolen's history is of relevance – not just in relation to the reviled Grandcourt, but as a susceptible and volatile subject.

From the early scenes of the novel, George Eliot sets about establishing Gwendolen as vulnerable to shock and terror. Her emotional volatility is prepared for in several references to her "susceptibility to terror" (51), introduced most memorably during the riveting scene in which she plays Hermione for a tableau. The "fits" of terror she experiences are like a "brief remembered madness," an "unexplained exception from her normal life" (51), a marked contrast to her usual fearlessness and high spirits and her desire to appear "daring in speech and reckless in braving dangers" (51). Along with triumph, Gwendolen also feels terror when Grandcourt resumes his pursuit of her: "Quick, quick, like pictures in a book beaten open with a sense of hurry, came back vividly, yet in fragments, all that she had gone through in relation to Grandcourt ... That unalterable experience made a vision at which in the first agitated moment, before tempering reflections could suggest themselves, her *native terror* shrank" (emphasis added; 247). Gwendolen's expectation of triumph is mixed with the "dread of a crisis" and her nature is one of those in which "exultation inevitably carries an infusion of dread ready to curdle and declare itself" (301). Later the narrator refers to Gwendolen's "disposition to *vague terror*" and "*vague*, ever visiting *dread*" (474; 362). Gwendolen is said to be "governed by many shadowy powers" and to invest with "shadowy omnipresence any threat of fatal power over her" (474).

Along with physiological and psychological investigations into the emotions, the Romantic fascination with terror, fear and awe in the sublime suggests itself as a pertinent context for George Eliot's representation of Gwendolen's dread and terror. We remember that Gwendolen doesn't like big wide spaces because they make her feel diminished.

Solitude in any wide scene impressed her with an undefined feeling of immeasurable existence aloof from her, in the midst of which she was helplessly incapable of asserting herself. The little astronomy taught her at school used sometimes to set her imagination at work in a way that made her tremble; but always when some one joined her she recovered her indifference to the vastness in which she seemed an exile; she found again her usual world in which her will was of some avail. (52)[77]

The sense here is of a Romantic or Kantian sublime that inspires trembling as it dwarfs and diminishes the subject. The sublime offered intimations of an immense and awful external power that provoked awe and terror, "intimations of a metaphysical force beyond rational knowledge and human comprehension."[78]

The way George Eliot figures dread is not dissimilar, I would argue further, from the Kierkegaardian understanding of it in *The Concept of Dread*, a work spelling out the idea of trembling at the void, the abyss, which is the underside of freedom and choice.[79] It is pertinent that whenever, in the early parts of the novel, Gwendolen feels power, or a sense of mastery and triumph, she also experiences a concomitant backlash or dread. Fear and trembling seem to follow her unconscious sense of the possibility that she may be denied freedom, that she is vulnerable and not powerful. Her fear of powerlessness makes her feel diminished and speck-like at times. Though she lays claim to power, as a woman and class outsider, she wields very little of it in the world and has quite circumscribed choices.

Even more cogent as an explanation for Gwendolen's dread and terror is her intimation of a dark, shadowy self beyond the control of her will. What Gwendolen fears is her own intrusive and uncontrollable unconscious. She experiences at times a "subjection to a possible self, a self not to be absolutely predicted ... [which] caused her some astonishment and terror" (114).[80] As Josephine McDonagh has pointed out, there is a pervasive emphasis in the novel on "a level of experience that is somehow beyond consciousness" and that "rather than a mechanism of harmonious unity, the individual memory is seen to be a disruptive, fracturing force, unsettling the surface of individual consciousness."[81] E. S. Dallas's "hidden soul" was conceived, we recall, as a repository that enables imagination and creativity. George Eliot seems here to explore the darker underside of Gwendolen's hidden soul as ungovernable and largely inaccessible. What it brings from the dark to the light are not the treasures of secret creativity, but the disruptive and corrosive freight of secret fear and dread. If Dallas expounds an aesthetics, a science of pleasure, grounded in the physiology of the unconscious, George Eliot elaborates its opposite – a violation and rending of the self – grounded nevertheless in a similar physiology.

A key episode in George Eliot's representation of Gwendolen's emotional state is her terrified response to the painting in the tableau scene, a reaction so incommensurate with its supposed cause as to demand readerly attention. The scene is particularly complex because the face and fleeing figure on the panel that springs open are premonitory of Gwendolen's later climactic experience on the boat with Grandcourt. By means of this episode George Eliot appears to be establishing Gwendolen as clairvoyant about her own disastrous fate with Grandcourt. Yet Gwendolen is not a visionary subject in the same way as Mordecai is, although, as I will go on to show, they are implicitly connected on a spectrum of what we may call heightened consciousness.[82] Gwendolen seems to produce the vision that haunts her and, in Grandcourt's drowning, to make real the dreaded specter of the white face and fleeing figure. To say that is to say (in post-Victorian terms) that she already has a labile image repertoire – akin to a symptom language – which expresses her feelings about Grandcourt. The image becomes part of Gwendolen's psychic vocabulary, speaking for her in ways she cannot consciously articulate. If the painting provokes an exaggerated response in the way it springs into view, it is also terrifying because it is a return of something that has already caused Gwendolen fear. In line with Bain's remarks on the powerful associations of past fear, and Carpenter's discussion of emotional memory, which I elaborated in the previous chapter, George Eliot shows how the reiteration of fearful images produces exponentially fearful responses. Having already seen the darkly suggestive painting, Gwendolen feels inexplicably haunted by it and so invests the face and fleeing figure with a kind of supernatural power. The panel that springs open functions like the unconscious that erupts with its fearful visions and unremembered memories into consciousness.

Like the young woman in Carpenter's example who had no memory of nearly drowning but showed great agitation at the sight of running water, Gwendolen's terror seems to signal some past dark experience. Critics have suggested a variety of imagined causes (abuse at the hands of her step-father, for example) to explain her sensitized consciousness, but George Eliot seems to me to be invoking a generalized emotional susceptibility, rather than an unnarrated but specific incident.[83] Her Latimer-like trembling and sensitivity is confined to discrete and largely private moments, however, for, unlike Latimer, she appears in "normal life" to be daring, reckless and conquering.

Rereading the tableau scene in relation to Gwendolen's anguish after the drowning, we see that it lodges in the reader's memory the image not just of Gwendolen's terror but of the face and fleeing figure. Indeed, Gwendolen's response to the painting works on a narrative level more to foreshadow future events than to replay past ones. Since Grandcourt's death is insistently prefigured in the image of the face and fleeing figure, George Eliot is clearly working rather heavy-handedly with the literary device of foreshadowing, but she cannot also escape the suggestion that Gwendolen may be prone to second sight. The latter's possible clairvoyance puts her in company with Mordecai, a visionary of a different kind. Mordecai and Gwendolen are linked in that both respond to urgings and promptings that well up into consciousness; both manifest what Lewes would call the "convergence of manifold activities" which make up consciousness. Indeed, George Eliot's famous observations in *Daniel Deronda* about second sight, though apparently about Mordecai, apply as well to Gwendolen:

"SECOND SIGHT" is a flag over disputed ground. But it is a matter of knowledge that there are persons whose yearnings, conceptions – nay, travelled conclusions – continually take the form of images which have a foreshadowing power: the deed they would do starts up before them in complete shape, making a coercive type; the event they hunger for *or dread* rises into vision with a seed-like growth, feeding itself fast on unnumbered impressions. They are not always the less capable of the argumentative process, or less sane than the commonplace calculators of the market: sometimes it may be that their natures *have manifold openings*, like the hundred-gated Thebes, where there may naturally be a greater and more miscellaneous inrush than through a narrow beadle-watched portal. (Emphasis added; 404)

George Eliot's narrator asserts that there are those who can visualize intensely and have the power to imagine what they yearn for. Mordecai is an example, particularly in his prefiguration of Daniel as his successor. But the passage introduces the question of dread as well as yearning. The clause "the deed they would do starts up before them in complete shape, making a coercive type" seems to apply less to Mordecai than to Gwendolen, who fantasizes Grandcourt's death and repeatedly sees the face and fleeing figure that so terrified her when the panel sprang open. In contrast to Mordecai, whose second sight is venerated, George Eliot pursues the inverse of prophetic vision in Gwendolen, whose narrow egotistic world contracts inward as much as Mordecai's widens out from his bodily suffering and personal circumstances. Gwendolen is one of those "quiveringly poised natures" prone to second sight through the promptings of dreaded visualizations. When the narrator speaks of natures with "manifold openings ... where there may naturally be a greater and more miscellaneous inrush than through a narrow beadle-watched portal," there is no specification of the source of the inrush, which could signify signs in the external world or promptings from deep within.[84] The "miscellaneous inrush" may contribute to Mordecai's special antennae for the friend through whom he will transmit himself, but in the case of Gwendolen's sort of "second sight" the "manifold openings" refer to what wells up from within – the intelligence carried by unconscious, emotional memory.

If Mordecai is a case of a heightened consciousness, attuned to its yearning for the "friend" who will continue his work, Gwendolen's consciousness is similarly sensitive, only her visions are shaped by dark fantasies and dread rather than yearning. "I saw my wish outside me," are Gwendolen's anguished words after Grandcourt's drowning, but they could just as well be uttered by Mordecai after encountering Daniel in the bookstore (596). Critics of the novel, most famously F. R. Leavis, have asserted that it falls into two halves, one dealing with Gwendolen's courtship and marriage, and the other with "the Jewish sections" and Daniel's discovery of his origins. Yet surely the connection between these parts – and particularly between Mordecai and Gwendolen, who seem worlds apart – resides in George Eliot's explorations of consciousness and the ways it is informed by unconscious fears and yearnings, memories and emotional evaluations. Rather than designating the unconscious as an entity or a separate place, George Eliot (like Lewes) emphasizes its continuity and connection with consciousness. This version of the unconscious thus accounts for both Mordecai's prophetic spirituality and Gwendolen's superstitious dread.

Because Gwendolen has so often been regarded by critics as a diseased sensibility, an hysteric, it is worth emphasizing that, although Gwendolen and Mordecai occupy different positions on the spectrum of "quiveringly" sensitive natures, in neither case is the condition presented as pathological. Indeed, Daniel does initially think that "Mordecai might be liable to hallucinations of thought – might have become a monomaniac on some subject which had given too severe a strain to his diseased organism" (423), but that view is subsequently abandoned; correspondingly, the narrator implicitly normalizes rather than pathologizes Gwendolen's disturbed consciousness. Athena Vrettos usefully points out that Gwendolen's visions "constitute a challenge to the privileged spiritual discourse of Mordecai, Mirah and Deronda," thereby threatening to undercut the novel's dominant narrative voice. Vrettos reasons that, if Gwendolen is diseased, the status of prophetic vision is called into question: "Eliot's rhetoric encodes the possibility that all visionary powers are functions of nervous disease."[85] This judgment seems to fly in the face of the well-known passage I quoted in which the narrator specifically insists on the sanity and rationality of those subject to visions. Rather than setting Gwendolen up as a diseased subject, the narrator calls her an "intense personality" (235), which suggests that certain ordinary tendencies are exaggerated or writ large in her make-up. I would argue that if Gwendolen's visions threaten to undercut the dominant narrative voice, they do so because they betray George Eliot's interest in Gwendolen's interior struggle, and her haunted and troubled consciousness, as ultimately more compelling and problematic – because more ordinary – than Mordecai's visionary spirituality.

The hidden wound

Having established Gwendolen's susceptibility to terror, prompted by both external and internal causes, and having put her in a situation of limited choice in which she harms herself by accepting Grandcourt's proposal after she has promised Lydia Glasher that she would reject him, George Eliot proceeds to explore her heroine's compounding mental anguish. In the context of this adumbration of psychic pain, the narrator refers to Gwendolen's anguish as a "hidden wound" (482). This is an important phrase, which has been much seized upon by critics of the novel. Whereas, for Louise Penner, the hidden wound has its roots in some putative past sexual abuse by Gwendolen's step-father, for Susan Weisser (and, earlier, Jacqueline Rose), responding to Freud's construction of sexuality, the wound is female sexuality itself.[86] Weisser explains that "to be sexual is to be wounded; to be woman is to be wounded; to be spiritually whole, one must be sexually lacking. Gwendolen's womanhood, then, is a wound that must remain hidden."[87] I suggest that "wound" be understood in a rather more literal way. In my reading of the novel's concern with consciousness and unconsciousness, the hidden wound seems to be a signification of psychic as opposed to physical injury. "Hidden" and "invisible" are often used to describe interior or psychic processes in George Eliot's work, but this novel particularly emphasizes the hidden mingling of conscious and unconscious motivations and decisions. The headnote to Chapter 16 surmises that, if the narrator of human actions were to do his work like the astronomer, he would "have to thread the hidden pathways of feeling and thought which lead up to every moment of action, and to those moments of intense suffering..." (139). "Hidden" and "invisible" also imply the work of the unconscious in consciousness, as in "dark rays doing their work invisibly in the broad light" of "more acknowledged consciousness" (518).

Gwendolen's hidden wound is most obviously the effect of terror in response to external events such as the panel that springs open, or the arrival of the "poisoned gems," which leaves her pallid and shrieking. But George Eliot places great emphasis in this novel on the power of what we may call internal events and the climate of reception they provide for what happens externally. Later in the novel, Daniel's mother voices a view particularly apposite to Gwendolen's distress. Without our consent, she complains, "events come on us like evil enchantments: and thoughts, feelings, apparitions in the darkness are events – are they not?" (540–41). The experience of our own unsolicited feelings may count as events that transfix or bind us, as if by spells. Like the Princess Halm-Eberstein, who implies that she feels guilty about concealing the nature of Daniel's origins from him, Gwendolen is plagued by a dread of wrongdoing, and, in the case of Lydia Glasher, the sting of remorse following the deliberate injury of another. The "poisoned gems" send her into a state of hysterical nervous shock because she is already primed internally by apparitions signifying her guilt and remorse. In Gwendolen's growing crisis of conscience and consciousness, George Eliot explores the notion of psychic injury as the confluence of internal and external events. Gwendolen is assailed both by external shocks and by internal hauntings to the point (after Grandcourt's drowning) that the distinction between internal fantasy and external occurrence becomes blurred.

Gothic haunting

I have been suggesting that George Eliot's representation of Gwendolen's interiority demonstrates the workings of unconscious feelings, sensations and images in accordance with Lewes's explanations of mind and consciousness. I want to argue further, however, that her exploration of psychic wounding as a haunted state is imaginatively and rhetorically aided by the tradition of gothic fiction and the ghost tale. While there is relatively little in the way of an established medical discourse of psychic shock in relation to memory disturbance at the time the novel is written, the discourse of literary terror and haunting was highly developed and could be enlisted to perform the work of psychological representation. As many critics have observed, the trajectory of the ghost story from the beginning of the nineteenth century to the end is the movement from external supernatural haunting to internal psychological haunting.[88]

George Eliot's use of gothic conventions looks back to an "already psychologized" gothic in the work of the Brontës and forward to Henry James, who, as David Trotter points out, used it as a way to talk about serious terror.[89] Think for a moment of the bare bones of Gwendolen's story: a young woman, usually self-possessed and imperious, is terrified, almost petrified, by the image of a face and fleeing figure. She is then courted by a powerful and well-placed man. His previous lover and mother of his children extracts a promise that she not marry him, but, pressed by her own needs, she eventually decides to break her promise and go ahead with the marriage. The Furies cross her threshold and the curse comes upon her when her predecessor sends her the family diamonds with an upbraiding letter. Coerced by her husband, she accompanies him on a yachting expedition during which he drowns and she sees, as predicted, his "white dead face" in the water. This is exactly the kind of plot one might find in the later Bulwer Lytton or Le Fanu. It hints at the power of presentiment, but stops short of asserting that anything supernatural has taken place. Just so, the narrator teases us with the possibility of a supernatural element at work in releasing the panel that terrifies Gwendolen, and reminds us of Gwendolen's presentiment of the uncanny face and fleeing figure.

Several critics have remarked on the affinities of *Daniel Deronda* with gothic fiction.[90] The insistent language of terror and dread, haunting, specter and apparition places Gwendolen's story in the tradition of the ghost tale and suggests her gothicized interior world. I have already shown the frequency with which George Eliot refers to Gwendolen's vague and native terror; these references to terror are linked increasingly to a discourse of the spectral and phantasmatic. When Grandcourt releases her from all financial worries, Gwendolen "had a momentary phantasmal love for this man who chose his words so well" (256), but, in her married life, she soon begins to experience "hidden rites" that go on in the "secrecy of [her] mind" that have the effect of "a struggling terror" (576). Phantasmal love gives way to phantasmagoria of fear, hate and revenge. Gwendolen's fantasies possess her like "phantoms," says the narrator: "[f]antasies moved within her like ghosts, making no break in her more acknowledged consciousness and finding no obstruction in it: dark rays doing their work invisibly in the broad light" (518). This passage also recalls Lewes's use of the darkness/light analogy and the idea of consciousness and unconsciousness as an unbroken stream. In the reference to fantasies and ghosts, along with "no break in her more acknowledged consciousness," and the images of light and dark, we see the convergence in George Eliot of the manifold discourses of Lewes's psychology and gothic terror.

Conflicting forces in Gwendolen are further dramatized as a contest between personified emotions: "In Gwendolen's consciousness Temptation and Dread met and stared like two pale phantoms, each seeing itself in the other – each obstructed by its own image; and all the while her fuller self beheld the apparitions and sobbed for deliverance from them" (577). Gwendolen's dreams are described in increasing detail, as if her terrified consciousness plays out its anxieties in them.[91] In the scene following Grandcourt's death, George Eliot's deployment of a gothic vocabulary intensifies: Gwendolen is like one of the "sheeted dead, shivering, with wet hair streaming, a wild amazed consciousness in her eyes" (587). When Daniel sees her the next morning, she looked like "the unhappy ghost of that Gwendolen Harleth whom Deronda had seen turning with firm lips and proud self-possession from her losses at the gaming-table" (590). What is distinctive about George Eliot's language of ghosts and apparitions is the third-person narrator who wields it. This eminently reasonable, sophisticated, wise and knowledgeable commentator, who moves in and out of the minds of her characters, is not herself colored by the heightened language she deploys. In this way she differs from the first-person narrators of *Jane Eyre*, *Villette*, Bulwer Lytton's *A Strange Story* or even *The Lifted Veil*. While the narrative is overtly propelled after Grandcourt's drowning by the ethical question of Gwendolen's guilt in not immediately attempting to save him, the narrator also necessarily focuses on consciousness and the registration of shock, states of abstraction, the absence or fragmentation of self, and the incessant reliving of the inassimilable moment.

Conscience and consciousness

The quotation about Temptation and Dread I cited earlier shows how the treatment of Gwendolen's troubled consciousness is simultaneously harnessed to a discourse of morality and conscience. George Eliot's fiction shows an abiding interest in consequences and particularly the laws of cause and effect. Deeds have "after-throbs" as she says in a headnote to Chapter 57 (598). Her interest in these "after-throbs" is part of her moral understanding of determinism, which urges us, because actions have consequences, to consider carefully how we act. George Eliot retains her focus on consequence as the inevitable result of action and reaction along with her interest in psychic suffering. There are two different, though related, discourses at work here – conscience and consciousness – the first of which tends ultimately to subsume and short-circuit the explanatory power of the second. That is, the narrative of psychic suffering is converted into an allegory of "Better" and "Worse" selves, or, as we saw in a previous passage, Temptation struggling with Dread. Lisbeth During, who writes about the relationship of dread to moral conscience, remarks astutely in passing that, with "the figure of Gwendolen Harleth, George Eliot has trespassed into areas of interior trauma and psychic unfreedom which her chosen secular morality cannot encompass."[92] I take issue with this formulation because it seems to me that George Eliot has not *trespassed* but deliberately staked out and gone forth into the area of psychic shock and injury. However, I would certainly concede that it is not an open-ended exploration. George Eliot is (at least overtly) less interested in Gwendolen's wounded psyche than in her potential guilt and responsibility for her own pain and suffering.

Gwendolen's confession of her fantasies of killing Grandcourt with the small sharp object in her cabinet, "like a long willow leaf in a silver sheath," seems to settle the question of her guilt in not aiding the rescue of her drowning spouse (592). She is haunted by the instrument, her fingers longing for it to the extent that she drops the cabinet key into the water to prevent herself from acting on her desires. Even after that preventative measure, she begins to fantasize how she can get to the weapon again. Yet along with her confession of guilty wishes, and even intention, Gwendolen vividly conveys both Grandcourt's emotional abuse through her description of his iron will – "sometimes I thought he would kill *me* if I resisted his will" – and her subjection, her sense of being a galley slave, a prisoner, denied even the fantasy of escape that comforted her as a child who objected to her step-father: "I used to fancy sailing away into a world where people were not forced to live with any one they did not like" (594, 596). Sailing now away from deliverance rather than towards it, she feels both powerful rage and powerless subjection. It is in this condition, which blots "everything else dim," that she suddenly becomes aware that he has fallen from the boat. Although the narrator does not focus on her absorbed, abstracted state as an alibi, Gwendolen is arguably rendered paralyzed, immobilized, by her abstraction from the present at the moment of the accident.[93] Instead, however, her immobility is rendered (by the narrator and Gwendolen herself) as purposeful withholding. She is wracked by guilt, and guilt too is Daniel's concern even as he dismisses its effect on her actions: "He held it likely that Gwendolen's remorse aggravated her inward guilt, and that she gave the character of decisive action to what had been an inappreciably instantaneous glance of desire" (597).

An ethical coach, Daniel advises her to see her "present suffering as a painful letting in of light" (388), a coming to consciousness, in terms of the novel's imagery, of that which has been operating in the darkness. He exhorts her to turn the promptings of her unconscious – her fear, dread and emotional memory – into conscious resolve:

"Keep your dread fixed on the idea of increasing that remorse which is so bitter to you. Fixed meditation may do a great deal towards defining our longing or dread. We are not always in a state of strong emotion, and when we are calm we can use our memories and gradually change the bias of our fear, as we do our tastes. Take your fear as a safeguard. It is like quickness of hearing. It may make consequences passionately present to you. Try to take hold of your sensibility, and use it as if it were a faculty, like vision." (388)

As often in George Eliot's work, emotion and sensibility are likened to senses such as hearing and seeing, sources of information about the internal world on which meditation can set to work in order to convert unconscious to conscious knowledge. No longer anarchic and destabilizing, unconscious fantasies and emotions become serviceable informants.

Underlining Daniel's advice, the morbid epigraph to the novel as a whole reads:

Let thy chief terror be of thine own soul:
There, 'mid the throng of hurrying desires
That trample o'er the dead to seize their spoil,
Lurks vengeance, footless, irresistible
As exhalations laden with slow death,
And o'er the fairest troop of captured joys
Breathes pallid pestilence.

The epigraph refers unmistakably to the way Gwendolen is desperately driven to break her promise to Lydia Glasher and is avenged by her own soul – an exemplification of the "ayenbite of inwyt," the sting of remorse. When Gwendolen betrays her promise to Lydia Glasher, "[t]he vision of her past wrong-doing, and what it had brought on her, came with a pale ghastly illumination over every imagined deed that was a rash effort at freedom, such as she had made in her marriage" (576). Here her vision and illumination dovetail with Daniel Deronda's story and highlight George Eliot's multifaceted conception of his role in the novel. For, as many critics have noted, Daniel's function as the eponymous central figure is not only to come to recognize who and what he is and accept the vocation that goes with that achieved identity: he also functions as a reluctant mentor and confessor for Gwendolen. In this role he is not just a listener, but a judge, focused on her guilt or innocence. His sympathy is at best grudging; that is, he responds to Gwendolen as a woman caught up in a salutary if painful crisis of conscience. His defensiveness against Gwendolen's needy confession signals his own movement away from subordinating himself to the needs of others, yet one cannot but feel the denial that Gwendolen encounters just when she requires a compassionate listener most. Ultimately, the narrative seems committed to Daniel's view that Gwendolen needs the experience of suffering and remorse to become a better woman. At the same time, therefore, as George Eliot travels some way on the interesting question of Gwendolen's susceptibility to fright and terror, and the convergence of external and internal shocks to the psyche, she also sets the exploration of psychic suffering and its effects in a discourse of conscience and morality.

George Eliot's representation of psychic shock, although arguably a precursor of later theories of trauma, differs significantly from them, perhaps most markedly in her emphasis on the responsibility and agency of the wounded subject. If trauma theory achieved prominence in the later twentieth century as a way of articulating the innocence of sufferers and as both a production and expression of "wound culture," the Victorian cultural need for a theory of emotional shock is rather different. While George Eliot shows Gwendolen's suffering from overwhelming emotional shock, the shock and horror is more about discovering what transgressions we may commit, and less about what is inflicted upon us from without: George Eliot's is less a "wound culture" than a conscience culture. In making the judgment that Gwendolen is not so much a witness to the cataclysms of history as to the fantasmatic power of the unconscious, we engage the oppositions in current trauma theory, which continue to structure debates over whether the mind is a passive registrant of or an active participant in the traumatizing event.[94]

Notwithstanding the emphasis on conscience and the focus in the final pages of the novel on a Gwendolen coming to her moral senses, George Eliot does give us an intimate and powerful representation of her heroine's psychic suffering in the aftermath of intense emotional experience. Interested in the relationship between consciousness and conscience, George Eliot has interpreted emerging theories of unconscious mental process (particularly those developed by Lewes) in terms of the motifs, language and accoutrements of the gothic tradition and ghost tale in order to delineate the psychic space of aftermath. In so doing she tells us what it means to live through an overwhelming experience that one cannot quite assimilate, and what kinds of effects that has on consciousness, memory and self-apprehension.

CHAPTER 5

Dissociation and multiple selves: memory, Myers and Stevenson's "shilling shocker"

In *The Strange Case of Dr Jekyll and Mr Hyde*, Dr Lanyon dies of shock after witnessing the grotesque morphing of Hyde into Jekyll. When Utterson, the lawyer, visits him, he is "shocked at the change which had taken place in the doctor's appearance. He had his death-warrant written legibly on his face." The effects of shock are both physical and mental: "The rosy man had grown pale; his flesh had fallen away … and yet it was not so much these tokens of a swift physical decay that arrested the lawyer's notice, as a look in the eye and quality of manner that seemed to testify to some deep-seated terror of the mind." Dr Lanyon confirms: "I have had a shock … and I shall never recover. It is a question of weeks."[1]

At the same time as the novella represents shock in Dr Lanyon straight-forwardly as a death-warrant, and seeks as a "shilling shocker" to subject its readers to a pleasurable form of terror, it also engages with emergent ideas about consciousness and its fragmented forms, which have bearing on formulations of psychic shock. Written at the moment when the concept of multiple personality was being articulated in medical and psychological circles, Stevenson's novella reflects on the central themes associated with this discourse. As part of a cluster of ideas about the way the mind responds to overwhelming or inassimilable experience, the discourse of multiple, alternating or split personality is dependent on assumptions about a non-unitary self, capable, under pressure, of switching from one strand of consciousness and memory to another, or indeed, several others. To read mid- to late-Victorian literary texts in relation to developing ideas about the non-unitary self is to illuminate both as mutually influential and also differently pre-occupied with the meanings of memory, inaccessible knowledge and layers of the self. This chapter explores one such case of the complex imbrication of literary and psychological discourse on the mind by looking at Stevenson's classic tale of self-severance in the context of contemporaneous ideas about the multiple self being developed by the Society for Psychical Research.

THE CASE OF LOUIS V AND THE MYERS DUO

In July of 1885, as Ian Hacking describes it in *Rewriting the Soul: Multiple Personality and the Sciences of Memory*, the discourse of multiple personality came into being. It did so through a variety of medical descriptions of the case of Louis Vivet. One of Vivet's doctors described the man as presenting a case of "doublement de personalité," but another declared that Vivet was more than a case of double personality – he had manifested eight distinct personalities between 1883 and 1885. What is important about Louis Vivet from Hacking's perspective is that a few of the many doctors studying his case linked each of his multiple personalities with a separate memory segment.[2]

The publication of the case in England followed some seven months after its description in France. Initially, it appeared in the "Psychological Retrospect" section of the *Journal of Mental Science* for January 1886 as a case of "Double or Multiple Personality" by one A. T. Myers. Also in January 1886, Robert Louis Stevenson published *The Strange Case of Dr Jekyll and Mr Hyde*. Accounts of the genesis of his story are legion; one of them concerns the possible influence of scientific discussions of the subconscious. In her prefatory note to the Tusitala Edition of Stevenson's works, Fanny Stevenson mentioned a possible source for the tale, suggesting tantalizingly that her husband was "deeply impressed by a paper he read in a French scientific journal on sub-consciousness."[3] For those of us interested in the complex and often mutually influential relationship between literary and psychological discourse in the later nineteenth century, this quotation has the status of a "hot clue." Did the paper that Stevenson purportedly read (it has never satisfactorily been identified) speak of alternating or multiple consciousness?[4] In a general way, Stevenson's novel is *the* literary expression of divided being: "Jekyll and Hyde" is a phrase that has entered common parlance as a synonym for the split self, and, as Stevenson explained later, he wanted to give voice in the tale to the "strong sense of man's double being." But what specifically is the relationship between Stevenson's classic allegory of the "devil within" and the discourse of the non-unitary self in late Victorian psychology? Certainly, the words Stevenson gives to Jekyll at the outset of his confession suggest that the author was aware of developments in the emergent psychology of multiple selves:

[M]an is not truly one, but truly two. I say two, because the state of my own knowledge does not pass beyond that point. Others will follow, others will outstrip me on the same lines; and I hazard the guess that man will be ultimately known for a mere polity of multifarious, incongruous and independent denizens. (61)

While Elaine Showalter has suggested that Stevenson may have read of the case of Louis V in the *Archives de Neurologie*, Stevenson denied that he had ever heard of it before the writing of his novel.[5] He told an interviewer in 1893 that he had never heard of any actual case of "double personality" when he wrote the book: "[a]fter the book was published I heard of the case of 'Louis V,' the man in the hospital at Rochefort. Mr. Myers sent it to me."[6]

If Stevenson did not take directly *from* this case, Robert Mighall has argued, "we can suspect that he might have given something to the writing up of it by Myers (1886)."[7] This would constitute a nice reversal of the common assumption that literature merely reflects developments in science and support the view, articulated with increasing frequency by literary critics, that the relation between literature and science is a two-way street. But if Myers and Stevenson did not yet know each other and each published his work in January, how could either have influenced the other? What needs to be explained is that Mighall is thinking of a later description of the case, which was published in November 1886, and could therefore have been influenced by Stevenson. It turns out that "Myers" published at least two versions of the case of Louis Vivet in the course of 1886. "Myers," however, is itself a multiple: the Myers who published the first version was not the same as the Myers who published the subsequent versions. This is not a strange case of "doublement de personalité," but of two brothers, A.T. and F. W. H. Myers. The former, A. T., wrote first on the Vivet case in January 1886.[8] Some months later, F. W. H. (not a doctor like his brother, but a Cambridge classics scholar, now best known as the author of *Human Personality* and a founder of the Society for Psychical Research) discussed the case at length in an article entitled "Multiplex Personality" which he published in the November 1886 issue of the periodical the *Nineteenth Century*. He also delivered this paper to the Society for Psychical Research and published it in the Society's *Proceedings* the following year.[9] Because F. W. H. is the better-known figure, he is usually considered the one responsible for introducing the concept of multiple personality to England – his is the dominant Myers personality: as it were, the primary state.[10]

In suggesting that Myers may have been influenced by Stevenson's tale in the writing up of the case in November 1886, Mighall points to similarities in language between "Multiplex Personality" and *The Strange Case of Doctor Jekyll and Mr Hyde*. Myers refers to Vivet's "monkey-like impudence" while Jekyll writes of Hyde's "apelike tricks"; Myers uses the phrase "polity of our being" which seems to echo Jekyll's characterization of man as a "mere polity of multifarious, incongruous and independent denizens" (61). While there may be a similarity in the language Myers and Stevenson use, discourse about the "primitive" or "savage" and its ape-like qualities was already well established by Darwin and Spencer.[11] Furthermore Myers had since at least the previous year been discussing and writing about alternations of personality, the non-unitary nature of the self, and the idea of personality as an aggregation. If Myers seems to echo Jekyll, Jekyll himself echoes phraseology and ideas which are to be found in Myers's earlier psychological writings. An 1885 report of Myers's address to the October meeting of the Society for Psychical Research read thus:

> Mr. Myers began by explaining the general position he was about to take up in the controversy now going on as to the true nature of man. The old view, he said, held both by ordinary common-sense and by most metaphysicians, maintains that each of us possesses a distinct and permanent personality – a self which is a unity and not *a mere aggregation* ... The new psychological view ... is to the effect that the only unity in us is the unity of our organism, and that our sense of personality depends merely on the temporary harmony of a sufficient number of the psychical elements which compose us. This view is supported by the physiological analysis, which tends to show how our higher physical processes may be mere developments of *the lower processes which we share with the brute.* (Emphasis added)[12]

Written before *Dr Jekyll and Mr Hyde* was published, this report refers to a "mere aggregation" and to the evolution of the "brute" within, both of which elements are present in Stevenson's descriptions, for example when Jekyll refers to a "mere polity" and writes of Hyde, "I still hated and feared ... the brute that slept within me" (73).

What is of interest here is less the question of who borrowed what phrase from whom than the fact that both literary and psychological texts are drawing on a developing discourse of multiple or hidden selves and the relationship among the diverse parts. Stevenson may have been influenced by contemporary discussions of the subconscious; Myers, who was to become the most vocal proponent of ideas about the subconscious, enthusiastically recognized a corroboration of his ideas in Stevenson's work. To read Stevenson's tale in the context of Myers's discussion of multiple personality is to see that both expose the illusion of a unitary self; both ponder the consequences of the idea that will and knowledge may be split and undermined as one state of consciousness gives way to another. Both question what implications the notion of a fragmented self may have for ethics, responsibility, self-possession and self-governance. The fact that the case of Louis Vivet is written up in English several times (by the Myers brothers) in the same year as Stevenson's tale comes out affirms that, by 1886, the question of "self-severance," multiplicity and its host of attendant problems for prevailing conceptions of mind were very much in the air.[13]

Before turning to Myers's relationship with Stevenson and the tale itself, I want first to outline some of the implications of Myers's work in the *Journal of the Society for Psychical Research* in the mid to late 1880s.

THE "FISSIPAROUS MULTIPLICATION OF THE SELF"

Fascinated by what he called "the mutability of personality," Myers spent many years exploring states of consciousness, and discontinuous and multiple selves. His magnum opus, *Human Personality and its Survival of Bodily Death*, published posthumously in 1903, was an extensive exploration of the nature of consciousness and whether personality persists after death.[14] On the one hand, then, Myers opposed the notion of a unitary self and patiently explained and defended (at the Society meetings and in the pages of the *Journal*) the idea of what he described richly as the "fissiparous multiplication of the self";[15] on the other hand, Myers believed in telepathy and was convinced of the perdurability of the self after death. Pamela Thurschwell has noted that the Society for Psychical Research aimed to

study objectively claims for the existence of supernatural phenomena, such as spiritualism, but ... its emotional impetus was towards countering the pessimism of a materialist and scientifically determined world view. For Frederick Myers, and others like him, the driving desire was to find a scientific proof of survival after death, and thus ally the claims of nineteenth-century positivist science with the older claims of religious faith.[16]

As Samuel Hynes has succinctly put it, Myers went forth in search of "the immortal soul" and found instead the "subconscious."[17]

Largely debunked in the last century as pseudoscientific, the Society for Psychical Research has only quite recently become an object of systematic academic scrutiny. As historians of science have come to acknowledge, its *Journal* and *Proceedings* constitute an important record of the issues debated in conjunction with ideas about dissociation, hypnotism and the multiplicity of the self.[18] Myers deals patiently and logically with many contemptuous respondents who assert the reality of spirit, soul and unity in contrast to his views, which fly in the face of the common sense encouraging us to think that each of us is a distinct and continuous personality rather than "a mere aggregation" of parts.[19] Hypnotism, Myers argued, has also shown the sense of free-will to be illusory; alternating memory, also evident through hypnosis, means that if we acquire "a second memory distinct from the first," we can hardly appeal to the "continuity of our memory as a proof of persistent personality."[20] In December, 1885, under the rubric "Further Notes on the Unconscious Self," Myers refers to his earlier paper on "Automatic Writing" in which he "endeavoured to explain certain phenomena – too often ignored (as I thought) by one school, too hastily referred to extra-human agencies by another – by the hypothesis of a second centre of mentation potentially existing without our own brains, and called into action by some underlying energy of our own."[21] The view about dreams which prevailed among many of Myers's readers was that "the dream-personages who converse with the sleepers are verily spirits."[22] In opposition, Myers insists on the dream as a device whereby internal manipulations are ascribed to external agencies. Dreams are a form of self-dramatization: "the personages who appear in our ordinary dreams are ... mere products of our own dramatic faculty; puppets whom we animate without being aware that it is ourselves who pull the strings."[23] Throughout this discussion of dreams, Myers's emphasis is on self-severance. In dreams we find a "fragment of our own mentation presenting itself to us as a message from *without;* we have a rudiment of what seems a second individuality entering into communication with our own." In the "rudimentary message" (a friend speaking in a dream) we have a "germ of externalisation" which is a "significant precursor of deeper secrets in the fissiparous multiplication of the self."[24] Dreams are a way of our sending messages to ourselves; we can make what goes on inside appear as if it comes from without.

The "fissiparous multiplication of the self" was not a concept to which Myers's readers gave happy assent. Letters to the *Journal of the Society for Psychical Research* written from the mid to late eighties express the anxiety about questions that plagued earlier discussions of the divided self: the existence of the soul and the notion of human responsibility. Myers hastened to assure such readers that one could assume the existence of a soul and still subscribe to the theory of multiplex personality. Thomas Barkworth, who later wrote an article for the *Journal* entitled "Duplex versus Multiplex Personality," argued that duplex personality was an allowable concept because the duality was to be understood in terms of animal or corporeal being, and spirit, but the concept of multiple personality was inadmissible because it appeared to assume that "the soul is a mere congeries of different conscious entities" without an "irreducible Ego."[25] Such readers complained that the concept "assails the existence of a soul; for it splits up our psychical being into a number of co-ordinate personalities, each of them closely dependent on a special state of the nervous system."[26] Myers responded by arguing that one could still preserve the idea of an underlying unity even in the face of a theory of multiplicity: "I should prefer to call our persistent being our individuality, rather than our personality; for this distinction of terms has become pretty general, and seems necessary for clearness."[27] He repeats the explanation that he had already penned in his article "Multiplex Personality," an explanation that depends largely on the metaphor of a manufactory. In the cerebral factory millions of looms work at different rates and in different groups. Groups exist that relate to the "conscious stream of existence," to "our underlying animal life," to our sleeping selves and to ourselves in the hypnotic trance. Each group weaves a strand of memory. What is important is that some of these strands or chains of memory are so discrete that we need to talk about an alternation of personality.[28] Myers attempts to convince his critics that this is not a fantastic conception: "We all know that a dying man will sometimes speak in the tongue which he learnt in infancy, but has forgotten in adult life. Why should we shrink from multiplying such interruptions and such *rapprochements*, or fear that the Ego behind the checkered lives of a Félida or a Léonie has lost by temporary diversification its pre-existing unity?"[29] As Myers explains, "[e]ach of us, we may say, contains within himself the potentiality of an unknown number of personalities, some at least of which may be educated to become so readily recurrent as his primary personality, although no one of them can – any more than his primary personality – be made to manifest itself in a really continuous manner."[30] In this scenario, memory becomes of prime importance as the essence of consciousness. Indeed, Myers goes so far as to suggest that we define consciousness as those acts and sensations that are memorable. Where memory is truncated or discontinuous, consciousness is similarly discontinuous.

Accordingly, Myers's discussion of Louis Vivet emphasizes the discontinuity of memory which follows a "sudden shock, falling on an unstable organisation."[31] Memory, he explains, is truncated and Louis can only remember such fragments of the past as have been linked with this abnormal state. The memories of successive stages are not lost, but juxtaposed, as it were, in separate compartments. When Louis passes into a different phase of personality, it is as if he has been "born again."[32] Myers admits that in cases like that of Louis Vivet it is difficult to tell "what epochs are intercalary or in what central channel the stream of his being flows."[33] That is, who, among the several personalities that Louis manifests, is the "real" Louis? In October, 1888, Myers reached the conclusion that the self with the highest order of memory is the real self. He read a paper on "French Experiments on Strata of Personality" reviewing Pierre Janet's experiments with Madame B. Janet was attempting "to observe the *unconscious actions* which the subject performs, in any phase of personality," in order to discover whether "these unconscious actions are recollected by her in any other phase."[34] Myers concluded that

> the most significant indication of differences in various hypnotic states is to be found in differences of the range of memory, and that the state in which the range of memory is the most extensive, – the state which includes the memories of other states, but is not included by them – has a *primâ facie* claim to be considered as the *profoundest* state of the subject, though it may not be the state best suited for the ordinary business of life.[35]

That last phrase is telling, as Myers was interested in using the conception of a multiplex self in practical ways – for the "ordinary business of life." While he recognized that most cases of "self-severance" as severe as that of Louis Vivet were to be found in the lunatic asylum, what absorbed Myers were the implications that this abnormal case had for knowledge of how the ordinary human mind works. In "Multiplex Personality" he attempts to move his readers beyond the conception that all changes in personality are pathological and retrogressive. Not only can personalities spontaneously adjust for the better but scientific practices such as hypnotism can induce or regulate nervous change "to effect physical and moral good." Myers had written in November, 1886, of "suggestive therapeutics" and was inspired by Dr. Voisin's experiments with hypnotized hysterics at Salpêtrière. He argues that personality change has the potential to be progressive rather than retrogressive. What if the altered state is an improvement on the original, such as in the case of Félida X, a young woman whose temperament and tractability were markedly improved when she was altered?[36] Her "secondary" self was labeled by her doctors as the "better" and they were all happy to see it become the dominant self. Myers suggests that medical practice might attempt to engender such spontaneous changes and aid in the "art of self-modification." After all, we do already in the ordinary course of things experience alterations of state from sleeping to waking. Hypnosis may be used to effect both moral and physical improvement: moral in the development of self-restraint and physical in the freedom from pain. Sounding very much like Stevenson, whose Jekyll dreams of dissociating the warring elements of his being and housing them in two different personalities, Myers noted that "cases [are] daily becoming more numerous where power is gained to dissociate the elements of our being in novel ways."[37] This pivotal sentence gestures also to early forms of psychoanalysis, where the possibility of relieving the patient of painful memories or reminiscences is based on assumptions about dissociation, and where the freedom from pain that hypnosis can effect is translated from the physical to the psychical sphere. Although Myers is mainly concerned here with the "moral progress ... attainable by physiological artifice,"[38] his insights suggest that, whether by physiological artifice or by chemical agency – which we use, for example, in the case of anesthesia – the self is mutable.[39]

MYERS AND STEVENSON

A number of issues from this review of Myers's work and the interests of the Society for Psychical Research bear on Stevenson's famous tale: the continuity and persistence of memory: self-severance and multiplicity; the question of beneficent self-modification; and the relation between the different phases of personality, which could also be figured as the struggle for dominance among discrete personalities. While many readers have regarded the transformation of Jekyll into Hyde as an instance of the fantastic – "impossible" and "absurd" – contemporary readers saw it as far closer to potential or even existing scientific practices. An unsigned review in *The Times* opined that the transformation through chemical agents, while amazing, was not beyond the realm of possibility: "[I]t is always possible that we may be on the brink of a new revelation as to the unforeseen resources of the medical art."[40] And Oscar Wilde (somewhat perversely but entirely characteristically) found the tale unhappily too close to fact, complaining in "The Decay of Lying" that "the transformation of Dr. Jekyll reads dangerously like an experiment out of the *Lancet.*"[41] The scientific and medical context of the story, clear to many readers from the start, was augmented by the fact that Stevenson's small cast of characters includes two doctors, neither of whom survives the horrors that unleashing the hidden elements of the self entails.

If Wilde thought the tale an instance of the "decay of lying" and evidence of "our monstrous worship of facts," Myers, who took the keenest interest in Stevenson's story, was very concerned that it did not sufficiently conform to "observed psychological fact."[42] Myers wrote enthusiastically to Stevenson shortly after the novel's publication, expressing his approbation of it and predicting (ultimately correctly) that Stevenson's reputation would come to rest on it. He took it upon himself, however, to offer several detailed suggestions for revisions. When Stevenson did not execute these, Myers wrote again in 1887 urging him to perfect his masterpiece and expressing concern lest he leave it for posterity with all its present infelicities upon it: "I do not want to be importunate, but I cannot but help reminding you that time is going on, and your masterpiece remains (so far as I know) without that final revision, the possible lack of which would be a real misfortune to English literature."[43] Stevenson never made the revisions. In his obituary for Stevenson in the *Journal of the Society for Psychical Research*, Myers noted that the novelist's death deprived the "muster-roll of our society" of one of its most brilliant names. He continued, lauding Stevenson especially for his keen sense of the subconscious or subliminal:

We cannot here survey the whole field of Mr. Stevenson's achievements. We must speak only of the actual link which interested him in our studies, and made his own literary history of such special value to the psychologist. He offered one of the most striking examples on record of the habitual uprush and incursion into ordinary consciousness of ideas or pictures conceived and matured in some subconscious region, without sense of effort or choice or will ... *Jekyll and Hyde* was itself a dream-inspiration; although here, as always, the self above the threshold co-operated skillfully and conscientiously with the self below; *and he had still proposed to himself,* if leisure came, to remodel some points in that appalling romance into closer accordance with observed psychological fact. (Emphasis added)[44]

A glance at the correspondence between Myers and Stevenson on the subject of Stevenson's tale shows that Myers is taking some license with pronouns in the sentence, "he had still proposed to himself"; he should rather have written, "I had proposed to him." It is true that Stevenson did respond to his suggestions with gratitude, writing in March, 1886: "I shall keep your paper; and if ever my works come to be collected, I will put my back into these suggestions,"[45] but it was certainly Myers who urgently proposed and Stevenson who was patently not at all urgent to dispose. Apparently the "closer accordance [between] observed psychological fact" and fictional representation was more important to Myers than to Stevenson. One reason was that Myers was by now convinced that discontinuous memory was a crucial aspect of multiple personality disorder and he was troubled by the fact that Jekyll and Hyde appeared to share memory. In his detailed and largely perceptive notes on a range of issues in the novel, Myers urged Stevenson to pay attention to this question, and to address the problem of the community of memory between Jekyll and Hyde. He thought that initially there should be two separate selves, each with his own discrete memory. "At first," Myers suggested, the "community [of memory] would be very imperfect; gradually the two memories would fuse into one; and in the last stage you might make an effective contrast of the increasing *fusion* of the two personalities in all except ethical temper, joined with the increasing revulsion ... of Jekyll against the ethical temper of Hyde."[46] Along similar lines, Myers informed Stevenson that by making the handwriting of Jekyll and Hyde the same he had missed something "for want of familiarity with recent psycho-physical discussions. Handwriting in cases of double personality (spontaneous ... or induced, as in hypnotic cases) *is not* and *cannot be* the same in the two personalities. Hyde's writing might look like Jekyll's done *with the left hand*, or done when partly drunk, or ill: that is the kind of resemblance there might be."[47] Myers noted in the *Journal of the Society for Psychical Research* in March 1886 that "I have good evidence of the production of handwriting resembling that of deceased persons – a better imitation than the writer can normally produce. It is, however, quite in accordance with analogy to suppose that our unconscious selves may be more skilful in mimicry than our conscious selves."[48] He is operating under the then-current state of opinion derived from cases such as that of Vivet that double or multiple personalities are quite discrete: handwriting and memory are instances of the difference between the personalities.

In the case of Jekyll and Hyde, however, Stevenson does not sever the memories or distinguish the handwriting of the two selves. In the course of the narrative Jekyll and Hyde appear to have a close (and possibly shameful) relationship and to know a great deal of each other. For instance, when Utterson says falsely that he has had a description of Hyde from Jekyll, Hyde accuses Utterson of lying. While such a response is typical of Hyde's rudeness, it does also imply that Hyde possesses in memory what Jekyll knows. It is only when we reach Jekyll's confession that the nature of their shared but different access to memory is explained: "Hyde was indifferent to Jekyll and remembered him but as the mountain bandit remembers the cavern in which he conceals himself from pursuit" (68). And Jekyll suffers great remorse because of his precise memories of what it is to be Hyde: "I sought with tears and prayers to smother down the crowd of hideous images and sounds with which my memory swarmed against me" (70). But Jekyll's account is not adequate to contain some of the complexities of memory sharing in Hyde and Jekyll. For example, the letter to Lanyon is written by Hyde, but, as Peter Garrett has noted, "its voice, as we can observe from its transcription in Lanyon's narrative ... seems entirely and convincingly Jekyll's. Whether we consider Hyde capable of extraordinary ventriloquism or rather suppose that much of Jekyll subsists in him, their relation hardly matches Jekyll's description."[49] And what of the words Hyde utters when the potion is ready and he binds Lanyon by saying "remember your vows: what follows is under the seal of our profession" (58)?

If Stevenson represents Hyde and Jekyll as sharing memory, albeit in a more complex way than Jekyll explains, Stevenson's fantastic narrative enacts in other ways the growing scientific sense that there may be such difference between phases of the self that they are for all intents and purposes different selves. And what makes fantastic transformation in *Jekyll and Hyde* so eerily appropriate is that late nineteenth-century mental physiologists did indeed look on the transformations of the self through hypnosis as magical.[50] In line with the fantastic transformations of gothic science fiction, Stevenson marks the difference of Hyde from Jekyll visually, corporeally, giving them very different physical appearances. This entails several useful implications: because of the physical metamorphosis brought about by the drug, no one who sees Hyde recognizes him as Jekyll. Hyde and Jekyll can go about as if they were entirely different people, because, in the physical sense, they are.[51] What science was beginning to know about multiple personality is that, while the body remains the same, the mind (and therefore memory) of the different personalities is recognizably different. Louis Vivet still looked like Louis Vivet when he manifested his multiple phases, even though each of these phases entailed discrete physical debilities as well as separate memories. As much as Vivet saw and felt himself to be different, the police and the psychiatric community had no trouble in recognizing him (physically) as himself. Stevenson reverses what would be a realist formulation. Instead of Jekyll's body staying constant while his memory splits and dissociates, Jekyll's body dissociates, as it were, and changes to become Hyde, while his memory endures.[52] Even as Stevenson recognizes the problem as one of split consciousness, the resultant dissociation is imagined in terms of a bodily split: "It was the curse of mankind that these incongruous faggots were thus bound together – that in the agonized womb of consciousness, these polar twins should be continuously struggling. How, then, were they dissociated?" (61). Psycho-physiology would soon come to formulate the psychic mechanisms of dissociation by which an agonized consciousness shuts out or cordons off incongruous or incompatible elements. Stevenson represents that dissociation physically; alternation is figured in terms of bodily alteration. Committed to the logic attendant on making Jekyll and Hyde corporeally different, Stevenson could not have given them entirely discrete memory because then they really would have been different people. Hyde needs to be able to remember that he can change himself back into Jekyll. And it is necessary that Jekyll and Hyde have the same handwriting so that when the former spontaneously changes into the latter, he can write to Dr Lanyon to procure the drugs he needs: "Then I remembered that of my original character, one part remained to me: I could write my own hand; and once I had conceived that kindling spark, the way that I must follow became lighted up from end to end" (72). Stevenson also uses the sameness of handwriting to make it look as if Henry Jekyll is forging on behalf of Hyde, thus making the dark relations between them even more suspect.

But the question of memory splitting is not jettisoned because Stevenson gives Jekyll and Hyde different corporeal selves. I would argue that Stevenson has cleverly structured the tale so that the state of splitting, or memory discontinuity, is invested in the reader. Of course, now that the story of Jekyll and Hyde has become part of our cultural mythology, almost no reader approaches the tale without knowing that Jekyll and Hyde are one and the same; yet the way Stevenson wrote the tale was that the reader should not know that Jekyll and Hyde were the same but should believe that they were totally different people for the majority of the story. Only when the implied reader reaches the end of Dr Lanyon's narrative does he or she know for sure what may have been dimly suspected: that Hyde is Jekyll, or as G. K. Chesterton put it, two men are one. By remarking on the difference between "one man is two" and "two men are one," Chesterton points implicitly to the readers' perspective and the surprise that what has been perceived as two separate beings is really one. It might be argued that even though today's readers may know at some level that Jekyll and Hyde are one, the story is not spoiled, because readers suppress or dissociate from what is known in order to read as if they were unknowing. What Stevenson does is to place the reader in the position of living the duality as if there were no connection between the two selves. Jekyll and Hyde appear to be different people, different identities, even though the relationship between them is figured as unspeakable. Is Jekyll being blackmailed? Is Hyde a sinister revival of some aspect of Jekyll's indiscreet past? The reader is therefore in the position of one who suffers the memory disjunction common in cases of double or multiple consciousness, where the self has no memory of the other selves or alters, who at one time or another dominate consciousness.

DUALITY VS. MULTIPLICITY

As we saw in the correspondence to the *Journal of the Society for Psychical Research*, the question of double as opposed to multiple selves was a vexed and charged one for Victorian religion. Duality was less threatening than multiplicity because it could be understood in terms of the animal or corporeal being, on the one hand, and the spiritual being or soul, on the other. Victorian readers like Barkworth, the respondent to Myers whom I discussed earlier, were more comfortable with admitting the idea of duplex personality because at least it was consonant with religious teachings and received wisdom about the duality of man. Stevenson's tale appears to be structured around several dualities. As Peter Garrett notes: "Good and evil, higher and lower, spirit and matter, body and soul: such are the oppositions from which Jekyll's philosophical discourse is constructed, and which for many readers have determined the meaning of the whole tale."[53] Yet these dualities or binaries are often undercut or qualified by an awareness of multiplicity.

Narrators and narrative are certainly multiple: Jekyll's confession, coming late in the tale, is part of a structure of multiple narratives, which perform the work of splitting knowledge and consciousness. The impersonal narrator introduces us to the lawyer Utterson and his friendships. Exchanges between Enfield and Utterson, communications from Dr Lanyon, and finally letters, and letters within letters, reveal the heart of the mystery. Jekyll's narrative, the final and posthumous revelation, is only a minor part (roughly one quarter) of the tale. Despite the multiplicity of narrators, at the outset of the narrative the language of doubleness, duality and couples is more insistent than that of multiplicity. Cain and his brother are mentioned in the description of Mr. Utterson (7) and later Lanyon makes reference to Jekyll's estrangement from him on account of his mad science, which he says would have estranged even Damon and Pythias (15). Jekyll talks of "polar twins" in the "agonized womb of consciousness." In Stevenson's tale there is initially a neat division of the double self into higher and lower, good and evil. If Hyde is, as Jekyll has said, like a "familiar, called up out of his own soul," the power structure is clear. Hyde may be a devil, but he is summoned to serve Jekyll, who is supposed to remain dominant and superior. The language of the "devil within" governs much of the tale's representation of Hyde's status. "My devil had been long caged" says Jekyll at one point, "[H]e came out roaring" (69). In an early moment of irony, Mr. Utterson is described as a man who subscribes to "Cain's heresy" and is tolerant enough to let his neighbor "go to the devil in his own way" (7). This is in accordance with a traditional discourse about the baser Adam. Thus the language of clear duality applies both to the Calvinist doctrines under which Stevenson grew up and to the evolutionary discourse of which he also makes use.[54] In both cases, the base, the brute, exists within and has to be controlled and dominated by the superior part.

But logical problems begin when Jekyll undertakes to dissociate the elements of which man is made. The discourse of duality is a discourse of superior and inferior parts of the self: while Hyde is the evil side, Jekyll ought to be purely the good. But he is still the mixture of the two, "that incongruous compound of whose reformation and improvement I had already learned to despair" (64). Hyde is the evil part given selfhood, but his manifestation does not rid Jekyll of the Hyde-like parts within. Even here, the notion of a simple duality is confounded as it is ostensibly enacted. Hyde is a part that becomes a person, but Jekyll is still left a man of many parts. It would be truer to say that Hyde is a manifestation of a part of Jekyll but Jekyll is still the sum of his parts despite, on occasion, the subtraction and manifestation of Hyde.

In addition, several critics have pointed to the plurality of voices in the tale, despite the neat division that a duality proposes. The use of pronouns is also erratic and complicated. When Hyde is on his rampage of cruelty, Jekyll notes, "I was suddenly, in the top fit of my delirium, struck through the heart by a cold thrill of terror. A mist dispersed; I saw my life to be forfeit; and fled from the scene of these excesses" (70). While Jekyll some-times refers to his other self as "Hyde," here he uses the pronoun "I," so that the sense of a unitary self with divisions is communicated, rather than two separate selves. Stevenson is trying to explore how a part becomes a person, ultimately a person who must be repudiated as other, as "he" rather than "I." And fittingly, the more Hyde "grows," the less efficacious is the technology Jekyll has devised to dissociate good and evil within himself. Like an addict, he is obliged on "more than one occasion" to "double, and once, with infinite risk of death, to treble the amount" of the powder he ingests (68).

At the peak of Jekyll's repudiation of Hyde, he switches to the third person and laments that he cannot say "I": "He, I say – I cannot say I. That child of Hell had nothing human; nothing lived in him but fear and hatred" (73). As his account proceeds, Jekyll is at times unable to invest himself in any use of the pronoun "I," talking about both Jekyll and Hyde as if they were two others, not himself: "The powers of Hyde seemed to have grown with the sickliness of Jekyll. And certainly the hate that now divided them was equal on each side. With Jekyll it was a thing of vital instinct. He had now seen …" (74). The instability of subject positions is seen in the following passage where third person switches back to first in Jekyll's indignation at Hyde's miscreant behavior with his cherished objects:

His terror of the gallows drove him continually to commit temporary suicide, and return to his subordinate station of a part instead of a person; but he loathed the necessity, he loathed the despondency into which Jekyll was now fallen and he resented the dislike with which he was himself regarded. Hence the apelike tricks he would play *me*, scrawling in *my* own hand blasphemies on the pages of *my* books, burning the letters and destroying the portrait of *my* father … (Emphasis added; 75)

The structure of multiple narratives is reinforced by images of fracture, refraction, repetition and multiplication. For example, the key that is to give access to the cellar and unlock the secret of Jekyll's identity is found to be fractured. When Utterson and Poole find the body of Hyde they immediately set about looking for Jekyll: "Hyde is gone to his account; and it only remains for us to find the body of your master" (49). Even at this point, the reader does not yet quite know the relation between Jekyll and Hyde and experiences them, as do Utterson and Poole, as different people. Searching the "dark closets" and the cellar, they find "[n]owhere … any trace of Henry Jekyll, dead or alive" (49), though they do find a key to the cellar which is fractured and looks as if a man has stamped upon it.

The image of the fractured key gives way to further images of breakdown and refraction. Utterson and Poole come upon a cheval glass, "into whose depths they looked with an involuntary horror. But it was so turned as to show them nothing but the rosy glow playing on the roof, the fire sparkling in a hundred repetitions along the glazed front of the presses, and their own pale and fearful countenances stooping to look in" (50). This is a telling image: looking for Jekyll in the depths of the mirror, the two men find the "fire sparkling in a hundred repetitions along the glazed front of the presses." The glass, which shows nothing but reflection, a multiplication of images, seems to presage the fracturing and multiplication of self that they do not yet understand as the key to Jekyll's case. In finding Hyde, they do not recognize that they have also found Jekyll. In this world of replication and multiplication, Stevenson seems to enjoy the *double entendre* that their ignorance allows. Later in the tale when Hyde comes to Dr Lanyon, the latter asks, "Are you come from Dr Jekyll?" meaning "Have you been sent by him?" but Hyde's more literal emanation from Jekyll is also implied as a pun to those in the know. In the scene with the mirror, Poole observes that the glass must have seen some strange things, to which Utterson responds "And surely none stranger than itself … what would Jekyll want with it?" (50). In the manuscript version, Stevenson wrote "This glass has seen some queer doings," which was then changed to "strange things" in the text.[55] The language of this statement is peculiar. How can the glass have seen itself, except in infinite reflections? And why should Jekyll's possession of a mirror be so strange? In order to understand what Utterson means, we need to know that a cheval glass is a special type of tall dressing mirror "suspended between two pillars, usually joined by horizontal bars immediately above and below the mirror and resting on two pairs of long feet. The cheval glass was first made toward the end of the 18th century."[56] Utterson is wondering why Jekyll would need a full-length mirror in his cabinet. The answer, we understand in hindsight, is so that he can see himself when he is not himself. The glass turns out to stand for Jekyll himself, who, like the mirror, has not only seen strange things, but is himself the strangest of them. What is eerily apposite, given the context of Stevenson's story, is that by the mid nineteenth century this kind of mirror had also became known as the Psyche. According to the *Oxford English Dictionary*, it was so called because of Raphael's full-length painting of the fabled Psyche. If Psyche is a metonym for "full-length," in the novel "full length" (the extent of corporeal change) is a metonym for psyche: Jekyll's transformation into Hyde is primarily about the mind's refraction which is then mirrored in the bodily change.

Further binaries of primary/secondary and dominant/subordinate are undercut as the good doctor's experiments in dissociation begin to defy his control. What starts out as an experiment that the doctor-scientist orchestrates becomes a case of spontaneous and unmanageable mutation – a voluntary change become involuntary, as Stevenson would later explain in "A Chapter on Dreams." Jekyll can no longer control his transformation into and out of Edward Hyde. After the murder of Carew, Jekyll has clearly decided to cease changing into Hyde, but soon finds that he transforms spontaneously. Unlike a mask that can be donned or doffed, the "separate self" that Jekyll has created begins to assume control of the joint enterprise Jekyll/Hyde. Hyde refuses to remain "hidden." According to Jekyll's narrative, the first spontaneous shift occurs when Jekyll is sitting in the sun on a bench in Regent's Park, his "spiritual side a little drowsed" (71), his conscience inactive, and his sense of himself complacent. The nature of his thoughts changes and he looks down to find he has become Hyde. Both Hyde and Jekyll are now of one mind, so to speak, because they both wish to return to the form of Jekyll: Hyde because he fears for his life, and Jekyll because what he hates most now is to be Hyde: "A change had come over me. It was no longer the fear of the gallows, it was the horror of being Hyde that racked me" (73). The next time Jekyll reverts, he is stepping "leisurely across the court ... drinking the chill of the air with pleasure" (74). Later, if he sleeps or dozes for a moment, he wakes as Hyde. It appears therefore that, as soon as his active conscience wavers or he relaxes vigilance, he is susceptible to becoming Hyde. As waking state gives way to trance state in hypnosis, so Jekyll gives way to Hyde. And as the shift from one personality to another occurs spontaneously and without mediation in cases of multiple personality like that of Louis V, so Jekyll can no longer orchestrate his alternations.

With the shift from voluntary to spontaneous transformation, the power relations between Jekyll and Hyde seem to change substantially. Stevenson represents Hyde as growing slightly in stature as the dominance of the original seems challenged by the double. The question of who is primary and who secondary – or as later psychologists would put it, who is dominant – is now a crucial one. When the transfers to Hyde begin to occur spontaneously, Jekyll notes that his lower side is growing stronger: "I was ... losing hold of my original and better self, and becoming slowly incorporated with my second and worse" (68). While many critics have placed these remarks in the context of evolutionary discourse about the anxiety of the primitive usurping the civilized, they can also be seen in the context of Myers's discussion of the modification of the self through substituting a preferred part for the previous dominant manifestation. Stevenson seems to echo the evaluative and judgmental language that both French and English doctors used in describing the alters of cases of double or multiple consciousness – Félida and Louis. In Félida's case, however, the second self was deemed to be the better and promoted as the dominant, which, we recall, prompted Myers to ponder the possibilities of self-improvement through installing a preferable secondary as the primary self. Stevenson's tale, however, dramatizes the horrifying prospect of "self-modification," in which the darker part of the self becomes dominant. In psychological discourse the idea is that knowledge and memory are apportioned among different selves. As William James points out in "The Hidden Self," a review of Janet's book *L'Automatisme psychologique*, "total possible consciousness may be split into parts which coexist, but mutually ignore each other and share the objects of knowledge between them, and – more remarkable still – are complementary."[57] What seems remarkable to James is the problem-solving logic of the apportionment: if total or integrated knowledge is insupportable, departments are set up to govern discrete bundles. At the same time, however, it may appear that the secondary self has usurped or been apportioned something of the primary and can, under conditions of hypnosis, be made to give up possession of its territory. In his discussion of Louis V's case, Myers had emphasized that the art of modification of the self was at stake. James reiterates that the goal of investigations such as Janet's is the reduction of human misery.

Jekyll, however, has modified himself and now cannot exorcize or subdue the "second personage" that has been given life, so to speak. The difference, once again, between Jekyll and Louis V, Léonie or Félida is that Jekyll has an agonized knowledge and memory of what it is to be Hyde. The basic point, as Myers and James understood dissociation, was not to have to know: ignorance may not be bliss, but it serves the psyche's purpose of not having to integrate actions and feelings that are contradictory and possibly repulsive or painful to the dominant self. Stevenson disallows this psychic strategy and can explore imaginatively the "double bind," the emotional and ethical consequences of having dissociation as a technology but keeping memory and knowledge integrated.

What is curious, however, is that the more Jekyll spontaneously reverts to Hyde, the more Hyde seems like Jekyll in his speech and even actions. The Hyde who visits Dr Lanyon is acting like Jekyll. His relief at the acquisition of the drug and his preparatory address to Lanyon before he takes the drug, are consistent with Jekyll rather than Hyde: "Lanyon, you remember your vows: what follows is under the seal of our profession. And now, you who have been so long bound to the most narrow and material views, you who have denied the virtue of transcendental medicine, you who have derided your superiors – behold!" (58). It is difficult therefore to characterize the relation between Jekyll and Hyde in terms of dominance or primacy, because, even though Hyde overtakes Jekyll spontaneously now and Jekyll slips into being Hyde as soon as he is relaxed or leisurely, Hyde does not revel in or enjoy his ascendancy. In fact, he is shown to be quite anxious to disappear – "to commit temporary suicide" – and have Jekyll once again in charge. There is no struggle on Hyde's part to subdue and annihilate Jekyll. So when Utterson and Poole are about to break down the door to Jekyll's cabinet, they hear Hyde beg for mercy and discover his still twitching body, and close by it the will of Jekyll in which Utterson has newly been named beneficiary. Indeed, Utterson thinks it very odd that Hyde, now occupying Jekyll's quarters, would not have destroyed the will displacing him (Hyde) and amended in Utterson's favor. Jekyll's narrative attempts to account for that: "Should the throes of change take me in the act of writing it, Hyde will tear it to pieces; but if some time shall have elapsed after I have laid it by, his wonderful selfishness and circumscription to the moment will probably save it once again from the action of his apelike spite" (76). Jekyll leaves off his narrative, wondering whether after Hyde has taken over again he will have the courage to commit suicide or whether he will die on the gallows. Once again, although suicide seems an implausible option for the aggressive and murderous Hyde, Jekyll's narrative attempts to rationalize Hyde's uncharacteristic actions. In so far as Hyde is the last remaining self manifested, he may be said to be the dominant state, a prospect that Jekyll foresees as he abdicates and lays down his pen at the end of the tale. He knows that he will now be reverting to Hyde and will never again appear as Jekyll. The power to dissociate the elements of his being results in a new association in which Jekyll finds himself increasingly powerless. Even the status of Henry Jekyll's full statement is compromised by his lack of control over the Hyde part of himself, for the fact that Jekyll disappears, leaving Hyde to decide whether he will live or die, denies the final piece of the narrative coherence and closure.

DISSOCIATIONS

I want to turn by way of concluding this discussion of memory and multiple selves to Stevenson's essay "A Chapter on Dreams." The essay, often read as an explanation of the creative process involved in producing *The Strange Case of Dr Jekyll and Mr Hyde*, is itself a document about disclaimers and dissociation. It is also an incidence of doubling in its relationship to *Dr Jekyll and Mr Hyde*, where the narrator of the account is in the position of Jekyll vis-à-vis his unconscious collaborators. In this essay, Stevenson places great emphasis on memory and the hidden self that reveals its treasures during sleep. Commissioned for *Scribner's Magazine*, where it was published in October, 1888, the essay is on the face of it a light-hearted and, indeed, self-ironic meditation on the creative powers of the unconscious mind and a description of the genesis of *Dr Jekyll and Mr Hyde*. Roger Swearingen has suggested that much of the essay was inspired by the kinds of questions enthusiasts asked Stevenson after the publication of the tale. What is significant for my scrutiny of the relations between literature and memory science is the fact that, by the time "A Chapter on Dreams" was written, Stevenson and Myers had corresponded on the case of Louis V and on the question of community of memory between Jekyll and Hyde.[58] I would like to argue that, at the time of writing the essay, Stevenson was even further exposed to and immersed in the discourse of the multiplicity of self, and the relation of the conscious self to its "unseen collaborators." Stevenson writes about knowledge held in the self beyond ordinary consciousness. He begins by asserting the power of memory to give us a sense of ourselves, introducing an explanatory analogy of entitlement and past claims: "There is scarce a family that can count four generations but lays a claim to some dormant title or some castle and estate; a claim not prosecutable in any court of law, but flattering to the fancy and a great alleviation of idle hours. A man's claim to his own past is yet less valid."[59] Without the "little thread of memory" that links us to the past, we would stand in "naked nullity" (198). All the more important then are dreams, which are "among the treasures of memory" (199). Stevenson moves on to discuss an "unusual" case in the world of dreamers, one who, after dreaming his fears as a child, goes on as a student to live a double life through dreaming. Once he becomes a writer of tales, this dreamer puts his sleeping self to work to produce wonderful tales for his waking self to transcribe. What is interesting about Stevenson's description of himself is not so much that it is written as if about someone else, in the third person, but that even the dreaming self is personified as "the little people" or the Brownies. Stevenson personifies – that is, dissociates – the elements of his creative or remembering self, as if to suggest that the Brownies are like the elves to the Shoemaker. He recalls here the explanation E. S. Dallas offers in *The Gay Science* of the work of the imagination: "The hidden efficacy of our thoughts, their prodigious power of working in the dark and helping us underhand, can be compared only to the stories of our folklore, and chiefly to that of the lubber-fiend who toils for us when we are asleep or when we are not looking."[60] Stevenson similarly creates a band of Dallas's "unknown and tricksy worker[s]," who do the work, while he is sleeping, for which he reaps all the benefit:[61]

Here is a doubt that much concerns my conscience. For myself – what I call I, my conscious ego, the denizen of the pineal gland unless he has changed his residence since Descartes, the man with the conscience and the variable bank-account, the man with the hat and the boots, and the privilege of voting and not carrying his candidate at the general elections – I am sometimes tempted to suppose he is no story-teller at all, but a creature as matter of fact as any cheesemonger or any cheese, and a realist bemired up to the ears in actuality; so that, by that account, the whole of my published fiction should be the single-handed product of some Brownie, some Familiar, some unseen collaborator, whom I keep locked in a back garret, while I get all the praise and he but a share (which I cannot prevent him getting) of the pudding. (207)

The ordinary man doesn't feel that he is the same one as the creator. Similarly, Jekyll, the good doctor, cannot possibly be Hyde, the antisocial miscreant. There are further similarities in language and formulation here to *The Strange Case of Dr Jekyll and Mr Hyde*: the unseen collaborators are kept in a back garret; Hyde has to come and go by the back entrance. The Brownies are described as "some Familiar"; Jekyll describes Hyde as a "familiar ... called up out of [his] own soul" and summoned to act out Jekyll's darker desires (65). In writing about his Brownies, Stevenson comically styles himself as an exploiter of the Familiar, who is the one behind the scenes doing all the real work. He himself is like one in a trance, writing automatically: "I hold the pen, too; and I do the sitting at the table..." (207). At this point, Stevenson explains the genesis of *Jekyll and Hyde*. He had for long been trying to write a story on "that strong sense of man's double being" (208). From the Brownies – in dream – came the "central idea of a voluntary change becoming involuntary" (208). What Stevenson doesn't say is that the very idea of the Brownies as an unseen part of the self is the idea behind *Dr Jekyll and Mr Hyde*, except, of course, that the Brownies are creative and collaborative rather than destructive, anarchic and self-serving.

Much of what Stevenson has to say in the chapter plays whimsically with the notion of dissociation.[62] The Brownies are a part of the self given separate being and can now take the rap for some of the criticism that the tale has drawn. "Will it be thought ungenerous, after I have been ... ladling out praise to my unseen collaborators, if I here toss them over, bound hand and foot, into the arena of the critics? For the business of the powders, which so many have censured, is, I am relieved to say, not mine at all but the Brownies'" (208). In a humorous way, Stevenson abdicates responsibility for the invention of an aspect of the story that has proved problematic. In a similar way, *The Strange Case of Dr Jekyll and Mr Hyde* explores the desire to abdicate responsibility for the self-indulgent, lawless, self, whose liberty, youth, "light step, leaping pulses and secret pleasures" Jekyll confesses to enjoying in the disguise of Hyde. In "A Chapter on Dreams," Stevenson casts into a comic key the discourse of splitting responsibility and knowledge that defines dissociation as William James, Myers and Janet are writing about it. As William James remarked in relation to one of Janet's subjects:

The primary self often has to invent an hallucination by which to mask and hide from its own view the deeds which the other self is enacting. Léonie 3 writes real letters, while Léonie 1 believes that she is knitting; or Lucie 3 really comes to the doctor's office while Lucie 1 believes herself to be at home ... Few things are more curious than these relations of mutual exclusion, of which all gradations exist, between the several partial consciousnesses.[63]

And as I have discussed above, Myers had argued in early 1886 that dreams are a device whereby internal manipulations are ascribed to external agencies, a form of self-dramatization: "the personages who appear in our ordinary dreams are ... mere products of our own dramatic faculty; puppets whom we animate without being aware that it is ourselves who pull the strings."[64] In dreams we find a "fragment of our own mentation presenting itself to us as a message from *without;* we have a rudiment of what seems a second individuality entering into communication with our own." If Stevenson's lightly ironic discussion of the creative parts of the self was influenced by Myers's in "A Chapter on Dreams," Myers was certainly pleased with the product, for, as we have seen, he praised Stevenson's essay in his obituary notice and acknowledged the debt owed by psychology to Stevenson's literary history. Rereading Stevenson's tale in the context of emergent memory science and ideas about dissociation highlights the close affinity and shared discourse of literature and psychology as they each endeavor to articulate and respond to the crisis of subjectivity and identity raised by the idea of the multiple self.

Afterword on afterwards

Central to Victorian thinking about consciousness and the effects on consciousness of overwhelming emotion, shock is a topic that engages a wide variety of Victorian writers, not least mental physiologists and novelists. The previous chapters of this book have attempted to excavate Victorian thinking around the concept of shock in order to show that it provides, at one and the same time, a significant "prehistory" of current conceptions of trauma and evidence of the role of literature in the cultural formation of trauma.

Late-modern theories of trauma imply and depend on assumptions about the unconscious mind and the way we process emotion that derive largely from Freud. Victorian theories about shock depend on rather different ideas about the architecture of the psyche and the nature of the unconscious mind. While it has not been the purpose of this book to compare Victorian and Freudian theories of the mind exhaustively, my excavation of earlier theories should provide a sharpened sense of the historical contingency of trauma theory. In principle, most critics would readily concede that contingency, but in practice a fairly limited set of propositions tends to be extracted from the field and applied as if they were universal and transcendent of culture and history. A more precise grasp of the pre-Freudian history of the wounded mind should dispel any universalized or transcendent notion of "the unconscious" and might also therefore broaden the current narrow focus on memory in contemporary approaches to trauma.

If I had gone forward on the (widely accepted) assumption that memory loss or dysfunction is the prime indicator of traumatic experience, I would have found *some* evidence of Victorian culture's engagement with emotional shock. A far richer and more compelling cache of ideas about the shocked psyche emerged from exploring Victorian theories of emotion and states of consciousness. The emphasis on memory as somehow the key to trauma has arisen in part as a result of the question: how does the experience of shock disrupt cognitive processes? As that question is answered in terms of unconscious rather than conscious registration, involuntary rather than voluntary recall, so the effect on memory has come to seem the most crucial result of the traumatic event. Although some critics and psychologists have disputed the primacy of memory as the *sine qua non* of trauma, a focus on this particular element continues to dominate literary and psychoanalytic articulations of trauma theory. Yet, as we have seen, the question of how memory is impacted by traumatic experience remains problematic, especially in explanations of the way memory is by-passed rather than simply avoided or forgotten or repressed. In nineteenth-century discourse, disturbances of memory as the result of overwhelming or shocking experience are only one aspect of a network of related ideas.

Among these, I have emphasized the importance of Victorian theories of emotion, and particularly the recognition that emotions occupy a peculiar status in being of the body as well as the mind. As such, they offer the nineteenth-century novelist a way of articulating what is known but not thought. The shocked somatic body also necessarily implicates the psyche and may indeed be deputized to "speak" for it. To the extent that emotions are cognitive, they carry knowledge that may not be consciously possessed and may thus cue the presence of thorns in the spirit. The idea of the wounded mind propelled Victorians to grapple on yet another front with "embodiedness" as a concept and to puzzle over the appropriate emphasis to be placed on mental as opposed to physical activity, a conundrum that continues in debates between neurobiological and psychoanalytic approaches to trauma. While the work of contemporary neurobiologist Bessel Van der Kolk draws attention to the way "the body keeps the score," neurobiological and psychoanalytic approaches to trauma are often represented as antithetical, the neurobiological seeming to discount the possibility of symbolic elaboration and unconscious agency. The longer history that I have attempted to plot reveals also what is enduring yet historically inflected about the significance of agency in relation to the unconscious mind. Issues about agency dominate Victorian debates about the unconscious – it is just that the frontiers of agency look rather different from how they do today.

This book has also attempted to show that Victorian fiction participated in a rich variety of ways in its culture's debates about the idea of the wounded psyche. It has been my purpose to demonstrate that reading the mid-Victorian novel in terms of the period's *own* theories about the relations of mind and body and the effects of shock on consciousness produces a historically nuanced understanding of the way fiction imagines and interrogates ideas about psychic wounding and suffering. The close readings of several literary texts have shown the signal place of the literary in formulations of psychic shock, and in "making up" the entranced, stunned and absent self.[1] Tracking the shifts in consciousness that follow overwhelming emotion, the texts we have discussed all focus on the abdication of ordinary volition, agency and consciousness. Theories of altered states of mind, of the unconscious and of emotional disruption contribute to an emergent category of self: one that is jolted out of ordinary consciousness, that is "not quite itself" or "beside itself." Powerful emotion is figured as a state of entrancement giving rise to a self that is dazed, stunned or numbed, transfixed, stupefied, amazed, fascinated, haunted, absent to itself, and even fragmented. The vocabulary of the haunted self has obvious affiliation to traditional folkloric and other explanations of the supernatural, possession, dreams and nightmare. Reworking literary traditions, such as melodrama, the gothic and tales of haunting and ghosts, mid- to late-Victorian fiction raises a host of nuanced questions about the mind in response to shock and terror. In thinking imaginatively about bodies and minds under siege, subject to stress, overwhelming experience, guilt and terror, these texts reveal the complex and various conceptions of emotion, memory and consciousness to which Victorian culture subscribed. While these texts share key assumptions with the medico-psychological discourse of their day, they also, by virtue of imaginative engagement with questions about memory and emotion, depart from and range beyond that discourse.

Moreover, these several readings endorse the view that the rise of twentieth-century trauma theory is by no means adequately explained by advances in neurology and psychology; one of the central findings of this study is that the emergence of trauma theory is dependent less on scientific discoveries than it is on cultural attitudes and ideology. Trauma as a concept is a *cultural* formation. As we have seen, Victorian ideas about the physical vulnerability of the mind and conceptions of shock in the second half of the nineteenth century were already capable of supporting a full-scale theory of mental shock in which powerful emotion could produce trance-like or dissociative effects and make affect regulation a consequent problem. Indeed, it would have been easier for the Victorians than it was for Freud to solidify such a theory, since in Freud's case the role of the unconscious in encoding traumatic memory proved to be an insoluble problem. Freud had to posit that the memory of the trauma falls into some other area than the unconscious, because it is not repressed in the same way as unconscious memories are repressed. Freudian trauma theory as it developed in response to shell-shocked soldiers is about the real, whereas the unconscious, as Freud conceived it, is a repository of fantasies that develop from forbidden knowledge. Freud's idea of disallowed and hence repressed memory (witnessing of the primal scene, seduction fantasies) entailed an encoding that was susceptible to unconscious elaboration and depended on the participation of the subject in creating the symbols and symptoms, which in turn became the only means of apprehending the unconscious. But war trauma was about unassimilated experience and had to involve a different kind of storage that by-passed memory and hence desire and fantasy – symbolic elaboration. Since Victorians did not generally think of the unconscious as formed by repression and taboo knowledge, their theories of memory and consciousness were actually less confounding when it came to understanding the way overwhelming experience is encoded. Why then did Victorian culture not produce a fully explicit and self-conscious theory of trauma?

Social and political events, not to mention the demands of gender theory, were instrumental in bringing early-twentieth-century trauma theory into being. Similarly, we need to look to the social context of Victorian ideas about mental shock in order to understand why the Victorians did not produce a fully formulated theory of trauma. The reason for this is that Victorian culture neither wanted nor needed it. I want briefly here to suggest why not.

I began this exploration of psychic shock by drawing attention to the generic category of "brain fever." A cursory survey of fictional accounts of brain fever reveals that they are often about penance or purification and mark a transition or transformation in the individual subject. They are about what we have done to ourselves, as opposed to what the world has done to us. Even in cases where brain fever is the result of overwork or undue taxing of the mind, it is often the subject's fault or responsibility that he or she becomes the sufferer. In the preceding chapters we have seen on several occasions that the realization of guilt is felt as a form of shock and its aftermath experienced as a fragmentation and discontinuity of consciousness. Stunned by her own lie to the policeman, Margaret Hale registers the shock of her dishonesty as prostration; agonized yet paralyzed responsibility in the Signalman propels him to his death. Gwendolen Harleth's hysterical collapse after seeing the diamonds betrays her guilt about having reneged on her promise to Lydia Glasher; her "lava-lit" memory and disruptions of consciousness after Grandcourt's death by drowning signal her remorseful and guilty conscience. Jasper's shock after hearing of Edwin and Rosa's broken engagement and his increasingly fragmented consciousness also speak to his guilt and murderous desires. The attempt to avoid guilt while experiencing pleasure animates the dissociative bodily split in Jekyll. Bound up with the idea of responsibility, Victorian investigations of the effects of shock are less concerned with *victimhood* than they are with *accountability*. Nevertheless, while the impetus towards justice never supersedes the discourse of conscience, atonement and penance, there is also detectable in fictive explorations of consciousness under emotional pressure a strong interest beyond the attribution of blame.

In a variety of ways, literature begins to imagine the aftermath of disaster for the victim and so to establish a discourse about the mind's vulnerability to overwhelming experience. A case in point is Mrs. Ellen Wood's short story "Lease, the Pointsman" (1869). It features a horrific train disaster in which several people are killed and many others damaged by shock because a pointsman apparently forgets to turn the points after a goods-train has passed, thereby setting the next train up for a collision. Everyone immediately turns on the pointsman, Harry Lease, to blame him for the accident. Agonized, he cannot remember whether he turned the points or not. The Squire, who was on the train with his wife and daughter, demands: "'Then how came you to neglect the points, Lease, and cause this awful accident?' 'I don't know, sir,' answered Lease, rousing up from his lethargy, but speaking like one in a dream. 'I can't think but what I turned them as usual.'"[2] Wood emphasizes the inability of the man to remember this habitual action: "[H]e only spoke aloud the problem that was working in his mind. Having shifted the points regularly for five years, it seemed just impossible that he could have neglected it now. And yet the man could not *remember* to have done it this evening" (52). He offers that, with all the confusion and distress around him, it is no wonder that his memory fails him, and hopes he will be able to remember what happened the next day. In response to the Squire's questions, Lease can only answer that "[t]here is such a thing as doing things mechanically, sir, without the mind being conscious of it" (52). Repeated questions as to whether Harry performed the action or not allow Wood to explore ideas about automatic or mechanical behavior. Lease describes how he usually winds up the clock at night but, because the action is habitual, he often cannot remember if he has done it or not: "I can't think but what it must have been just in that way that I put the points right to-night" (52). The Squire is incensed by this talk and fulminates:

Killing men and women and children; breaking arms and shins and bones; putting a whole trainful into mortal fright; smashing goods and property and engines to atoms; turning the world, in fact, upside down, so that nobody knows whether they stand on their heads or their heels! You may think you can do this with impunity perhaps, but the law will soon teach you better. I shouldn't like to go to bed with human lives upon my soul. (52)

To this Lease "listened mechanically – closed his eyes and put his head back against the top ledge of the palings, like one who has got a shock" (52–53). When he tells his wife about his inability to remember turning the points and emphasizes what a frantically busy day it had been, she realizes with a start that *she* may also be indirectly responsible for the accident, not having taken tea to her husband that day. Wood traces the causes back from the accident itself to his wife's poor management of the household. Because she is disorganized she used to send their small child with the tea but on one occasion the child was harassed, which led to Harry's insistence that she not continue this errand. In tracing the circumstances around Harry's exhaustion and lack of tea, Wood questions how far away from the action, how indirectly, its causes may lie. At the same time, the story focuses on the question of blame in the aftermath of the disaster. Indeed, Harry is so wracked with guilt and disabled by shock that he soon falls ill and dies. While he is off work and ailing, his wife and children starve, shunned and shamed by the community, along with him, until the narrator of the story takes pity on them. As the narrator surmises:

You can't always make things fit into one another; I was thinking so as I left Lease ... It was awful carelessness not to have set the points; causing death, and sorrow, and distress to many people. Looking at it from their side, the pointsman was detestable, only fit, as the Squire said, for hanging. But, looking at it side by side with Lease, seeing his sad face, and his self-reproach, and his patient suffering, it seemed altogether different; and the two sides would not by any means fit in together. (57–58)

Others, like the Squire, whose daughter now suffers nightmares, focus largely on the consequences of the accident for the victims, and feel only the desire to have Lease punished: "Every time Lena wakes up from sleep in a fright, fancying it is another accident, his anger returns" (60).

Drawing attention to the shock Lease experiences as similar to that suffered by the victims of the accident, Wood teases out the complexity of the aftermath. By the end of the story, the focus shifts from the blame of Harry Lease to the disastrous results of the accident for everyone involved, victims as well as apparent perpetrator. The story can be seen to explore questions about agency and passivity, volition and responsibility. Though there is still an emphasis on confession and expiation, it marks too a querying of accountability in the unconscious subject and even a relocation of the idea of responsibility from the individual to the collective.

What is especially pertinent about the story is that it enacts exactly the scenario that William Carpenter would use as an example seven years later in the fourth preface to the *Principles of Mental Physiology* (4th edition, 1876), where, as I have noted in Chapter 3, he discusses the question of responsibility in relation to automatic action.

> [W]e blame the man whom we believe to have been in fault ... [I]f the pointsman can excuse himself by showing that he had been on duty for eight-and-forty hours continuously, and did not know what he was about, we shift the blame on the Directors who wrongly overtaxed his brain, whilst, if it turns out that his inattention was due, neither to drunkenness nor to over-fatigue, but to sudden illness, we cannot say that any one was in fault.[3]

Carpenter's point is that agency is at the heart of responsibility and the exercise of will. If we give up the idea of agency, we open the door to admitting that consciousness is epiphenomenal and we are essentially automata.

Also in 1876, English courts returned an unprecedented verdict of "not guilty on the ground of unconsciousness." The acquittal marks a shift in legal understanding of defenses built on the idea of mental aberration. Moving beyond the insanity plea of the McNaughtan case, jurors found that a defendant who was absent to himself, who acted in a "state of mental life inaccessible to the waking person," could not be deemed guilty.[4] This is an important decision because it means that no longer did the subject have to be insane or deranged but merely absent or unconscious. Whether absent from himself or herself by virtue of opium use, trance and dream states, or automaton-like behavior, the subject could not be held accountable. The effect of this ruling was to recognize altered rather than pathological states as sufficient to vitiate intention and agency. Despite their different approaches and purposes, Carpenter and the Old Bailey find problems of consciousness most meaningful in so far as they bear on volition, resolve and the commission (or omission) of a deed. Wood is interested in the same questions but seems, however, prepared to explore how the self that goes missing may not just be "not guilty," but can even come to occupy the position of victim. As Lease suffers a similar kind of shock to the victims of the railway accident, his position seems to shift, at least in the eyes of the narrator, from putative agent towards suffering victim.

Comparing novels such as George Eliot's *Silas Marner* (1861) and Wilkie Collins's *The Moonstone* (1866), we can bring the idea of the missing agent into sharper focus. Silas experiences occasional trances, also described as cataleptic fits, in which his normal state of consciousness is entirely suspended. He is "missing" in this way when the theft of the deacon's money takes place, just as he will be "absent" later when his own hoarded gold is stolen: "'I must have slept,' said Silas. Then, after a pause, he added, 'Or I must have had another visitation like that which you have all seen me under, so that the thief must have come and gone while I was not in the body, but out of the body.'"[5] In that novel, the thief is (on both occasions) indeed someone other than Silas. But what if the thief, who came and went while Silas was "out of the body," were himself? The thief becomes Silas himself in fictions such as *The Moonstone* (1866), where Franklin Blake steals the diamond under the influence of the opium he has unknowingly ingested. Again, in such cases, the questions of guilt, intention and detection are foregrounded in the exploration of the unconscious agent.

Although Victorian culture is focused largely on questions of culpability, I want to argue further that the very constructions of mind allowing for a "missing" perpetrator could also support theories of a "missing" victim, whose consciousness was suspended as a result, and in the aftermath, of the event. A transitional figure, conflating the positions of perpetrator and victim, is the perpetrator who goes missing to himself as the result of guilt or conscience, a scenario which, I have argued, underlies the troubled consciousness of Jasper in *The Mystery of Edwin Drood* (1870). In explorations of this kind, the self is bifurcated and fragmented by its guilt. The idea of "missing in aftermath" is starkly demonstrated in the Erckmann-Chatrian novel *Le Juif polonais*, which was translated into English by Leopold Davis Lewis and became a popular melodrama, *The Bells*. It opened at the London Lyceum in 1871 and played for 150 performances, making the career of the lead actor, Henry Irving. The play features a respected burgomaster, Mathias, who is tormented by the sound of bells and accompanying visions of the murder he committed some twenty years previously. Having seen a Parisian mesmerist at a fair, Mathias is alerted to the idea that the mesmerist can send a man to sleep and make him tell all the things that weigh on his conscience. In the climactic scene of the play, Mathias dreams that he has come before the court, charged with the murder, and that the President of the court compels him to subject himself to the mesmerist, whose role shifts from that of entertainer to forensic expert and who soon puts him into mesmeric sleep. Mathias duly confesses the murder and the disposition of the body in his lime-kiln. The mesmerist then wakes him from his trance and the court sentences him to hang. While the tableau behind him enacts the waking and sentencing as the substance of his dream, Mathias, it should be noted, continues to sleep and dream. The dreaming Mathias now staggers forward, begging for the rope to be cut from his neck. He collapses and, clutching at his neck, dies. In this shocking final scene, Mathias experiences the fantasy of punishment as a reality to the extent that his unconscious (dreaming) state, in which he is hung, actually kills him. Through its tableaux, the play reveals the power of a projected state of mind, in which memory and fantasy become the lived (and fatal) reality.[6]

In accordance with the ethos of culpability in relation to the missing self, the fantasy in *Jekyll and Hyde* of a self whose elements may be dissociated is a dream of impunity, an alibi. On reflection, we see that it is not a great leap from there to understanding the mentally dissociated self as a different form of alibi. If an alibi offers proof that the suspect of a crime is accounted for by being elsewhere, fragmentation or dissociation is not dissimilar in that it offers the victim an opportunity not to feel the pain of having been "there" at the unspeakable and inassimilable event. In this context, an alibi becomes a mechanism of defense, a shutting down of affect in the aftermath of overload, the unconsciousness of a too painful memory. Victorian texts provide ample evidence that the idea of the psychic wound is becoming culturally important; they hover, however, on the brink of formulating a discourse about the "missing" victim. The story of the medical, legal and financial factors, as well as the moral and ethical dispositions, that propelled that construction to the fore has been told in terms of modernist technology, the shell-shock of warfare, sexual seduction and early-twentieth-century psychology and psychoanalysis. What I have attempted here is to open up to scrutiny the way Victorian literary texts, in the context of the "New Psychology" and changing conceptions of mind, emotion and memory, begin to imagine the psychic wound and its social and personal implications. While not discounting the forces of technology, war, imperialism and industrialization as contributing to the emergence of theories of mental shock, I have sought to complicate existing histories and genealogies of trauma by reaching further back than such histories usually do and by concentrating pre-eminently on the literary text. In its complex representations of the mind in shock, overwhelmed, stunned and arrested, Victorian fiction shapes an incipient discourse of trauma. Rather than applying contemporary trauma theory to Victorian texts in order to reveal their unwitting representation of the traumatized subject as twentieth-century theory defines it, we can better use the fiction of this period in order to understand the historical production of trauma theory and to critique that theory's universalist tendencies.

Notes

INTRODUCTION: THE PSYCHE IN PAIN

1. Charlotte Brontë, *Jane Eyre*, Oxford World's Classics (Oxford: Oxford University Press, 2000), 20.
2. Ibid., 21.
3. Charles Dickens, *Little Dorrit*, Oxford World's Classics (Oxford: Oxford University Press, 1999), 543.
4. See, for example, Jenny Bourne Taylor, *In the Secret Theatre of Home: Wilkie Collins, Sensation Narrative, and Nineteenth-Century Psychology* (London: Routledge, 1988); and her "Obscure Recesses: Locating the Victorian Unconscious," in *Writing and Victorianism*, ed. J. B. Bullen (London: Longman, 1997), 137–79; and Jonathan Miller, "Going Unconscious," in *Hidden Histories of Science*, ed. Robert B. Silvers (New York: New York Review, 1995), 1–35.
5. Mark Seltzer, "Wound Culture: Trauma in the Pathological Public Sphere," *October* 80 (Spring 1997): 5 n. 6.
6. Tim Armstrong, "Two Types of Shock in Modernity," *Critical Quarterly* 42:1 (2000): 64.
7. Ibid., 60.
8. Ibid., 62.
9. Seltzer, "Wound Culture," 5 n. 6.
10. Ibid., 5.
11. Bill Bynum, "Phrenitis: What's in a Name?," *The Lancet* 356:9245 (December 2, 2000): 1936. Bynum notes that it was a common Victorian lay diagnosis; his example of brain fever is, significantly, drawn from literature: "In George Eliot's great medical novel *Middlemarch*, for instance, the reprobate John Raffles suffers from the alcoholic variant of brain fever, recognised by Lydgate from recent descriptions by the American physician John Ware."
12. Audrey C. Peterson, "Brain Fever in Nineteenth-Century Literature: Fact and Fiction," *Victorian Studies* 19:4 (1976): 445–64, notes that "brain fever was not a fictional invention ... both physicians and laymen believed that emotional shock or excessive intellectual activity could produce a severe and prolonged fever" (449).
13. Charles Dickens, *Great Expectations*, Oxford World's Classics (Oxford: Oxford University Press, 1998), 455.

14. Alisa Webb, "Constructing the Gendered Body: Girls, Health, Beauty, Advice, and the *Girls' Best Friend*, 1898–99," *Women's History Review* 15:2 (April 2006): 256–57.

15. William Benjamin Carpenter, *Principles of Human Physiology: With Their Chief Applications to Psychology, Pathology, Therapeutics, Hygiene, & Forensic Medicine*, 5th edn. (London: John Churchill, 1855), 558.

16. See Mark Seltzer, *Serial Killers: Death and Life in America's Wound Culture* (New York: Routledge, 1998).

17. See, for example, Mark Micale and Paul Lerner, eds., *Traumatic Pasts: History, Psychiatry, and Trauma in the Modern Age, 1870–1930* (Cambridge: Cambridge University Press, 2001), whose essays explore the rise of psychological trauma as a disease entity dependent on the growth of technological modernity. Although the editors emphasize the cultural dimensions of trauma, and the importance of truly interdisciplinary studies, the essays in this volume do not focus to a significant extent on the role of literature. See also Roger Luckhurst, *The Trauma Question* (London: Routledge, 2008), who asserts the role of literary culture as integral to the formation of the concept of trauma – but only since 1980. Although Luckhurst provides a genealogy of trauma reaching back to the 1870s, he too does not discuss Victorian literature.

18. See, for example, Roger Smith, "The Physiology of the Will: Mind, Body, and Psychology in the Periodical Literature, 1855–1875," in *Science Serialized: Representations of the Sciences in Nineteenth-Century Periodicals*, ed. Geoffrey Cantor and Sally Shuttleworth (Cambridge, Mass: The MIT Press, 2004), 98.

19. See Nicholas Rand, "The Hidden Soul: The Growth of the Unconscious in Philosophy, Psychology, Medicine, and Literature, 1750–1900," *American Imago* 61:3 (2004): 284.

20. E. S. Dallas, *The Gay Science*, 2 vols. (London: Chapman & Hall, 1866), 1:207.

21. *Oxford English Dictionary*, 2nd edn., *s.v.* "trauma."

22. Dallas, *The Gay Science*, 1:316.

23. I am aware that while I use the term "the unconscious" in my title and throughout the book, Victorian writers refer to unconsciousness as opposed to consciousness, the "unconscious working of the mind," "unconscious mental processes" and that quaint Victorian formulation, "unconscious cerebration." I want to emphasize that my use of the term "the unconscious" is *not* referring to the Freudian unconscious, which is specifically contrasted with Victorian formulations in Chapter 1.

24. Arthur Schopenhauer, *Fragments* (1818), quoted in Rand, "The Hidden Soul," 257.

25. See Joel Peter Eigen, *Unconscious Crime: Mental Absence and Criminal Responsibility in Victorian London* (Baltimore: Johns Hopkins University Press, 2003), 10. While his focus is on what crimes are committed by the missing self and mine is on what causes the self to go missing, the history of legal decisions he provides is extremely useful.

26. See Helen Small, ed., *Literature, Science and Psychology, 1830–1970: Essays in Honour of Gillian Beer* (Oxford: Oxford University Press, 2003), 7.

27. Alan Bewell, *Romanticism and Colonial Disease* (Baltimore: Johns Hopkins University Press, 1999), 23.

28. Freud, for example, was a great admirer of George Eliot; he read *Middlemarch* and *Daniel Deronda*, referred to *Adam Bede* in the *Interpretation of Dreams*, and gave George Eliot's novels as gifts to friends. George Eliot's treatment of questions of consciousness and psychic injury may therefore have been part of a climate of thinking that influenced the way the Freudian concept of trauma developed. On Freud and George Eliot, see Carl T. Rotenberg, "George Eliot – Proto-Psychoanalyst," *The American Journal of Psychoanalysis* 59:3 (1999): 257. See also Nicholas Dames, *Amnesiac Selves: Nostalgia, Forgetting and British Fiction 1810–1870* (Oxford: Oxford University Press, 2001), 167–206, who claims that the sensation fiction of Collins predated the discussion of amnesia in nineteenth-century psychology and physiology.

29. See Helen Small's account of the influence of literary texts on eighteenth-century conceptions of madness in *Love's Madness: Medicine, the Novel, and Female Insanity: 1800–1865* (Oxford: Clarendon Press, 1996).

30. William Benjamin Carpenter, *Principles of Mental Physiology*, 4th edn. (1876; New York: Appleton, 1890), 455.

31. Jessie Chambers, *D. H. Lawrence: A Personal Record*, 2nd edn. (London: Frank Cass and Co., 1965), 105; see also Keith Oatley and Jennifer Jenkins, who discuss George Eliot's "experiments in life" in their text book on the emotions, *Understanding Emotions* (Oxford: Blackwell, 1996), 18–22. George Levine refers indirectly to Lawrence in his discussion of the inside action in the introduction to *The Cambridge Companion to George Eliot* (Cambridge: Cambridge University Press, 2001), 9.

32. See Lisa Rodensky, *The Crime in Mind: Criminal Responsibility in the Victorian Novel* (Oxford: Oxford University Press, 2003), 6–7, who argues for the special powers of the realist novel's third-person narrator in disclosing a character's interiority but does not discuss other kinds of literature which may creatively represent movements of mind using other modes of narration.

33. Ronald Thomas, *Dreams of Authority: Freud and the Fictions of the Unconscious* (Cornell: Cornell University Press, 1990), 133.

34. I am here paraphrasing Freud's comments in the case of Fraulein Elisabeth von R in *Studies in Hysteria* in the *Standard Edition of the Complete Psychological Works of Sigmund Freud*, ed. and trans. James Strachey (London: Hogarth Press and the Institute for Psychoanalysis, 1955–72), 11:160–61, quoted in Thomas, *Dreams of Authority*, 133.

35. George Henry Lewes, *Problems of Life and Mind*, 5 vols. (London: Trübner, 1874–79); first series, *The Foundations of a Creed* (1874), 1:127–28. Also quoted in Sally Shuttleworth and Jenny Bourne Taylor, eds., *Embodied Selves: An Anthology of Psychological Texts 1830–1890* (Oxford: Oxford University Press, 1998), 69.

36. The phrase is from Ruth Leys, *Trauma: A Genealogy* (Chicago: University of Chicago Press, 2000), 10.

37. Charles Dickens, *Dombey and Son*, Oxford World's Classics (Oxford: Oxford University Press, 1982), 52.

38. Even the concept of pleasurable shock, such as the thrills and purposeful terror induced by tales of horror and roller-coasters alike, is dependent on burgeoning science and technology. See Jeffery T. Schnapp, "Crash (Speed as Engine of Individuation)," *Modernism/Modernity* 6:1 (1999): 1–49.
39. See, for example, Keith Oatley, *Emotions: A Brief History* (Oxford: Blackwell, 2004), 70. But as Martha Nussbaum and others have noted, early Freudian analysis draws on a hydraulic conception of emotion; see *Upheavals of Thought: The Intelligence of Emotions* (Cambridge: Cambridge University Press, 2001), 96.
40. [J. Fitzjames Stephen], "A Letter to a Saturday Reviewer," *Cornhill Magazine* 8 (1863): 443.
41. Robert Tracy, introduction to *In a Glass Darkly* by Sheridan Le Fanu, Oxford World's Classics (Oxford: Oxford University Press, 1999), viii.
42. Terry Castle, *The Female Thermometer: Eighteenth-Century Culture and the Invention of the Uncanny* (New York: Oxford University Press, 1995), 15–20.
43. See Thomas, *Dreams of Authority*, 6; he looks broadly at the project of the nineteenth-century novel and sees in it many similarities to Freud's objective for *The Interpretation of Dreams*: both replace religious authority with forms of treatment (20).
44. Elton E. Smith and Robert Haas, eds., *The Haunted Mind: The Supernatural in Victorian Literature* (Lanham: The Scarecrow Press, 1999), viii.
45. Samuel Hynes, *The Edwardian Turn of Mind* (Princeton: Princeton University Press, 1968), 146, 138.

1 HISTORICIZING TRAUMA

1. For a discussion of the very broad range of experience covered by the term "trauma," see the introduction to Leys, *Trauma: A Genealogy*.
2. E. Ann Kaplan, *Trauma Culture: The Politics of Terror and Loss in Media and Literature* (New Brunswick, NJ: Rutgers University Press, 2005), 24.
3. Walter Benjamin influentially drew attention to the "traumatophile" in his essay "On Some Motifs in Baudelaire." See Walter Benjamin, *Illuminations*, ed. Hannah Arendt, trans. Henry Zohn (New York: Schoken Books, 1988), 155–200.
4. Benjamin drew particular attention to the way Baudelaire and Poe register the shock of city life; as later chapters will show, there are many British writers of the mid to late nineteenth century (for example Dickens, George Eliot, Elizabeth Gaskell) attentive in different ways to similar accumulating pressures.
5. See Richard McNally, *Remembering Trauma* (Cambridge, Mass.: Harvard University Press, 2003), 8–9.
6. More recent formulations offer further distinctions among different kinds of dissociative disorders. There are four main categories of dissociative disorders now defined in the standard catalogue of psychological diagnoses used by mental health professionals in North America, the *Diagnostic and Statistical Manual of Mental Disorders, Text Revision (DSM-IV-TR)*, 4th edn. (Washington, DC: American Psychiatric Association, 2000): Dissociative Amnesia, Dissociative Fugue, Dissociative Identity Disorder and Depersonalization Disorder.

7. Leys, *Trauma: A Genealogy*, 6; Leys is quoting Allan Young, *The Harmony of Illusions: Inventing Post-Traumatic Stress Disorder* (Princeton: Princeton University Press, 1995), 5.
8. See generally Leys, *Trauma: A Genealogy;* see also the critique of Leys in E. Ann Kaplan, *Trauma Culture*, 36–37.
9. Leys, *Trauma: A Genealogy*, 7.
10. For an informative discussion of the differences between contemporary trauma theory's emphasis on the unassimilable event and psychoanalytic emphasis on the mediation of the unconscious in traumatic memory, see Susannah Radstone, "Screening Trauma: *Forrest Gump*, Film and Memory," in *Memory and Methodology*, ed. Susannah Radstone (Oxford: Berg Press, 2000), 89.
11. Leys, *Trauma: A Genealogy*, 10.
12. E. Ann Kaplan, *Trauma Culture*, 35.
13. Radstone, "Screening Trauma: *Forrest Gump*," 89.
14. See E. Ann Kaplan, *Trauma Culture*, 38. It should be noted here that Kaplan's sources for this claim are slight: she quotes from a yet unpublished paper by Martin Hoffman, which relies on the work of Joseph LeDoux, ostensibly allowing not only for unremembered trauma or dissociation, in which the trauma is unavailable to cognition or memory, but also for a combination of dissociation and cognition which allows the trauma to be in conscious memory. LeDoux's *The Emotional Brain: The Mysterious Underpinnings of Emotional Life* (New York: Simon and Schuster, 1996), 239–65, does indeed discuss neurobiological imaging of hippocampal shrinking in traumatized patients, and the effects of intense emotion on the amygdala, but does not specifically address how these findings would reconfigure current trauma theory.
15. Recent studies dispute the idea that the traumatic event can leave an indelible engraving on the mind without leaving a trace in ordinary memory. See, for example, McNally, *Remembering Trauma*, who claims that "there is no reason to postulate a special mechanism of repression or dissociation to explain why people may not think about disturbing experiences for long periods. A failure to think about something does not entail an inability to remember it (amnesia)" (2).
16. See Joseph LeDoux, *The Emotional Brain*, 239–65.
17. Thomas H. Huxley, "On the Hypothesis that Animals Are Automata and Its History," in *The Collected Essays of T. H. Huxley* (London: Macmillan, 1894), 1:240; see also the discussion of Huxley in Thomas Dixon, *From Passions to Emotions: The Creation of a Secular Psychological Category* (Cambridge: Cambridge University Press, 2003), 144.
18. Huxley, "On the Hypothesis," 242.
19. William Benjamin Carpenter, *Principles of Mental Physiology*, 4th edn. (New York: Appleton, 1890), vii–viii.
20. Dixon, *From Passions to Emotions*, 142.
21. See Roger Smith, "The Physiology of the Will: Mind, Body, and Psychology in the Periodical Literature, 1855–1875," in *Science Serialized: Representations of the Sciences in Nineteenth-Century Periodicals*, ed. Geoffrey Cantor and Sally

Shuttleworth (Cambridge, Mass.: The MIT Press, 2004), 84. Smith surveys the periodical literature, providing a useful map of the scientific discourse of non-academic writers and readers.

22. Edward Reed, *From Soul to Mind: The Emergence of Psychology from Erasmus Darwin to William James* (New Haven: Yale University Press, 1997), 3.

23. Rick Rylance, *Victorian Psychology and British Culture 1850–1880* (Oxford: Oxford University Press, 2000), 25.

24. Reed, *From Soul to Mind*, 5.

25. Dixon, *From Passions to Emotions*, 9. He argues that it is important "to distinguish between Christian, merely theistic, and Idealist versions of psychology and their relationships to science" (235).

26. Smith, "The Physiology of the Will," 82.

27. Catherine Crowe, *Spiritualism and the Age we Live in* (London: Newby, 1859), 7.

28. William Benjamin Carpenter, *On Mesmerism and Spiritualism, &c.: Historically and Scientifically Considered* (London: Longman, 1877).

29. Smith, "The Physiology of the Will," 81.

30. Ibid., 82.

31. Ibid., 93.

32. On the question of reassurance, see generally ibid., 81–110.

33. Gilbert Ryle, *The Concept of Mind* (London: Hutchinson and Co., 1949), 11.

34. Daniel Hack Tuke, *Illustrations of the Influence of the Mind upon the Body in Health and Disease: Designed to Elucidate the Action of the Imagination*, 2nd edn. (1872; Philadelphia: Henry C. Lea's Son & Co., 1884), 33.

35. See Smith, "The Physiology of the Will," who lists the following: "mental science, mental physiology, the physiology of the will, unconscious cerebration, the physiology and pathology of the mind, moral insanity, and lesion of the will" (81).

36. Alan Richardson, *British Romanticism and the Science of the Mind* (Cambridge: Cambridge University Press, 2001), 12.

37. See Christopher Hilton, "Gaskell and Mesmerism: An Unpublished Letter," *Medical History* 39 (1995): 226; [James Martineau], "Mesmeric Atheism. *Letters on the Laws of Man's Nature and Development.* By Henry George Atkinson F.G.S., and Harriet Martineau. London: J. Chapman, 1851," *Prospective Review* 7:26 (1851): 224–62.

38. See Dixon's discussion of "dual-aspect monism" in *From Passions to Emotions*, 142–43.

39. See Robert H. Wozniak, who suggests that "dual-aspect monism was the brain child of George Henry Lewes (1817–1878)," "Mind and Body: René Descartes to William James," in *Serendip* (Pennsylvania: Bryn Mawr College, 1995), http://serendip.brynmawr.edu/Mind/19th.html/ (accessed March 24, 2007); originally published in 1992 at Bethesda, MD, and Washington, DC, by the National Library of Medicine and the American Psychological Association.

40. See William B. Carpenter, *Principles of Human Physiology: With Their Chief Applications to Psychology, Pathology, Therapeutics, Hygiene, & Forensic Medicine*, 5th edn. (London: John Churchill, 1855), 547.

41. Ibid., 548.
42. Ibid., 549. See also Taylor, *In the Secret Theatre of Home*, for a discussion of the increasing importance Carpenter placed on "Volition" and "Will" in his later work.
43. Carpenter, *Principles of Human Physiology*, 549.
44. See Herbert Spencer, *The Principles of Psychology*, 2nd edn. (London: Williams and Norgate, 1870), 1:125, 128. I am indebted here to Thomas Dixon's discussion of Spencer's dual-aspect monism in *From Passions to Emotions*, 142–43.
45. See Jonathan Miller, "Going Unconscious," 24.
46. For further examples, see Dixon, *From Passions to Emotions*, 181, 190.
47. Frances Power Cobbe, "Dreams as Illustrations of Unconscious Cerebration," *MacMillan's Magazine* 23:138 (1871): 523. See also her earlier article "Unconscious Cerebration: A Psychological Study," *MacMillan's Magazine* 23:133 (1871): 24–37.
48. G. H. Lewes, *Problems of Life and Mind* (1874–79) third series, *The Study of Psychology: Its Object, Scope, and Method* (London: Trübner, 1879), 74.
49. Ian McEwan, *Saturday* (London: Jonathan Cape, 2005), 254–55.
50. Gordon S. Haight, ed., *The George Eliot Letters*, 9 vols. (New Haven: Yale University Press, 1954–78) III:227. As Reed, *From Soul to Mind*, has suggested, the idea of the soul was not necessarily contradicted by a "broadly evolutionary view of the world" as is evident in the theory "that God had arranged for human beings to evolve a soul or had simply implanted souls in certain animal lineages" (175).
51. See Steven Pinker's *The Blank Slate: The Modern Denial of Human Nature* (New York: Viking-Penguin, 2002), 1–72.
52. Robert Chambers, *Vestiges of the Natural History of Creation and Other Evolutionary Writings*, ed. James Secord (London: University of Chicago Press, 1994), 334–35; quoted in Rick Rylance, *Victorian Psychology*, 35.
53. Alison Winter, *Mesmerized: Powers of Mind in Victorian Britain* (Chicago: University of Chicago Press, 1998), 35.
54. The fiction of the period provides many examples of similar reconciliations. Given that light and electricity were powers that had to be material but were invisible and hence seemed also spiritual, the Irish master of the ghost tale, Sheridan Le Fanu, could construct the following explanation for his doctor-narrator in "Green Tea," a story of profound mental disturbance: "You know my tract on The Cardinal Functions of the Brain. I there, by the evidence of innumerable facts, prove, I think, the high probability of a circulation arterial and venous in its mechanisms, through the nerves. Of this system, thus considered, the brain is the heart. The fluid, which is propagated hence through one class of nerves, returns in an altered state through another and the nature of that fluid is spiritual, though not immaterial, any more than, as I remarked, light or electricity are so." See Sheridan Le Fanu, "Green Tea," *All the Year Round* 2 (1869): 576; reprinted in Le Fanu, *In a Glass Darkly*, ed. Tracy, 38–39. In "The Haunters and the Haunted, or The House and the Brain" (originally published in *Blackwood's Edinburgh Magazine*, 1859, in the same

volume as George Eliot's *The Lifted Veil*), Edward Bulwer Lytton writes of the power of mind as a material force: "Nor, supposing it true that a mesmerized patient can respond to the will or passes of a mesmerizer a hundred miles distant, is the response less occasioned ... by a material fluid – call it Electric, call it Odic, call it what you will – which has the power of traversing space and passing obstacles, that the material effect is communicated from one to the other." See Edward Bulwer Lytton, "The Haunters and the Haunted, or The House and the Brain," *Blackwood's Edinburgh Magazine* 86 (August, 1859): 231.

55. See Catherine Gallagher, *The Body Economic: Life, Death, and Sensation in Political Economy and the Victorian Novel* (Princeton: Princeton University Press, 2006), 1.
56. Kurt Danziger, *Naming the Mind: How Psychology Found its Language* (London: Sage, 1997), 9.
57. Ibid., 13. Studies such as Reed's history of psychological thought, *From Soul to Mind*, and Rylance's *Victorian Psychology* focus less on concepts than important figures, but Rylance, especially, offers a thorough account of the various discourses (the soul, philosophy, physiology and medicine) that went into making up the field of psychology, as well as a lengthy engagement with the psychological writing and its reception of Herbert Spencer, George Henry Lewes and Alexander Bain. Although not specifically focused on the relations between literature and science, *Victorian Psychology* turns frequently to George Eliot's work as an example of the ways in which literature engages with and critically evaluates emergent psychological discourse.
58. See, for example, Londa Schiebinger, *The Mind has No Sex: Women and the Origins of Modern Science* (Cambridge, Mass.: Harvard University Press, 1989), and Elaine Showalter, *The Female Malady: Women, Madness and English Culture: 1830–1980* (New York: Pantheon Books, 1985).
59. Taylor, *In the Secret Theatre of Home*; Michael Davis, *George Eliot and Nineteenth-Century Psychology: Exploring the Unmapped Country* (Aldershot: Ashgate, 2006).
60. Other recent anthologies of Victorian science and medicine that include psychological writing are Laura Otis, ed., *Literature and Science in the Nineteenth Century: An Anthology* (Oxford: Oxford University Press, 2002), and Lilian Furst, ed., *Medical Progress and Social Reality: A Reader in Nineteenth-Century Medicine and Literature* (Albany: State University of New York Press, 2000).
61. Samuel Taylor Coleridge, *The Collected Works of Samuel Taylor Coleridge*, ed. Kathleen Coburn (London: Routledge and Kegan Paul, 1983), VII:112–13.
62. William Hamilton, "Three Degrees of Mental Latency," in Shuttleworth and Taylor, eds., *Embodied Selves*, 81.
63. Nicholas Rand, "The Hidden Soul: The Growth of the Unconscious in Philosophy, Psychology, Medicine, and Literature, 1750–1900," *American Imago* 61:3 (2004): 262–63.
64. See ibid., 262. For broad histories of the unconscious, see Henri Ellenberger, *The Discovery of the Unconscious: The History and Evolution of Dynamic*

Psychiatry (New York: Basic Books, 1970), and L. L. Whyte's *The Unconscious Before Freud* (London: Tavistock, 1962).

65. Miller, "Going Unconscious," 34.

66. Ibid., 17, 18.

67. Ibid., 24.

68. Ibid., 25.

69. Ibid., 29.

70. See Athena Vrettos, "Defining Habits: Dickens and the Psychology of Repetition," *Victorian Studies* 42:3 (1999/2000): 399–426, on Victorian conceptions of the mechanized mind and habit, their relation to associationist philosophy, and their challenge to theories of the human capacity for moral transformation.

71. Taylor, *In the Secret Theatre of Home*; see her discussion of the "lost parcel or hidden soul," 184–88.

72. See Joel Peter Eigen, *Unconscious Crime: Mental Absence and Criminal Responsibility in Victorian London* (Baltimore: Johns Hopkins University Press, 2003).

73. George Eliot, *Adam Bede* (Oxford: Clarendon Press, 2001), 162.

74. Taylor, "Obscure Recesses," 141.

75. Ibid., 161.

76. Ibid., 164.

77. In part, the association of trauma with memory (loss, dysfunction, forgetting) reflects the degree to which the work of Cathy Caruth has been influential among literary critics. See, for example, Rosemarie Bodenheimer's *Knowing Dickens* (Ithaca: Cornell University Press, 2007), 69, whose chapter on "Memory" relies primarily on Caruth in its discussion of trauma theory. See also Christopher Herbert's *War of No Pity: The Indian Mutiny and Victorian Trauma* (Princeton: Princeton University Press, 2008), which is dependent largely on twentieth-century articulations of psychological trauma in analyzing the Indian uprising and its cultural aftermath as trauma. He relies almost exclusively on Caruth's *Unclaimed Experience: Trauma, Narrative, and History* (Baltimore: Johns Hopkins University Press, 1996). His assumption is that trauma is an ahistorical and transhistorical phenomenon – although "no name yet existed" for the condition of Post-Traumatic Stress Disorder, it dominates the "postwar moment" (18). My own work on trauma prior to the historicizing project of this book is also evidence of the tendency among literary critics to rely on Caruth's formulations; see Jill Matus, *Toni Morrison* (Manchester: Manchester University Press, 1998).

78. Thomas De Quincey, "Animal Magnetism," *Tait's Edinburgh Magazine* 4 (1834): 473.

79. John Elliotson, quoted in Jonathan Miller, "Going Unconscious," 11.

80. Ekbert Faas, *Retreat into the Mind: Victorian Poetry and the Rise of Psychiatry* (Princeton: Princeton University Press, 1988), 40. Faas cites "Animal Magnetism and Neurohypnotism" (*Fraser's Magazine* 29 [Jan.–June 1844]: 681–99): "[A] patient may be taught any thing during the nervous sleep if

impressed upon the mind at the proper stage, and ... he will be able to repeat his task with verbal accuracy whenever he be thrown into that state again, but shall have no consciousness or knowledge whatever of the act performed when in the ordinary waking condition" ("Animal Magnetism," 697).

81. "Animal Magnetism," 695, quoted in Faas, *Retreat into the Mind*, 40.
82. Faas, *Retreat into the Mind*, 40, 41.
83. See Daniel Pick's discussion of the hypnotist in *Svengali's Web: The Alien Enchanter in Modern Culture* (New Haven: Yale University Press, 2000), 1–15, 127–65.
84. Harriet Martineau, *Letters on Mesmerism*, 2nd edn. (London: Edward Moxon, 1850); excerpted in Shuttleworth and Taylor, eds., *Embodied Selves*, 56.
85. See Robert Young, *Darwin's Metaphor: Nature's Place in Victorian Culture* (Cambridge: Cambridge University Press, 1985), for an exploration of the relations between the history of psychology and debates on evolutionary theory; he suggests it is curious that the history of phrenology should have been sequestered from that of evolutionary thought, given the implications of the former for evolutionary theory (63).
86. Adam Crabtree, *From Mesmer to Freud: Magnetic Sleep and the Roots of Psychological Healing* (New Haven: Yale University Press, 1993), 290; see Ian Hacking's discussion of Crabtree in *Rewriting the Soul: Multiple Personality and the Sciences of Memory* (Princeton: Princeton University Press, 1995), 149.
87. Hacking, *Rewriting the Soul*, 5.
88. Ibid., 198.
89. Ibid., 6.
90. Ibid., 232–33.
91. Ibid., 189.
92. Dames, *Amnesiac Selves: Nostalgia, Forgetting, and British Fiction, 1810–1870* (Oxford: Oxford University Press, 2001), 171.
93. Ibid., 172; he sees the amnesia of Austen, Brontë and Dickens as a willed forgetting of what is not useful in order to integrate the self or present a self that is integrated. In the 1860s, however, Collins is inaugurating something new. Memory becomes nervous – as it is seen increasingly as a function of the nervous system, so it can be seen to break down: it becomes pathologized.
94. Henry Holland, *Chapters on Mental Physiology* (London: Longman, 1852), 185, 187; see also Sally Shuttleworth's discussion of Holland in "'The Malady of Thought': Embodied Memory in Victorian Psychology and the Novel," in *Memory and Memorials 1789–1914: Literary and Cultural Perspectives*, ed. Matthew Campbell, Jacqueline M. Labbe and Sally Shuttleworth (New York: Routledge, 2000), 49.
95. Hacking, *Rewriting the Soul*, 183.
96. "A Novel or Two," *National Review* (October 1855): 349–50.
97. Danziger, *Naming the Mind*, 40.
98. Thomas Brown could write that "[e]very person understands what is meant by an *emotion*" and what they understood was that emotions were non-intellectual states of mind. See ibid., 41–42.

99. Dixon, *From Passions to Emotions*, 3. This statement does not, however, do justice either to the debate surrounding the nature of emotion in the nineteenth century or to the vigorous and ongoing 21st-century forms of that debate.
100. Ibid., 244, 245.
101. Ibid., 244. See Max Rosenkrantz's critique of Dixon's claim that Christian thinkers can reveal what was missed by their secular counterparts: *Journal of the History of Philosophy* 43:2 (2005): 214–15.
102. Dixon, *From Passions to Emotions*, 143–44.
103. Alexander Bain, *Mind and Body: The Theories of their Relation* (London: Henry King, 1873), 132. See Dixon's discussion of this passage, *From Passions to Emotions*, 144.
104. William Reddy, *The Navigation of Feeling: A Framework for the History of Emotions* (Cambridge: Cambridge University Press, 2001), 15.
105. Ibid., 16, 17.
106. See Adam Frank's review essay, "Some Avenues for Feeling," *Criticism* 46:3 (Summer 2004): 511–24, for an account of contemporary affect theory and in particular the work of Silvan Tomkins which counters appraisal or intentionalist theory by arguing for the distinction between affective and cognitive capacities (514). Tomkins proposes that the affects are a separate system whose primary evolutionary function is to amplify the drives (515). See Ruth Leys's trenchart critique of affect program theory, forthcoming in *Representations* (2010) and in Jan Plamper and Benjamin Lazier, eds., *Fear: Across the Disciplines* (Pittsburgh: Pittsburgh University Press, 2010).
107. Reddy, *The Navigation of Feeling*, x.
108. Barbara H. Rosenwein, "Worrying About Emotions in History," *The American Historical Review* 107:3 (June 2002): 836, 837. See also Daniel Gross, *The Secret History of Emotion: From Aristotle's Rhetoric to Modern Brain Science* (Chicago: University of Chicago Press, 2006), 5, who argues that emotions are not only social; they are constituted by scarcity and power differentials.
109. See Wolfgang Schivelbusch, *The Railway Journey: The Industrialization of Time and Space in the Nineteenth Century* (Berkeley: University of California Press, 1986), for an account of the medical treatment of shock in relation to railway accidents.
110. See Christopher Herbert, *War of No Pity*, who describes the phantasmagoric and hallucinatory quality of much writing on the uprising. Drawing mainly on Cathy Caruth's definitions, he interprets the mutiny as a cultural trauma, which engendered a large-scale schism in the "British psyche." He does not focus on Victorian psychological theories of mental shock. See 137, 274–78.
111. Edgar Jones and Simon Wessely, "Case of Chronic Fatigue Syndrome after Crimean War and Indian Mutiny," *British Medical Journal* 319 (1999): 1645–47. See also their *Shell-Shock to PTSD: Military Psychiatry from 1900 to the Gulf War* (Hove: Psychology Press, 2006).

112. Jones and Wessely, "Case of Chronic Fatigue Syndrome," 1647.

113. Ibid.

114. Edgar Jones and Simon Wessely, "Psychiatric Battle Casualties: An Intra- and Interwar Comparison," *The British Journal of Psychiatry* 178 (2001): 242.

115. The authors here (ibid., 246) cite G.W. Beebe and M. E. DeBakey, *Battle Casualties: Incidence, Mortality, and Logistic Considerations* (Springfield: Charles C. Thomas, 1952), 77.

116. Jones and Wessely, "Psychiatric Battle Casualties," 246.

117. Colonel Atwell Lake, CB, *Kars and Our Captivity in Russia* (London: Richard Bentley, 1856), 27.

118. Ibid., 26.

119. Ibid., 263.

120. Ibid., 245.

121. Alexander Kinglake, *The Invasion of Crimea: Its Origin, and an Account of its Progress Down to the Death of Lord Raglan*, vol. IV, *The Winter Troubles* (New York: Harper & Brothers, 1881), 152.

122. James Gibson, *Memoirs of the Brave: A Brief Account of the Battles of the Alma, Balaklava, and Inkerman, with Biographies of the Killed and A List of the Wounded* (London: The London Stamp Exchange, 1889), 27.

123. Tuke, *Illustrations of the Influence of the Mind upon the Body*, 386.

124. Ibid., 164.

125. Maria Luddy, ed., *The Crimean Journals of the Sisters of Mercy: 1854–56* (Dublin: Four Courts Press, 2004), 28.

126. Ibid., 135.

127. Andrew Ward, *Our Bones are Scattered: The Cawnpore Massacres and the Indian Mutiny of 1857* (New York: Henry Holt, 1996); Ward depends on Mowbray Thomson in noting that "many of the most frail and frantic of the women and children had died of shock and exhaustion" (203). For a description of the terror of the women and children, see also Mowbray Thomson, *The Story of Cawnpore* (London: Richard Bentley, 1859), 66.

128. Hacking, *Rewriting the Soul*, 188, points out that French statisticians themselves prepared reports on the psychological effects of the war; a "thick volume of 1874, *On the Influence of Great Commotions on the Development of Mental Illness*, presented accounts of 386 civilians who experienced long-term distress from some wartime event."

129. "The War," *The Lancet* (January 21, 1871): 99.

130. Alex Boggs, "Paris after the Double Siege," *The Lancet* (July 8, 1871): 75.

131. Anonymous, "Effects of Fright on the Mind," *Journal of Mental Science* 18 (July 1872): 234.

132. Ibid., 235.

133. Herbert Page, "Shock from Fright," in *A Dictionary of Psychological Medicine*, ed. Daniel Hack Tuke (Philadelphia: P. Blackiston, 1892), II:1157.

134. Edwin Morris, *A Practical Treatise on Shock* (London: Robert Hardwicke, 1867), v–vi. Contrast Page's view, some twenty-five years later, that "the early and amicable settlement of the claim for compensation on account of the

injuries sustained" is one of the best treatments for disorders following railway shock; see Page, "Shock from Fright," 1160.

135. Morris, *A Practical Treatise on Shock*, 1.

136. Ibid., 88.

137. See Danuta Mendelson, *The Interfaces of Medicine and Law: The History of the Liability for Negligently Caused Psychiatric Injury (Nervous Shock)* (Aldershot: Ashgate, 1998), 1–4. See also her discussion of *Coultas et uxor* v. *The Victorian Railway Commissioners*, 60–70.

138. This topic has received attention in histories of accident and trauma; see Ralph Harrington, *The Railway Accident: Trains, Trauma and Technological Crisis in Nineteenth-Century Britain*, http://york.ac.uk/inst/irs/irshome/papers/rlyacc. html/; see also Herbert Page, *Injuries of the Spine and Spinal Cord Without Apparent Mechanical Lesion, and Nervous Shock, in their Surgical and Medico-Legal Aspects* (London: Churchill, 1883); and *Railway Injuries, With Special Reference to Those of the Back and Nervous System, in Their Medico-Legal and Clinical Aspects* (London: Griffin, 1891); Ruth Leys, *Trauma: A Genealogy*; Hacking, *Rewriting the Soul*.

139. George Eliot, *Middlemarch*, ed. David Carroll, Oxford World's Classics (Oxford: Oxford University Press, 1998), 190.

140. Ibid., 191.

141. On the historicity and constructedness of trauma as a concept, see particularly Young, *The Harmony of Illusions*; Hacking, *Rewriting the Soul*; and Leys, *Trauma: A Genealogy*.

142. Janet Oppenheim points to the way scientists and doctors are "moulded, too, by systems of values, ethical codes, religious beliefs, and all manner of preconceived opinion." See *"Shattered Nerves": Doctors, Patients and Depression in Victorian England* (New York: Oxford University Press, 1991), 4.

143. Herbert Spencer, *The Principles of Psychology* (1855), 2nd edn. (London: Williams and Norgate, 1870–72), 1:151. Although Michael Maher asserts that Spencer sees "all forms of consciousness ... [as] resolvable into elementary units of feeling akin to electric-shocks," Spencer does not specifically refer to the shock as electric. See Maher's anti-materialist *Psychology Empirical and Rational*, 8th edn. (London: Longmans, Green, 1915), also available online at http://maritain.nd.edu/jmc/etext/psycho23.htm (accessed April 23, 2009).

144. Spencer, *Principles of Psychology*, 1:152.

145. Alexander Bain, *The Emotions and the Will*, 3rd edn. (London: Longmans, 1880), 4.

146. Ibid., 10.

147. Alexander Bain, *Mind and Body: The Theories of their Relation* (London: Henry King, 1873), 40.

148. Tuke, *Illustrations of the Influence of the Mind upon the Body*, 246.

149. Ibid., 230.

150. George Eliot, *Daniel Deronda*, ed. Graham Handley, Oxford World's Classics (Oxford: Oxford University Press, 1998), 402. George Henry Lewes was actively involved in experiments with frogs and electricity as he explored the

physiology of consciousness; see Richard Menke, "Fiction as Vivisection: G. H. Lewes and George Eliot," *ELH* 67:2 (2000): 617–53.

151. See Keith Oatley, *Emotions: A Brief History* (Oxford: Blackwell, 2004), 70–71.

152. Sidney Ochs, *A History of Nerve Functions: From Animal Spirits to Molecular Mechanisms* (Cambridge: Cambridge University Press, 2004), 112.

153. William B. Carpenter, *Principles of Mental Physiology* (New York: Appleton, 1874), 14.

154. Ochs, *A History of Nerve Functions*, 108; I am summarizing here from Ochs's more detailed account of this history, 108–21. See also Edwin Clarke and L. S. Jacyna, *Nineteenth Century Origins of Neuroscientific Concepts* (Berkeley: University of California Press, 1987), 157, who suggest that the "history of concepts of nerve function is ... one of the longest in the evolution of neurosciences." They classify the first period as preceding Galvani (1791); the second dates from 1791 to 1840; and the third from Emil du Bois-Reymond in the 1840s to the present day.

155. *Researches in Animal Electricity* was published over many years, the first part appearing in 1848, the last in 1884. Clarke and Jacyna, *Nineteenth Century Origins of Neuroscientific Concepts*, credit Du Bois-Reymond with placing the discipline of electrophysiology of nerve and muscle on a firm scientific basis (157). See also Danziger, *Naming the Mind*, 62.

156. Bain, *Mind and Body*, 37, 73.

157. Morris, *A Practical Treatise on Shock*, 11.

158. Arrhenius's theory was that, even in the absence of an electric current flowing through a solution, electrolytes (substances able to dissolve in water to yield a solution that conducts electricity) can dissociate into ions, which are electrically charged particles.

159. Bain, *Mind and Body*, 41.

160. Eliot, *Middlemarch*, 382–83. See Michael Davis, *George Eliot and Nineteenth-Century Psychology: Exploring the Unmapped Country* (Aldershot: Ashgate, 2006), 151–52, who discusses this and other passages in which George Eliot uses electricity to analogize internal processes.

161. Martha N. Nussbaum, *Upheavals of Thought: The Intelligence of Emotions* (Cambridge: Cambridge University Press, 2001), 25.

162. See, for example, LeDoux, *The Emotional Brain*, and Jaak Panksepp, *Affective Neuroscience : The Foundations of Human and Animal Emotions* (Oxford: Oxford University Press, 1998).

163. See "Thinking through the Body: An Interview with Allan Schore," interview by Roz Carroll, http://thinkbody.co.uk/papers/interview-with-allan-s.htm (accessed April 27, 2009); and Allan N. Schore, *Affect Regulation and the Repair of the Self* (New York: Norton, 2003).

164. See Dames, *Amnesiac Selves*; on Victorian theories of memory in relation to psychic shock, see also Chapter 3 below.

165. See, for example, José Brunner, "Identifications, Suspicions, and the History of Traumatic Disorders," *Harvard Review of Psychiatry* 10:3 (2002):179–84. Brunner notes that "the symptoms of [late nineteenth-century] disorders

encompassed a wide range of phenomena from emotional instability, hallucinations, hyperarousal, physical and mental numbness, auditory disturbances,
'tunnel vision,' and partial paralyses to trembling, nightmares, loss of concentration, persistent headaches, and compulsive vomiting" (176).

2 DREAM AND TRANCE: GASKELL'S *NORTH AND SOUTH* AS A "CONDITION-OF-CONSCIOUSNESS" NOVEL

1. Critics have also focused on female authority, gender relations and the dominance of the marriage or domestic plot over the industrial themes.
2. Other critics who have focused to some extent on the emotional economy of
the novel include Rosemarie Bodenheimer, "*North and South*: A Permanent
State of Change," *Nineteenth-Century Fiction* 34:3 (December 1979): 281–301;
and Terence Wright, *Elizabeth Gaskell: "We are not Angels": Realism, Gender,
Values* (Houndmills: MacMillan Press, 1995), who observes that the novel is "a
book full of pain … of stress and disturbance, of pangs of conscience and sexual
torment" (105).
3. Elizabeth Gaskell, *Mary Barton*, ed. Edgar Wright, Oxford World's Classics
(Oxford: Oxford University Press, 1998), xxxvi, 398.
4. See Wright, *Elizabeth Gaskell*, 107, who focuses on the dailiness of suffering in
the novel.
5. Gaskell to Charles Dickens, 17 December 1854, in *The Letters of Mrs Gaskell*, ed.
J. A. V Chapple and Arthur Pollard (Manchester: Manchester University Press,
1997), 324.
6. Elizabeth Gaskell, *North and South*, ed. Angus Easson, intro. Sally
Shuttleworth, Oxford World's Classics (Oxford: Oxford University Press,
1998), 245. Further references are to this edition and will be made parenthetically in the text.
7. See Shuttleworth, introduction to ibid., xvi. Gaskell herself referred to him in a
letter of 1855 as "weak and vacillating."
8. Mathew Thomson, "Neurasthenia in Britain: An Overview," in *Cultures of
Neurasthenia: From Beard to the First World War*, ed. Marijke Gijswijt-Hofstra
and Roy Porter (Amsterdam: Rodopi, 2001), 77.
9 Lecture by Frederick Braithwaite, *Proceedings of the [British] Institute of Civil
Engineers*, 13:463 (1854); quoted in Wolfgang Schivelbusch, *The Railway
Journey: The Industrialization of Time and Space in the Nineteenth Century*
(Berkeley: University of California Press, 1986), 124–25.
10. Edwin Morris, *A Practical Treatise on Shock After Surgical Operations and
Injuries: With Especial Reference to Shock Caused by Railway Accidents*
(London: Hardwicke: 1867), 19.
11. Ibid., 23.
12. Ibid., 23.
13. Ibid., 29–30.

14. George Beard, "A New Theory of Trance and its Bearings on Human Testimony," *The Journal of Nervous and Mental Disease* 4:1 (January 1877): 6.
15. Ibid., 8.
16. Ibid., 9. Emphasis added.
17. Herbert Page, "Shock from Fright," in *A Dictionary of Psychological Medicine*, 2 vols., ed. Daniel Hack Tuke (Philadelphia: P. Blackiston, 1892), II:1159.
18. On Gaskell's tolerant attitude towards but scant knowledge of mesmerism, see Christopher Hilton, "Elizabeth Gaskell and Mesmerism: An Unpublished Letter," *Medical History* 39 (1995): 219–35. Gaskell did not appear to know much about or be particularly interested in mesmerism or hypnosis, and this in spite of the fact that Manchester was her home and, one might say, the birthplace of hypnotism in 1845. James Braid was a Manchester doctor who induced hypnotic states by means of mechanical activity and intense concentration rather than mesmeric passes, and who made mesmerism scientifically respectable as "neurypnology." In 1854 Gaskell wrote a letter to Ann Scott worrying about the state of a sick friend and asking whether mesmerism was really known to have therapeutic effects in the management of disease. See ibid., 234. Gaskell makes one remark about mesmerism in *Mary Barton*, where it appears synonymous with the power of one mind over another (284).
19. The dying Bessy thinks Margaret's coming to her has been prefigured in a dream (*North and South*, 149).
20. See Shuttleworth and Taylor, eds., *Embodied Selves*, 69.
21. See Terence Wright's discussion of Margaret's response to Thornton's proposal, which suggests that nightmare is brought into a daytime experience (*Elizabeth Gaskell*, 107).
22. See Carpenter, *Principles of Mental Physiology* (New York: Appleton, 1874), 26.
23. Ibid., 24.
24. See Louise Henson, "'The Condition-of-England' Debate and the 'Natural History of Man': An Important Scientific Context for the Social-Problem Fiction of Elizabeth Gaskell," *Gaskell Society Journal* 16 (2002): 30–47; Henson finds Gaskell in agreement with the representation of excess of passion in Holland and Carpenter (38–40). While Henson claims that "we can see Gaskell utilizing ethnological and physiological concepts in her social-problem fiction," her brief discussion of *North and South* does not focus on the ways Gaskell departs from Carpenter and the mid-Victorian emphasis on order and control.
25. For a contrasting view, see Louise Henson, "Mesmeric Delusions: Mind and Mental Training in Gaskell's Writings," in *Victorian Literary Mesmerism*, ed. Martin Willis and Catherine Wynne (Amsterdam: Rodopi, 2006), 83–103. Henson sees Gaskell as typically Unitarian in her discomfort with mesmerism as a state of mind that "disabled the judgement and undermined responsibility for moral conduct" (103). She does not, however, discuss *North and South*.
26. I am grateful to Stephanie Lougheed, my student in ENG 458 at the University of Toronto (2005), for making this point in a seminar discussion.
27. Wright, *Elizabeth Gaskell*, 110.

28. See Bodenheimer, "*North and South*: A State of Permanent Change," 295–96, for an excellent discussion of these instances, which focuses on Margaret's foray into the public realm; while I am indebted to her discussion, my own focus is more on the altered states of consciousness produced in the aftermath of powerful emotional experience.

29. See Patsy Stoneman's discussion of shame in relation to sexuality in *Elizabeth Gaskell* (Sussex: Harvester Press, 1987), 128–30. But shame is not only associated with sexuality. At its base it is a sense of a diminishment of self – thus Margaret is ashamed of her diminished status in Mr. Thornton's eyes and burns with shame when she remembers her high-handed approach to honesty and deceit in their discussion of buying and selling in the markets.

3 MEMORY AND AFTERMATH: FROM DICKENS'S "THE SIGNALMAN" TO *THE MYSTERY OF EDWIN DROOD*

1. Peter Ackroyd, *Dickens* (London: Minerva, 1991), 1013.

2. Biographers have not generally connected Dickens's symptoms to those listed in definitions of Post-Traumatic Stress Disorder. Peter Ackroyd, for example, says only that "[t]he great conceiving power of Charles Dickens was ... turned into a medium for recurrent and conscious nightmare." See ibid., 1017.

3. My account here draws on the fuller treatment of this incident and Dickens's reactions offered in ibid, 1017 and Edgar Johnson, *Charles Dickens: His Tragedy and his Triumph*, 2 vols. (London: Gollancz, 1953), II:1021.

4. Robin Atthill, "Dickens and the Railway," *English* 13 (1961): 134.

5. Extending Robin Atthill's analysis, David Seed suggests that "from the very first the railway was for Dickens associated with violence and mystery"; see Seed, "Mystery in Everyday Things: Charles Dickens' 'Signalman,'" *Criticism* 23:1 (1981): 47.

6. *Standard Edition of the Complete Psychological Works of Sigmund Freud*, 24 vols., ed. and trans. James Strachey (London: Hogarth Press and the Institute for Psychoanalysis, 1955–72), XVIII:12. All references are to this edition and will be cited hereafter as *SE*. Freud repeatedly gives the railway accident as an example of the disaster that produces trauma. See, for example, *Studies in Hysteria*, *SE*, II:213.

7. Among the historians of medicine, psychoanalysis and technology who have focused on the pre-Freudian history of trauma and the railway, see especially Hacking, *Rewriting the Soul*; Ralph Harrington, "The Railway Accident: Trains, Trauma and Technological Crisis in Nineteenth-Century Britain," www.york.ac.uk/inst/irs/irshome/papers/rlyacc.htm/ (accessed April 25, 2009); Wolfgang Schivelbusch, *The Railway Journey: The Industrialization of Time and Space in the Nineteenth Century* (Berkeley: University of California Press, 1986); Eric Caplan, "Trains, Brains and Sprains: Railway Spine and the Origins of Psychoneuroses," *Bulletin of the History of Medicine* 69:3 (1995): 387–419; George Drinka, *Birth of Neurosis: Myth, Malady and the Victorians*

(New York: Simon & Schuster, 1984); Young, *The Harmony of Illusions*. See also the essays by Harrington and Caplan in *Traumatic Pasts: History, Psychiatry, and Trauma in the Modern Age, 1870–1930*, ed. Mark Micale and Paul Lerner (Cambridge: Cambridge University Press, 2001), 31–77.

8. For a general overview of Victorian theories of the unconscious memory, see Chapter 1; see also Taylor, "Obscure Recesses," 153–58.

9. Hacking, *Rewriting the Soul*, 185.

10. Henri Ellenberger, *The Discovery of the Unconscious: The History and Evolution of Dynamic Psychiatry* (New York: Basic Books, 1970), 245.

11. Schivelbusch, *The Railway Journey*, 134, 135.

12. Schivelbusch charts this movement, drawing on testimony from Dickens himself, after the Staplehurst crash, and that of other nineteenth-century passengers who escaped unscathed but suffered shock.

13. Thomas Buzzard, "On Cases of Injury from Railway Accidents," *The Lancet* 1 (1867): 624.

14. Herbert Page, *Railway Injuries, with Special Reference to Those of the Back and Nervous System in their Medico-Legal and Clinical Aspects* (London: Griffin, 1891), 44.

15. Herbert Page, *Injuries of the Spine and Spinal Cord Without Apparent Mechanical Lesion, and Nervous Shock, in Their Surgical and Medico-Legal Aspects*, 2nd edn. (London: Churchill, 1885), 168.

16. Ibid., 174.

17. Ibid., 163–64.

18. William James, review, *The Psychological Review* 1 (1894): 197.

19. Freud, *SE*, XVIII:12.

20. Ibid.

21. Ibid., XVIII:13.

22. Cathy Caruth, *Trauma: Explorations in Memory* (Baltimore: Johns Hopkins University Press, 1995), 4–5, 7.

23. Geoffrey Hartman, "On Traumatic Knowledge and Literary Studies," *New Literary History* 26:3 (1995): 537.

24. Jane Austen, *Mansfield Park*, Oxford World's Classics (Oxford: Oxford University Press, 1998), 188.

25. James, review, 199.

26. See, for example, William Carpenter, *Principles of Mental Physiology* (New York: Appleton, 1874), 443–44. This treatise was an expansion of the fourth and fifth editions of *Principles of Human Physiology* (1852 and 1855).

27. Forbes Winslow, *On Obscure Diseases of the Brain, and Disorders of the Mind: Their Incipient Symptoms, Pathology, Diagnosis, Treatment, and Prophylaxis* (London: John Churchill, 1860), 407. For further cases, see ibid., 465–66.

28. Theodule Ribot, *Diseases of Memory: An Essay in the Positive Psychology*, trans. William Huntingdon Smith (1881; New York: Appleton, 1887), 176.

29. Ibid., 178.

30. Carpenter, *Principles of Mental Physiology*, 429.

31. Ibid., 429–30.

32. E. S. Dallas, *The Gay Science* (London: Chapman & Hall, 1866), 1:207.
33. Charles Dickens, *Dombey and Son*, Oxford World's Classics (Oxford: Oxford University Press, 1982), 449.
34. Frances Power Cobbe, "The Fallacies of Memory," from *Hours of Work and Play*, in Shuttleworth and Taylor, eds., *Embodied Selves*, 151. For further discussion of Cobbe, see Jenny Taylor's essay "Fallacies of Memory in Nineteenth-Century Psychology: Henry Holland, William Carpenter and Frances Power Cobbe," *Victorian Review* 26:1 (2000): 98–118.
35. Leys, *Trauma: A Genealogy*, 7.
36. Carpenter, *Principles of Mental Physiology*, 453–54.
37. Ibid., 455.
38. Ibid., 454.
39. Caruth argues therefore that trauma can be seen as a symptom of history rather than a symptom of the unconscious. See Chapter 1 for a discussion of Ruth Leys and others, who critique Caruth's dependence on Bessel van der Kolk's neurobiological explanations of the mechanism by which traumatic experience is recorded but unremembered.
40. Carpenter, *Principles of Mental Physiology*, 440.
41. Ibid., 466.
42. Ibid., 469.
43. See Sally Shuttleworth's useful overview of the changes in fictional and psychological representations of memory in the period in "'The Malady of Thought': Embodied Memory in Victorian Psychology and the Novel," in *Memory and Memorials, 1789-1914: Literary and Cultural Perspectives*, ed. Matthew Campbell, Jacqueline M. Labbe and Sally Shuttleworth (New York: Routledge, 2000), 50.
44. Carpenter, *Principles of Mental Physiology*, 463.
45. Ibid., 464.
46. Ibid., 465; acknowledging the work of the German metaphysicians and more recently that of William Hamilton, he reviews also John Stuart Mill's *Examination of William Hamilton's Philosophy* and quotes frequently from Frances Power Cobbe's essays on "Unconscious Cerebration."
47. Carpenter, *Principles of Mental Physiology*, 515.
48. Ibid., 532–33.
49. Ibid., 535.
50. "And I find myself quite unable to conceive that when I am consciously attempting, whether by speech or by writing, to excite in the minds of my readers the ideas which are present to my consciousness at the moment, it is *not* my Mind which is putting my lips or my hand in motion, but that (as Professor Huxley maintains) it is my Body which is moving *of itself*, and simply keeping my mind informed of its movements." See the 1876 Preface to Carpenter, *Principles of Mental Physiology*, 4th edn., xxii–xxiii.
51. Ibid., xix; Cooke and Wheatstone first demonstrated the use of the electric telegraph in 1837 and received the Albert Award for their work in 1867.

52. Ibid., xxxv. See Ellen Wood's story "Lease, the Pointsman" (1869), which I discuss in the Afterword.

53. Ibid., 4th ed. xxxv–xxxvi.

54. William James, "Are we Automata?" *Mind* 4:13 (January 1879): 8, http://psychclassics.yorku.ca/James/automata.htm (accessed April 2, 2007).

55. The story has attracted a wide variety of interpretations. See Gary Day, "Figuring out 'The Signalman': Dickens and the Ghost Story," in *Nineteenth-Century Suspense: From Poe to Conan Doyle*, ed. Clive Bloom (London: Macmillan, 1988), 26–45; David Greenman, "Dickens' Ultimate Achievements in the Ghost Story: 'To be Taken with a Grain of Salt' and 'The Signalman,'" *The Dickensian* 85 (Spring 1989): 40–48; Ewald Mengel, "The Structure and Meaning in Dickens's 'The Signalman,'" *Studies in Short Fiction* 20:4 (1983): 271–80; Seed, "Mystery in Everyday Things"; John Stahl, "The Sources and Significance of the Revenant in Dickens's 'The Signalman,'" *Dickens Studies Newsletter* 11 (1980): 98–101; Graeme Tytler, "Charles Dickens's 'The Signalman': A Case of Partial Insanity?" *History of Psychiatry* 8 (1997): 421–32.

56. Alison Winter, *Mesmerized: Powers of Mind in Victorian Britain* (Chicago: University of Chicago Press, 1998), 148.

57. Fred Kaplan, *Dickens and Mesmerism: The Hidden Springs of Fiction* (Princeton: Princeton University Press, 1975), 77.

58. Page, "Shock from Fright," 1159.

59. Caruth, *Trauma*, 5.

60. Quoted in Paul Schlicke, ed., *Oxford Reader's Companion to Charles Dickens* (Oxford: Oxford University Press, 1999), 249.

61. Karen Petroski, "The Ghost of an Idea: Dickens's Uses of Phantasmagoria, 1842–44," *Dickens Quarterly* 16:2 (June 1999): 71–93, links early descriptions of the advent of the railway train into the station with phantasmagoria, a term originally associated with magic-lantern shows and subsequently with hallucinations, dreams and nightmare. See also Edward Stanley, "Opening of the Liverpool and Manchester Railroad," *Blackwood's Edinburgh Magazine* 28 (1830): 823–30; cited in Richard Altick, *The Shows of London* (Cambridge and London: Belknap, 1978), 219.

62. As the editor of popular journals, Dickens had often featured articles on the railway and on railway safety. His essay "Need Railway Travellers be Smashed?," which appeared in the November, 29 1851, issue of *Household Words*, is a vigorous and strident argument for reforms in railroad safety mechanisms. See also Ewald Mengel, *The Railway Through Dickens's World* (Frankfurt: Peter Lang, 1989), a useful anthology of railway literature.

63. Charles Dickens, "The Signalman," in Dickens, *Christmas Stories* (London: Oxford University Press, 1956), 531. References are to this edition and will hereafter be made parenthetically in the text.

64. Young, *The Harmony of Illusions*, 7.

65. The identity of the narrator has been variously construed by critics. Seed, for example, in "Mystery in Everyday Things," sees him as one of the Barbox

Brothers, who narrated the earlier parts of "Mugby Junction"; Greenman argues that the narrator should be taken as an independent in "Dickens' Ultimate Achievements," 47. See also Stahl, "The Sources and Significance of the Revenant in Dickens's 'The Signalman,'" and Day, "Figuring out 'The Signalman': Dickens and the Ghost Story."

66. Graeme Tytler, "Charles Dickens's 'The Signalman,'" 421.

67. See Harrington, "The Railway Accident," paras. 1–2; he is referring here to the work of Roger Cooter, "The Moment of the Accident: Culture, Militarism and Modernity in Late-Victorian Britain," in *Accidents in History: Injuries, Fatalities and Social Relations* (Amsterdam: Rodopi, 1997), 107–57.

68. Charles Dickens, *The Mystery of Edwin Drood*, ed. Margaret Cardwell, Oxford World's Classics (Oxford: Oxford University Press, 1999), 2. References are to this edition and will hereafter be made parenthetically in the text.

69. For a discussion of attitudes towards detective fiction, see Gerhard Joseph, "Who Cares Who Killed Edwin Drood?, or, on the Whole, I'd Rather Be in Philadelphia," *Nineteenth-Century Literature* 51:2 (September 1996): 161–75.

70. Kate Perugini, "*Edwin Drood* and the Last Days of Charles Dickens," *Pall Mall Magazine* 37 (June 1906): 646; quoted in David Paroissen, introduction to Charles Dickens, *The Mystery of Edwin Drood* (London: Penguin, 2002), xx.

71. Doris Alexander "Solving the Mysteries of the Mind in *Edwin Drood*," *Dickens Quarterly* 9:3 (2002): 130. See 126, where Alexander argues that "from the time of his involvement in the Stapleton [*sic*] railway accident, Dickens had taken an especially keen interest in derangements of consciousness." Recalling the incident of Albert Smith, who suffered a lapse in memory, Alexander surmises that Edwin, perhaps transported to Egypt, may have suffered "some Albert-Smith style of partial amnesia from the shocking events of that night" (130). Alexander develops a theory that Jasper has mistakenly murdered one of the tramps mentioned twice in the novel. In so doing she unwittingly demonstrates how the pursuit of questions of consciousness becomes the reconstruction of the plot and what happened. In contrast, Elsie Karbacz and Robert Raven, "The Many Mysteries of *Edwin Drood*," *The Dickensian* 90:1 (1994): 5–18, minimize questions of consciousness; they argue that the explanation for Jasper's "behaviour must lie elsewhere than in the further reaches of morbid psychology" (9). They discount the idea of "some sort of double or divided nature" in Jasper, which would account for Jasper's love for Edwin along with his murderous intentions towards him, pointing instead to the "backstory" of the connection between the Bud and Drood families that has resulted in the engagement of Edwin and Rosa.

72. Michael Hollington, "'To the Droodstone:' Or, from *The Moonstone* to *Edwin Drood* via *No Thoroughfare*," *Q/W/E/R/T/Y* 5 (1995): 148.

73. Ibid., 148.

74. In this way, as I will argue, the novel anticipates popular twentieth-century detective novels like *Falling Angel*, or postmodern films like *Memento*, in which the detective or avenger unwittingly pursues himself as he closes in on the perpetrator of a heinous crime.

75. Freud, *Introductory Lectures on Psycho-Analysis, SE*, xv:27.
76. Several critics have touched on the question of the fragmented non-unitary self; see Hollington who agrees with Harry Stone that the "core idea of Edwin Drood is 'probably the notion of Jasper's split personality, and his unconscious self-pursuit and self-conviction.'" See Hollington, "'To the Droodstone,'" 144, quoting Harry Stone, ed., *Dickens' Working Notes for his Novels* (Chicago: University of Chicago Press, 1987), 377.
77. Although Dickens's *Great Expectations* may not seem overtly engaged with the same questions of consciousness that occupy *The Mystery of Edwin Drood*, Catherine Gallagher has shown that discourses of "the apparition," the "emanation," the spirit world and hallucination are repeatedly invoked in it. See Catherine Gallagher and Stephen Greenblatt, "The Novel and Other Discourses of Suspended Belief," in *Practicing the New Historicism* (Chicago: University of Chicago Press, 2000), 163–210. Written in 1861, *Great Expectations* was dedicated to Chauncey Hare Townsend, whose book *Facts in Mesmerism* was regarded as a balanced perspective on that perplexing phenomenon.
78. See Jeremy Tambling, *Dickens, Violence and the Modern State: Dreams of the Scaffold* (Houndmills: MacMillan, 1995), 169, who says that Dickens was "perhaps responding to the slow process by which everything in the text comes to a point of conclusion that could have been guessed from its origin, and there is no difference between the content of the conscious and unconscious mind." For a thorough discussion of the similarities between *Edwin Drood* and *The Moonstone*, see Hollington, "'To the Droodstone,'" 141–49.
79. See Karbacz and Raven, "The Many Mysteries of *Edwin Drood*," 9, who develop a complicated argument that Jasper is after Rosa's inheritance; they suggest that Jasper is Edwin's paternal uncle, and as such will inherit from Edwin after he dies. He is shocked at the news of the severed engagement because Edwin's marriage to Rosa is part of his scheme.
80. John Forster, *The Life of Charles Dickens*, 2 vols. (London: J.M. Dent and Sons, 1966), II:366.
81. Emily Jolly, "An Experience," *All the Year Round* n.s. 2 (August, 1869): 282.
82. Ibid., 288.
83. Paul Hernadi, "Dual Perspective: Free Indirect Discourse and Related Techniques," *Comparative Literature* 24:1 (1972): 32–43; Dorrit Cohn, "Transparent Minds: Narrative Modes for Presenting Consciousness in Fiction," in *Theory of the Novel: A Historical Approach*, ed. Michael McKeon (Baltimore: Johns Hopkins University Press, 2000), 493–514.
84. The opening paragraph of the novel is a notable exception, but arguably at this point Dickens wishes the reader to experience the blur between reality and fantasy and the disorientation of time and space occasioned by the opium vision.
85. Forster, *The Life of Charles Dickens*, II:366. Emphasis added.
86. In their concentration on plot and putative backstory, Karbacz and Raven dismiss the idea of Jasper's troubled consciousness. Of the end of the novel and

Forster's comments on the dissociated nature of Jasper's narrative, they remark: "Forster says that the last chapters would be written in the condemned cell, perhaps by way of a narrative by Jasper in which he describes his life and crimes" ("The Many Mysteries of *Edwin Drood*," 16). As we see, however, what Forster wrote was rather different. See Wendy Jacobson, *The Companion to the Mystery of Edwin Drood* (London: Allen and Unwin, 1986), 134, who suggests that Dickens may have meant that, when the murderer confesses, it will in fact have been "the act of another man."

87. Fred Kaplan, *Dickens and Mesmerism*, 224 n. 6, has noted "the complexities and divisions of Jasper's consciousness dominate the novel," but I wish further to draw attention to the ubiquity of problems of consciousness in the novel as a whole.

88. The irascible and passionate Neville is, for example, in a minor way, a figure like Jasper, except that he loses his temper more obviously. See *Edwin Drood*, 82; after he has fulminated against Edwin, his sister Helena recalls him to himself and he is once more sensible of having lost the guard he had set upon his passionate tendency.

89. This is not itself a new strategy for Dickens, but I am arguing for the cumulative effect of several strategies in this novel that register the self as an objectified other.

90. Charles Dickens and Wilkie Collins, *No Thoroughfare*, in Dickens, *Christmas Stories*, 570. See Hollington's excellent discussion of this text in relation to *The Moonstone* and *The Mystery of Edwin Drood* in "'To the Droodstone,'" 143–45.

91. Jasper is often "not himself," it is initially implied, because he is an opium addict. From Dickens's representation of the opium den and its users in the opening chapter, and in line with contemporary Victorian stereotypes of its effects, opium is figured as a personality- and mind-altering drug. Still, it is important to note that Jasper went to opium in order to "still a pain," when he could not bear his life, which suggests that opium is a contributory factor in his degeneration and not its clear cause.

92. The question of undue influence or supernatural power is also carried out in a minor key is relation to Grewgious and his clerk, who is described as a Familiar, once summoned but now unable to be dispatched.

93. John Milton, *Comus: A Masque*, scene 1, lines 205–9.

94. See Karbacz and Raven, "The Many Mysteries of *Edwin Drood*," 9. They surmise that Jasper may already have committed a murder last year around the same time and now, having drugged Durdles, plans to pour quicklime over the body.

95. See Tambling, *Dickens, Violence and the Modern State*, 179, who sees "a schizophrenia at work in Jasper." Such a retrospective diagnosis is unnecessary given the discourses of memory and the unconscious from which Dickens could extrapolate Jasper's discontinuous states.

96. See Edmund Wilson, "Dickens: The Two Scrooges," in *The Wound and the Bow: Seven Studies in Literature* (New York: Oxford University Press, 1965), 69–85, as an example of several critics who propose that the novel deals with

the duality of good and evil. I agree with Philip Collins, *Dickens and Crime*, 3rd edn. (New York: St. Martin's Press, 1994), 303, who notes that "Jasper certainly leads a double life, but that does not mean he has a dual consciousness." See also 306, where he argues that Jasper's association with the Cathedral is by his own admission a "gross hypocrisy; his appearance of loving Edwin may be the same." On the question of Jasper's bestiality and savagery, the novel provides several further instances and also compares his real predatory qualities to those imputed to other characters, such as Neville or Deputy (an incarnation surely of Trabb's boy and a more important character than Collins's Gooseberry in *The Moonstone*). Durdles tells Jasper to "recollect" himself when he threatens to kill the stone-throwing Deputy, who may have observed the goings-on in the crypt when Jasper drugs Durdles and takes the key. While Deputy is described by Durdles as the "own brother to Peter the Wild Boy," the boy is self-preservatory and disdainful of propriety, rather than feral. Similarly, Neville owns up to his heated "tigerish blood" but it is Jasper who, with the "snarl of a wolf," admits to Princess Puffer his murderous desire to kill Edwin.

97. See Nancy E. Schaumburger, "The 'Gritty Stages' of Life: Psychological Time in *The Mystery of Edwin Drood*," *The Dickensian* 86:3 (1990): 158–63, who focuses on the multiple references to *Macbeth* in the novel.

98. See Hollington, "'To the Droodstone,'" 144, who discusses the importance of Doctor Candy's unintelligible memories.

4 OVERWHELMING EMOTION AND PSYCHIC SHOCK IN GEORGE ELIOT'S *THE LIFTED VEIL* AND *DANIEL DERONDA*

1. Keith Oatley and Jennifer Jenkins, *Understanding Emotions* (Oxford: Blackwell, 1996), 18–22.

2. Eliot, *Middlemarch*, 163.

3. Haight, ed., *The George Eliot Letters*. IX:220. References to the letters are to this edition and will be cited hereafter as *GEL* with volume and page number.

4. *GEL*, III:111.

5. George Eliot, *Daniel Deronda*, ed. Graham Handley, Oxford World's Classics (Oxford: Oxford University Press, 1998), 362. All references are to this edition and will hereafter be cited parenthetically in the text.

6. Beryl Gray, "Pseudoscience and George Eliot's 'The Lifted Veil,'" *Nineteenth Century Fiction* 36:4 (1982): 415. See 422, where Gray does note that Latimer's pursuit of reckless self-devotion "culminates in the alienation of all affections," but does not otherwise pay attention to the novella's engagement with emotion.

7. Kate Flint, "Blood, Bodies and *The Lifted Veil*," *Nineteenth-Century Literature* 51:4 (1997): 455–73. Flint focuses on the relationship of the novella to physiological psychology and the importance of the body and visuality.

8. The coupling of "thought and emotion" is not confined to *The Lifted Veil*; see, for example, George Eliot's famous statement about the project of her fiction: "[M]y writing is simply a set of experiments in life – an endeavour to see what

our *thought and emotion* may be capable of – what stores of motive, actual or hinted as possible, give promise of a better after which we may strive" (emphasis added). See *GEL*, VI:216–17.

9. On the view of emotions as "noncognitive, nonintentional subjective feeling-states," see Martha Nussbaum, *Upheavals of Thought: The Intelligence of Emotions* (Cambridge: Cambridge University Press, 2001), 112.

10. *GEL*, II:165.

11. George Eliot, *The Lifted Veil and Brother Jacob*, ed. Helen Small, Oxford World's Classics (Oxford: Oxford University Press, 1999), 4. Hereafter references are to this edition and will be cited parenthetically in the text.

12. Helen Small, introduction to ibid., xii–xxiii, for example, focuses on George Eliot's knowledge of and interest in mesmerism.

13. J. Gill Holland, "George Henry Lewes and 'Stream of Consciousness': The First Use of the Term in English," *South Atlantic Review* 50:1 (1986): 31–39.

14. Alexander Bain, *The Emotions and the Will* (London: Parker and Son, 1859), 50.

15. Nussbaum, *Upheavals of Thought*, 108.

16. R. S. Lazarus, *Emotion and Adaptation* (New York: Oxford University Press, 1991), 6–7; quoted in Nussbaum, *Upheavals of Thought*, 108.

17. Nussbaum, *Upheavals of Thought*, 32.

18. Ibid., 33. Her exploration of emotion belongs to a group of theories opposed to the view of emotions as automatic, non-cognitive and physiological, and participates in ongoing debates in 21st-century emotion theory about the status of emotion in cognitive process.

19. Ibid., 23.

20. Ibid., 33.

21. Dixon, *From Passions to Emotions*, 178–79.

22. Herbert Spencer, *The Principles of Psychology*, 2nd edn. 2 vols. (London: Williams and Norgate, 1870), 1:472–75.

23. George Henry Lewes, *The Physiology of Common Life* (New York: Appleton, 1860), II:130–31.

24. Ibid., II:105–6.

25. Ibid., II:104–5.

26. See Malcolm Bull, "Mastery and Slavery in 'The Lifted Veil,'" *Essays in Criticism* 48:3 (July 1998): 244–61.

27. Lewes was, however, rather critical of the use of the electrode and battery analogy because it allowed the idea to persist that the force in the nerves was derived from some other source outside the nerve itself. See Lewes, "Origin of Nerve-Force," in *The Physical Basis of Mind* (London: Trübner, 1877), 179. This volume is the third volume and second series of *Problems of Life and Mind*: first series: [1] *The Foundations of a Creed* (1874); [2] *The Foundations of a Creed* (1875); second series: [3] *The Physical Basis of Mind* (1877); third series [4] *The Study of Psychology: Its Object, Scope and Method* (1879); [5] *Mind as a Function of the Organism; The Sphere of Sense and Logic of Feeling; The Sphere of Intellect and Logic of Signs* (1879). The last two volumes were published posthumously.

28. *Oxford English Dictionary*, 2nd edn., *s.v.* "Telepathy," notes "1882 MYERS in *Proc. Soc. Psychical Research* I. II. 147. We venture to introduce the words *Telæsthesia* and *Telepathy* to cover all cases of impression received at a distance without the normal operation of the recognised sense organs": http://dictionary. oed.com.myaccess.library.utoronto.ca/cgi/entry/50248456?single=1&query_ty pe=word&queryword=telepathy&first=1&max_to_show=10 (accessed October 10, 2008).

29. Jenny Uglow points out that it is a nice twist of the plot that Latimer's father believes a dose of scientific education would correct the boy's over-sensitivity. Science is not devoid of imagination; it depends on it. See *George Eliot* (London: Virago, 1987), 118.

30. Lewes, *Physiology of Common Life*, II:347.

31. Ibid., II:348.

32. Ibid., II:353.

33. Ibid., II:354.

34. See *GEL*, III:227.

35. I therefore disagree with Helen Small, in her introduction to *The Lifted Veil*, xxvi, who discusses Lewes's chapter and concludes that the blood transfusion scene eradicates the mystery.

36. See Kate Flint's discussion of visuality in "Blood, Bodies, and *The Lifted Veil.*"

37. See John Picker, *Victorian Soundscapes* (Oxford: Oxford University Press, 2003), on the debates around street musicians of the 1850s.

38. See Carolyn Marvin, *When Old Technologies were New: Thinking About Electric Communication in the Late Nineteenth Century* (New York: Oxford University Press, 1988).

39. George Eliot wrote excitedly to Barbara Bodichon in January, 1878, about the new invention of the phonograph, "which can report gentlemen's bad speeches in all their stammering." Shortly after, she and Lewes went into town "to have the Telephone explained and demonstrated" at Bell's Telephone office. See Rosemary Ashton, *George Eliot: A Life* (London: Hamish Hamilton, 1996), 359; George Henry Lewes's diary March 21, 1878, quoted in *GEL*, VII:16 n. 3.

40. George Eliot, *Felix Holt, the Radical*, ed. Lynda Mugglestone (London: Penguin, 1995), 10.

41. George Eliot, "Shadows of a Coming Race," in *Impressions of Theophrastus Such*, ed. Nancy Henry (London: Pickering, 1994), 138; quoted in Picker, *Victorian Soundscapes*, 4.

42. Spencer, *The Principles of Psychology*, 1:152–53; see Chapter 1 for a fuller discussion of shock as the unit of consciousness.

43. Ibid., 1:184.

44. Lewes, *The Physical Basis of Mind*, 359, 366.

45. Ibid., 359.

46. See Richard Menke, "Fiction as Vivisection: G. H. Lewes and George Eliot," *ELH* 67:2 (2000): 617–53. He notes that "[t]he squirrel's heartbeat, after all, would not only be audible with a stethoscope (a French invention imported to England by the real-life Lydgates of the 1820s); its internal pulsations, motions,

and secretions were also becoming graphically recordable with machines such as the sphygmograph and the kymograph, staples of the physiological laboratory by the 1870s." See ibid., 636.

47. Thomas Pinney, ed., *Essays of George Eliot* (London: Routledge and Kegan Paul, 1963), 126.

48. Ibid., 271.

49. *GEL*, III:III.

50. Alan Palmer, *Fictional Minds* (Lincoln: Nebraska University Press, 2004), 10, quoting George Poulet, "Phenomenology of Reading," *New Literary History* 1:1 (1969): 56.

51. Among critics who have raised the question of trauma in this novel, Louise Penner, "Unmapped Country: Uncovering Hidden Wounds in *Daniel Deronda*," *Victorian Literature and Culture* 30 (2002): 77–97, argues that Gwendolen has been traumatized by sexual abuse on the part of her stepfather; my view is that this claim is of dubious validity because there is insufficient evidence in the novel to support it and that a Freudian narrative has been problematically imposed on the representation of Gwendolen's terror and dread. Lisbeth During and Adrian Poole both make references to trauma but neither explores the idea of trauma in the novel in a sustained way; see Lisbeth During, "The Concept of Dread: Sympathy and Ethics in *Daniel Deronda*," in *Renegotiating Ethics in Literature*, ed. Jane Adamson, Richard Freadman and David Parker (Cambridge: Cambridge University Press, 1998), 65–83; and Adrian Poole, "'Hidden Affinities' in *Daniel Deronda*," *Essays in Criticism* 33:4 (1983): 294–311, whose astute analysis of affinities in the novel nevertheless draws on an unhistoricized notion of trauma: *The Winter's Tale* tableau scene is described as a traumatic violation and Gwendolen's final parting from Deronda is referred to as a trauma. There have been several studies of Gwendolen in terms of madness, hysteria, monomania, nervous disorder and agoraphobia: see Marlene Tromp, "Gwendolen's Madness," *Victorian Literature and Culture* 28:2 (2000): 451–67; Simon During, "The Strange Case of Monomania: Patriarchy in Literature, Murder in *Middlemarch*, Drowning in *Daniel Deronda*," *Representations* 23 (Summer 1988): 86–104; Athena Vrettos, *Somatic Fictions: Imagining Illness in Victorian Culture* (Stanford: Stanford University Press, 1995), 69–75; Carol Stone, "George Eliot's *Daniel Deronda*: The Case of Gwendolen H," *Nineteenth Century Studies* 7 (1993): 57–68; and David Trotter, "The Invention of Agoraphobia," *Victorian Literature and Culture* 32:2 (2004): 463–74.

52. Hacking, *Rewriting the Soul*, 183, notes that the idea of trauma "was already in circulation in 1885, sometimes under the name of moral trauma – *traumatisme moral* – when Freud arrived in Paris to study under Charcot".

53. T. O. Ward, "Case of Double Consciousness Connected with Hysteria," *Journal of Psychological Medicine and Mental Pathology* 2 (1849): 457.

54. Ibid., 458.

55. Alexander Bain, *The Emotions and the Will*, 3rd edn. (London: Longmans, Green, and Co., 1880), 19.

56. Ibid., 20.
57. Ibid., 21, 22.
58. Ibid., 159.
59. Ibid., 157.
60. Alexander Bain, *The Senses and the Intellect*, 3rd edn. (London: Longmans, Green, and Co., 1868), 603.
61. James Sully, Preface to George Henry Lewes, *The Physical Basis of Mind* (London: Kegan Paul, Trench, Trübner, 1893), vii.
62. Lewes, *The Physiology of Common Life*, II:II.
63. Ibid., II:12.
64. Ibid., II:59.
65. Ibid., II:53.
66. Ibid., II:54.
67. Ibid., II:50.
68. Lewes, *The Physical Basis of Mind*, 356–57.
69. Ibid., 357.
70. Ibid., 364.
71. Ibid., 358. See J. A. V. Chapple's discussion of this passage in relation to *Daniel Deronda*, in *Science in the Nineteenth-Century Novel* (Basingstoke: Macmillan, 1986), 120.
72. Lewes, *The Foundations of a Creed*, 1:145 (1874).
73. Lewes, *Problems of Life and Mind*, third series, *Mind as a Function of the Organism*, II:365; see the discussion of this passage by Holland, "George Henry Lewes and 'Stream of Consciousness,'" 36; see also Sally Shuttleworth's discussion of Claude Bernard and Comte in the development of Lewes's thought. "The Language of Science and Psychology in George Eliot's *Daniel Deronda*," in *Victorian Science and Victorian Values: Literary Perspectives*, ed. James Paradis and Thomas Postlewait (New York: New York Academy of Sciences, 1981), 284.
74. Lewes, *The Physiology of Common Life*, II:54.
75. Ibid., II:65.
76. Menke, "Fiction as Vivisection: G. H. Lewes and George Eliot," 636. Menke's fine essay discusses Lewes's experiments on frogs, which led to his fascination with the nature of pain and its relationship to consciousness. If analgesics were administered to experimental subjects then sensation continued but no pain was felt. Indeed, from his studies, Lewes concluded that "the characteristics of pain are coextensive with those of consciousness itself." See ibid., 623. His discussion of *Daniel Deronda* draws attention to Grandcourt's torture of Gwendolen, and to George Eliot's focus on Gwendolen's pain as a means of anatomizing her consciousness. He argues that Gwendolen's mental torture yields the "dynamic" psychology and consciousness George Eliot wishes to explore (645), and that consciousness for Gwendolen "has properties acutely reminiscent of pain" (640). My own interpretation is that Gwendolen's psychic pain is not only an occasion for anatomizing and revealing consciousness in general, but is represented also as a subject in its own right – a special kind of consciousness that registers the effect of shock and terror.

77. See Trotter, "The Invention of Agoraphobia," for a reading of Gwendolen in relation to the developing discourse of agoraphobia.

78. See Fred Botting, *Gothic* (London: Routledge, 1996), 4; see also Jerrod E. Hogle's discussion of the Burkean sublime in the introduction to *The Cambridge Companion to Gothic Fiction* (Cambridge: Cambridge University Press, 2002), 14.

79. Published in the 1840s, Kierkegaard's study of dread was most likely unknown to George Eliot. I cite it here not to suggest direct influence but to point to the larger historical context of the way emotions such as dread and terror could be understood.

80. Shuttleworth, "The Language of Science and Psychology in George Eliot's *Daniel Deronda*," 280, quotes this passage, arguing that in this novel George Eliot was rejecting "modes of thought that presume that all life can be known and strictly defined or quantified."

81. See Josephine McDonagh, *George Eliot* (Plymouth: Northcote House, 1997), 88, 89.

82. For a recent discussion of the novel that focuses on Gwendolen and Mordecai in terms of "second sight," see Pamela Thurschwell, "George Eliot's Prophecies: Coercive Second Sight and Everyday Thought Reading," in *The Victorian Supernatural*, ed. Nicola Brown, Carolyn Burdett and Pamela Thurschwell (Cambridge: Cambridge University Press, 2004), 87–105.

83. See, particularly, Penner, "Unmapped Country."

84. Several critics have noted that the novel seems responsive to the climate in which psychic investigations are beginning to take place. When read in relation to Mordecai and the vexing question of second sight, the passage gestures towards the Victorian contexts in which spiritualism, telepathy and clairvoyance were debated and discussed. See, for example, Roger Luckhurst, *The Invention of Telepathy: 1870–1901* (Oxford: Oxford University Press, 2002), 43; Nicholas Royle, *Telepathy and Literature: Essays on the Reading Mind* (Oxford: Blackwell, 1991), 64–110; and McDonagh, *George Eliot*, 88. At the same time as George Eliot hints at the possibility of prophetic and visionary powers in Mordecai, she also allows that subliminal promptings (as Frederic W. H. Myers, one of the founders of the Society for Psychical Research, would call them) rather than supernatural or predestined forces are at work. The context of telepathic powers of communication is less important here, I would suggest, than the account of unconscious informants of feeling, volition and thought developed by Lewes.

85. Vrettos, *Somatic Fictions: Imagining Illness in Victorian Culture*, 69, 75.

86. See Louise Penner, "Unmapped Country," and Susan Ostrov Weisser, "Gwendolen's Hidden Wound: Sexual Possibilities and Impossibilities in *Daniel Deronda*," *Modern Language Studies* 20:3 (Summer 1990): 3–13.

87. Weisser, "Gwendolen's Hidden Wound," 11.

88. See the introduction for a discussion of critical views on the trajectory of the ghost story during the nineteenth century.

89. On Brontë's use of the gothic, see Alison Milbank, "The Victorian Gothic in English Novels and Stories, 1830–1880," in Hogle, ed., *The Cambridge*

Companion to Gothic Fiction, 153–55; see also Trotter, "The Invention of Agoraphobia," 468.

90. See, for example, Peter K. Garrett, *Gothic Reflections: Narrative Force in Nineteenth-Century Fiction*. (Ithaca: Cornell University Press, 2003), and Thurschwell, "George Eliot's Prophecies: Coercive Second Sight and Everyday Thought Reading."

91. Although this seems ordinary enough from a post-Freudian perspective, George Eliot's apprehension of dream is far more sophisticated than much contemporary nineteenth-century dream theory.

92. During, "The Concept of Dread: Sympathy and Ethics in *Daniel Deronda*," 72.

93. In this regard, it is interesting that 1876, the year in which the novel was published, marks the first time an English court delivered a verdict of "not guilty on the ground of unconsciousness." See Joel Peter Eigen, *Unconscious Crime: Mental Absence and Criminal Responsibility in Victorian London* (Baltimore: Johns Hopkins University Press, 2003), 10.

94. See Chapter 1 for a more detailed discussion of contemporary debates in trauma theory.

5 DISSOCIATION AND MULTIPLE SELVES: MEMORY, MYERS AND STEVENSON'S "SHILLING SHOCKER"

1. Robert Louis Stevenson, *The Strange Case of Dr Jekyll and Mr Hyde*, Oxford World's Classics (Oxford: Oxford University Press, 1987), 36. Further references are to this edition and will be made parenthetically in the text.

2. See Hacking, *Rewriting the Soul*. In much the same way that Foucault disclosed the ideological agenda behind concepts of insanity, or put the "politics" into "bio," Hacking seeks to uncover the ideological and professional implications of the rise of memory science. See my discussion of Hacking's approach in Chapter 1.

3. See Emma Letley's introduction to *The Strange Case of Dr Jekyll and Mr Hyde*, ix–x. Letley is quoting Mrs. Stevenson's Prefatory Note to *The Works of Robert Louis Stevenson*, Tusitala Edition, 35 vols. (London: William Heinemann, 1923–24), v:xvi.

4. See R. G. Swearingen, *The Prose Writings of Robert Louis Stevenson: A Guide* (London: MacMillan Press, 1980), 101, on the lack of identification of this article.

5. Elaine Showalter, "Dr. Jekyll's Closet," in *The Haunted Mind: The Supernatural in Victorian Literature*, ed. Elton E. Smith and Robert Haas (London: The Scarecrow Press, 1999), 67. While Showalter begins with the case of Louis V and ends with that of the multiple, Miss Beauchamp, her emphasis on repressed sexuality and gender in relation to multiple personality is rather different from mine.

6. Swearingen, *The Prose Writings of Robert Louis Stevenson*, 101.

7. See Robert Mighall, ed., *The Strange Case of Dr Jekyll and Mr Hyde and Other Tales of Terror* (London: Penguin, 2002), 175 n. 5. His introduction focuses

mainly on the tale in the context of criminal psychiatric theory. The context in which I wish to situate the tale is that of Myers's interest in the implications of the multiple self for the ordinary rather than pathological individual.

8. See Hacking, *Rewriting the Soul*, who correctly distinguishes the brothers and dates of publication in his text, but whose notes and bibliography incorrectly give 1896 as the date of publication for both A.T. and F. W. H.

9. See *Journal of the Society for Psychical Research* 2 (November, 1886): 443, where Myers apologizes "for the fact that the paper in question had appeared that morning in print in the *Nineteenth Century* for November, some days before the nominal date of issue of that review." Both of Frederick Myers's versions of "Multiplex Personality" make reference to earlier accounts of the case in the *Proceedings of the Society for Psychical Research* 4 (1886): 496–514.

10. F. W. H. Myers, "Multiplex Personality," *The Nineteenth Century* 20 (Nov., 1886): 648–66; reprinted in Shuttleworth and Taylor, eds., *Embodied Selves*, 132–38.

11. See Christine Persak, "Spencer's Doctrines and Mr. Hyde: Moral Evolution in Stevenson's 'Strange Case,'" *Victorian Newsletter* 86 (1994): 15.

12. *Journal of the Society for Psychical Research* 2 (November, 1885): 90–91.

13. In this regard, I differ from Anne Stiles, " Robert Louis Stevenson's *Jekyll and Hyde* and the Double Brain," *Studies in English Literature, 1500–1900* 46:4 (Autumn 2006): 879–900, who argues that theories of the dual brain, discussed in the 1870s, influenced Stevenson. I am less interested in a specific scientific influence than a context in which ideas about multiplicity and the questions it raises about memory and self-knowledge shape both scientific inquiry and literary creation.

14. On Myers's contributions and the significance of his concept of consciousness, see William James, "Frederic Myers' Services to Psychology," *Proceedings of the Society for Psychical Research* (1901): 17; reprinted in William James, *Memories and Studies* (London: Longmans, 1911), 145–70.

15. *Journal of the Society for Psychical Research* 2 (April, 1886): 243.

16. Pamela Thurschwell, *Literature, Technology and Magical Thinking: 1880–1920* (Cambridge: Cambridge University Press, 2001), 15.

17. Samuel Hynes, *The Edwardian Frame of Mind* (Princeton: Princeton University Press, 1968), 143.

18. C. S. Alvarado, "Dissociation in Britain During the Late Nineteenth Century: The Society for Psychical Research, 1882–1900," *Journal of Trauma and Dissociation* 3:2 (2002): 9 33. See also Pamela Thurschwell, *Literature Technology and Magical Thinking*, and Luckhurst, *The Invention of Telepathy: 1870–1901*.

19. *Journal of the Society for Psychical Research* 2 (November, 1885): 91.

20. Ibid.

21. *Journal of the Society for Psychical Research* 2 (December, 1885): 122.

22. Ibid. (April, 1886): 239.

23. Ibid., 240.

24. Ibid., 243.

25. Ibid., 4 (April, 1889): 60.

26. Ibid., 61.

27. Ibid., 60–61.

28. Ibid., 62.

29. Myers is referring to the subjects of well-known case histories of multiple or double consciousness. Félida and Léonie are the subjects discussed by Eugene Azam and Pierre Janet respectively. See below my discussion of William James, "The Hidden Self," *Scribner's Magazine* 7 (1890): 361–73, who assesses these cases; see *Journal of the Society for Psychical Research* 4 (April, 1889): 63.

30. *Journal of the Society for Psychical Research* 4 (May, 1889): 77.

31. F. W. H. Myers, "Multiplex Personality," 651.

32. Ibid., 652.

33. Ibid.

34. *Journal of the Society for Psychical Research* 3 (October, 1888): 306.

35. Ibid. See, for example, Morton Prince's difficulty with the different manifestations of Miss Beauchamp, and the discussion of his attempt to rid his patient of her most antisocial and yet coherent self in Leys, *Trauma: A Genealogy.*

36. Myers, "Multiplex Personality," 655.

37. Ibid., 663.

38. Ibid., 665.

39. For a discussion of the story in the context of mental chemistry, see Michael Davis, "Incongruous Compounds: Re-reading *Jekyll and Hyde* and Late-Victorian Psychology," *Journal of Victorian Culture* 11:2 (Autumn 2006): 207–25.

40. See Paul Maixner, ed., *Robert Louis Stevenson: The Critical Heritage* (London: Routledge and Kegan Paul, 1981), 206; see also Persak, "Spencer's Doctrines and Mr. Hyde," 14.

41. Oscar Wilde, "The Decay of Lying," *The Nineteenth Century: A Monthly Review* 25 (January–June, 1889), 38.

42. F. W. H. Myers, "Obituary," *Journal of the Society for Psychical Research* 7 (January, 1895): 6.

43. See Maixner, ed., *Critical Heritage*, 222. Several critics have focused with different emphasis from mine on Myers's critique. See, for example, Irving Saposnik, *Robert Louis Stevenson* (New York: Twayne, 1974), 151, who sees Myers flat-footedly reading the story as a "realistic portrayal of specialized psychic phenomena"; and, more recently, Stephen Arata, *Fictions of Loss in the Victorian Fin de Siècle* (Cambridge: Cambridge University Press, 1996), 36–38, who focuses on the way Myers reads Hyde as a member of the bourgeoisie.

44. Myers, "Obituary," 6.

45. R. L. Stevenson to F. W. H. Myers, March 1, 1886, in *The Letters of Robert Louis Stevenson*, ed. Bradford A. Booth and Ernest Mehew (New Haven: Yale University Press, 1995), V:217.

46. Maixner, ed., *Critical Heritage*, 221.

47. Ibid., 215.

48. *Journal of the Society for Psychical Research* 2 (March, 1886): 224.

49. See Peter K. Garrett, "Cries and Voices: Reading *Jekyll and Hyde*," in *Dr Jekyll and Mr Hyde After One Hundred Years*, ed. William Veeder and Gordon Hirsh (Chicago: University of Chicago Press, 1988), 66.
50. Ruth Leys makes this point in her discussion of Morton Prince's pioneering study of multiple personality in *Trauma: A Genealogy*, 42.
51. For a summary of different accounts of the novel's genesis, see Letley's introduction to the Oxford World's Classics edition, viii–x; and Swearingen, *The Prose Writings of Robert Louis Stevenson*, 99–101.
52. In this regard, the tale can be profitably compared with *The Mystery of Edwin Drood*, discussed in Chapter 3. Jekyll takes a drug, a potion which he swallows, to "dissociate the elements of his being" and literally change himself into someone else. Similarly, Jasper takes a drug – he smokes opium – in order to escape from himself, undertaking the journey, exorcizing for a time the murderous desire, and then experiencing the transporting visions that opium brings.
53. Peter K. Garrett, *Gothic Reflections: Narrative Force in Nineteenth-Century Fiction* (Ithaca: Cornell University Press, 2003), 104. While Garrett acknowledges (106–7) that Stevenson's "radically disunified model of the self displaces traditional disunities," his emphasis is not, like mine, on the psychological discourse of the time which was also proposing and considering the implication of multiplicity over duality.
54. See Hilary J. Beattie, "Father and Son: The Origins of *The Strange Case of Dr Jekyll and Mr Hyde*," *Psychoanalytic Study of the Child* 56 (2001): 317–60; see also Christine Persak, "Spencer's Doctrines and Mr. Hyde," 16–17, on the theme of evolution.
55. See Showalter's discussion of this in "Dr. Jekyll's Closet," 71. See also William Veeder in "Collated Fractions of the Manuscript Drafts of *Strange Case of Dr Jekyll and Mr Hyde*," in Veeder and Hirsh, eds., *Dr Jekyll and Mr Hyde after One Hundred Years*, 55.
56. *Encyclopaedia Britannica Online*, s.v. "cheval glass," www.britannica.com// article?tocId=9023899 (accessed October 14, 2008).
57. James, "The Hidden Self," 369.
58. See Glenda Norquay, ed., *R. L. Stevenson on Fiction: An Anthology of Literary and Critical Essays* (Edinburgh: Edinburgh University Press, 1999), 126–27, who cites J. C. Furnas, *Voyage to Windward*. Furnas was of the opinion that Stevenson's thinking in the essay owed something to his relationship with Myers.
59. "A Chapter on Dreams" was originally published in *Scribner's Magazine* 3 (January, 1888): 122–28; see Appendix B in *The Strange Case of Dr Jekyll and Mr Hyde*, 198. All further references are to the Oxford edition and will be cited parenthetically in the text.
60. Dallas, *The Gay Science*, 1:201.
61. Ibid.
62. Today there are four main categories of dissociative disorders as defined in the *DSM*. See chapter 1, n. 6.

63. James, "The Hidden Self," 371.

64. *Journal of the Society for Psychical Research* 2 (April, 1886): 240.

AFTERWORD ON AFTERWARDS

1. I follow Ian Hacking here in using the term "making up," which is the way he characterizes PTSD – the "making up" of a certain kind of person that individuals can conceive themselves as being and on the basis of which they can become eligible for insurance-reimbursed therapy, or compensation, or can plead diminished responsibility in courts of law. See Hacking, "Making Up People," in *Reconstructing Individualism: Autonomy, Individuality, and the Self in Western Thought*, ed. Thomas C. Heller, Morton Sosna and David E. Wellberyal (Stanford: Stanford University Press, 1986), 222–36.

2. Wood, "Lease, the Pointsman," 51–52. Further references will be made parenthetically in the text.

3. Carpenter, *Principles of Mental Physiology*, 4th edn., xxxv–xxxvi. This edition reprints the 1874 and 1876 prefaces.

4. Daniel McNaughtan, tried for political assassination, was acquitted on the grounds of insanity, his case giving rise to the McNaughtan rules, which outlined the criteria defining the failure of the accused to understand the nature of the crime and the difference between right and wrong. See Eigen, *Unconscious Crime*, 6, 13.

5. George Eliot, *Silas Marner: The Weaver of Raveloe*, ed. Terence Cave, Oxford World's Classics (Oxford: Oxford University Press, 1998), 11.

6. See Philip Davis, *The Oxford English Literary History*, vol. VIII, *1830–1880: The Victorians* (Oxford: Oxford University Press, 2002), 261, who discusses Lewis's "experiments with mental externalization" in depicting the protagonist's inner guilt. See also Carolyn Williams's discussion of the melodramatic tableau in *The Bells* in "Moving Pictures: George Eliot and Melodrama," in *Compassion: The Culture and Politics of an Emotion*, ed. Lauren Berlant (London: Routledge, 2004), 107.

Selected bibliography

"A Novel or Two." *National Review* (October, 1855): 336–50.

Ackroyd, Peter. *Dickens.* London: Minerva, 1991.

Alexander, Doris. "Solving the Mysteries of the Mind in *Edwin Drood.*" *Dickens Quarterly* 9:3 (2002): 125–31.

Altick, Richard. *The Shows of London.* Cambridge and London: Belknap, 1978.

"Animal Magnetism and Neurohypnotism." *Fraser's Magazine* 29 (Jan.–June, 1844): 681–99.

Anonymous. "Effects of Fright on the Mind." *Journal of Mental Science* 18 (July, 1872): 234–35.

Arata, Stephen. *Fictions of Loss in the Victorian Fin de Siècle.* Cambridge: Cambridge University Press, 1996.

Armstrong, Tim. "Two Types of Shock in Modernity." *Critical Quarterly* 42:1 (2000): 60–73.

Ashton, Rosemary. *George Eliot: A Life.* London: Hamish Hamilton, 1996.

Atthill, Robin. "Dickens and the Railway." *English* 13 (1961): 130–35.

Bain, Alexander. *The Emotions and the Will.* 3rd edn. London: Longmans, 1880.

   Mind and Body: The Theories of their Relation. London: Henry King, 1873.

Beard, George. "A New Theory of Trance and its Bearings on Human Testimony." *The Journal of Nervous and Mental Disease* 4:1 (January, 1877): 1–47.

Beattie, Hilary J. "Father and Son: The Origins of *The Strange Case of Dr Jekyll and Mr Hyde.*" *Psychoanalytic Study of the Child* 56 (2001): 317–60.

Benjamin, Walter. *Illuminations.* Ed. Hannah Arendt. Trans. Henry Zohn. New York: Schoken Books, 1988.

Bodenheimer, Rosemarie. *Knowing Dickens.* Ithaca: Cornell University Press, 2007.

   "*North and South*: A Permanent State of Change." *Nineteenth-Century Fiction* 34:3 (December, 1979): 281–301.

Boggs, Alex. "Paris after the Double Siege." *The Lancet* (July 8, 1871): 74–75.

Booth, Bradford A., and Ernest Mehew, eds. *The Letters of Robert Louis Stevenson.* 8 vols. New Haven: Yale University Press, 1994–95.

Botting, Fred. *Gothic.* London: Routledge, 1996.

Buzzard, Thomas. "On Cases of Injury from Railway Accidents." *The Lancet* 1 (1867): 389–91, 453–54, 509–10, 623–25.

Caplan, Eric. "Trains, Brains and Sprains: Railway Spine and the Origins of Psychoneuroses." *Bulletin of the History of Medicine* 69:3 (1995): 387–419.

Carpenter, William Benjamin. *On Mesmerism and Spiritualism, &c.: Historically and Scientifically Considered.* London: Longman, 1877.

Principles of Human Physiology: With their Chief Applications to Psychology, Pathology, Therapeutics, Hygiene, & Forensic Medicine. 5th edn. London: John Churchill, 1855.

Principles of Mental Physiology. 1876; 4th edn. New York: Appleton, 1890.

Caruth, Cathy. *Unclaimed Experience: Trauma, Narrative, and History.* Baltimore: Johns Hopkins University Press, 1996.

Castle, Terry. *The Female Thermometer: Eighteenth-Century Culture and the Invention of the Uncanny.* New York: Oxford University Press, 1995.

Chapple, J. A. V., and Arthur Pollard, eds. *The Letters of Mrs Gaskell.* Manchester: Manchester University Press, 1997.

Clarke, Edwin, and L. S. Jacyna. *Nineteenth Century Origins of Neuroscientific Concepts.* Berkeley: University of California Press, 1987.

Cobbe, Frances Power. "Dreams as Illustrations of Unconscious Cerebration." *MacMillan's Magazine* 23:138 (1871): 512–23.

"The Fallacies of Memory," From *Hours of Work and Play.* In *Embodied Selves: An Anthology of Psychological Texts 1830–1890.* Ed. Sally Shuttleworth and Jenny Bourne Taylor. Oxford: Oxford University Press, 1998, 150–54.

"Unconscious Cerebration: A Psychological Study." *MacMillan's Magazine* 23:133 (1871): 24–37.

Cohn, Dorrit. "Transparent Minds: Narrative Modes for Presenting Consciousness in Fiction." *Theory of the Novel: A Historical Approach.* Ed. Michael McKeon. Baltimore: Johns Hopkins University Press, 2000, 493–514.

Coleridge, Samuel Taylor. *The Collected Works of Samuel Taylor Coleridge.* Ed. Kathleen Coburn. 16 vols. London: Routledge and Kegan Paul, 1969–2002.

Collins, Philip. *Dickens and Crime.* 3rd edn. New York: St. Martin's Press, 1994.

Conan Doyle, Sir Arthur. "The Adventure of the Cardboard Box." *Sherlock Holmes: The Complete Novels and Stories,* Volume II. New York: Bantam Books, 1986, 321–40.

Cooter, Roger. "The Moment of the Accident: Culture, Militarism and Modernity in Late-Victorian Britain." *Accidents in History: Injuries, Fatalities and Social Relations.* Amsterdam: Rodopi, 1997, 107–57.

Crabtree, Adam. *From Mesmer to Freud: Magnetic Sleep and the Roots of Psychological Healing.* New Haven: Yale University Press, 1993.

Crowe, Catherine. *The Night Side of Nature, or Ghost and Ghost Seers.* London: George Routledge, 1904.

Spiritualism and the Age we Live in. London: Newby, 1859.

Dallas, E. S. *The Gay Science.* 2 vols. London: Chapman & Hall, 1866.

Dames, Nicholas. *Amnesiac Selves: Nostalgia, Forgetting, and British Fiction 1810–1870.* Oxford: Oxford University Press, 2001.

Danziger, Kurt. *Naming the Mind: How Psychology Found its Language.* London: Sage, 1997.

Davis, Michael. *George Eliot and Nineteenth-Century Psychology: Exploring the Unmapped Country.* Aldershot: Ashgate, 2006.

"Incongruous Compounds: Re-reading Jekyll and Hyde and Late-Victorian Psychology." *Journal of Victorian Culture* 11:2 (Autumn 2006): 207–25.

Davis, Philip. *The Oxford English Literary History, Volume VIII, 1830–1880: The Victorians.* Oxford: Oxford University Press, 2002.

Day, Gary. "Figuring out 'The Signalman': Dickens and the Ghost Story." *Nineteenth-Century Suspense: From Poe to Conan Doyle.* Ed. Clive Bloom London: Macmillan, 1988, 26–45.

De Quincey, Thomas. "Animal Magnetism." *Tait's Edinburgh Magazine* 4 (1834): 456–73.

Diagnostic and Statistical Manual of Mental Disorders, Text Revision (DSM-IV-TR). 4th edn. Washington, DC: American Psychiatric Association, 2000.

Dickens, Charles. "Need Railway Travellers be Smashed?" (November 29, 1851): 88–221.

Dickens, Charles, and Wilkie Collins. *No Thoroughfare.* In Dickens, *Christmas Stories.* London: Oxford University Press, 1956, 537–659.

Dixon, Thomas. *From Passions to Emotions: The Creation of a Secular Psychological Category.* Cambridge: Cambridge University Press, 2003.

Drinka, George. *Birth of Neurosis: Myth, Malady and the Victorians.* New York: Simon & Schuster, 1984.

Du Maurier, George. *Trilby.* Ed. Dennis Denisoff. Oxford World's Classics. Oxford: Oxford University Press, 1998.

During, Lisbeth. "The Concept of Dread: Sympathy and Ethics in *Daniel Deronda.*" *Renegotiating Ethics in Literature.* Ed. Jane Adamson, Richard Freadman and David Parker. Cambridge: Cambridge University Press, 1998, 65–83.

During, Simon. "The Strange Case of Monomania: Patriarchy in Literature, Murder in *Middlemarch*, Drowning in *Daniel Deronda.*" *Representations* 23 (Summer 1988): 86–104.

Eigen, Joel Peter. *Unconscious Crime: Mental Absence and Criminal Responsibility in Victorian London.* Baltimore: Johns Hopkins University Press, 2003.

Ellenberger, Henri. *The Discovery of the Unconscious: The History and Evolution of Dynamic Psychiatry.* New York: Basic Books, 1970.

Faas, Ekbert. *Retreat into the Mind: Victorian Poetry and the Rise of Psychiatry.* Princeton: Princeton University Press, 1988.

Flint, Kate. "Blood, Bodies and *The Lifted Veil.*" *Nineteenth-Century Literature* 51:4 (1997): 455–73.

Forster, John. *The Life of Charles Dickens.* 2 vols. London: J. M. Dent and Sons, 1966.

Freud, Sigmund. *Standard Edition of the Complete Psychological Works of Sigmund Freud.* Ed. and trans. James Strachey. 24 vols. London: The Hogarth Press and the Institute for Psychoanalysis, 1953–72.

Furst, Lilian, ed. *Medical Progress and Social Reality: A Reader in Nineteenth-Century Medicine and Literature.* Albany: State University of New York Press, 2000.

Gallagher, Catherine. *The Body Economic: Life, Death, and Sensation in Political Economy and the Victorian Novel.* Princeton: Princeton University Press, 2006.

Gallagher, Catherine, and Stephen Greenblatt. "The Novel and Other Discourses of Suspended Belief." *Practicing the New Historicism*. Chicago: University of Chicago Press, 2000, 163–210.

Garrett, Peter K. "Cries and Voices: Reading Jekyll and Hyde." *Dr Jekyll and Mr Hyde After One Hundred Years*. Ed. William Veeder and Gordon Hirsh. Chicago: University of Chicago Press, 1988, 59–72.

Gothic Reflections: Narrative Force in Nineteenth-Century Fiction. Ithaca: Cornell University Press, 2003.

Gaskell, Elizabeth. *Cousin Phillis and Other Tales*. Oxford World's Classics. Oxford: Oxford University Press, 1981.

Gibson, James. *Memoirs of the Brave: A Brief Account of the Battles of the Alma, Balaklava, and Inkerman, with Biographies of the Killed and A List of the Wounded*. London: The London Stamp Exchange, 1889.

Gray, Beryl. "Pseudoscience and George Eliot's 'The Lifted Veil.'" *Nineteenth Century Fiction* 36:4 (1982): 407–23.

Greenman, David. "Dickens' Ultimate Achievements in the Ghost Story: 'To be Taken with a Grain of Salt' and 'The Signalman.'" *The Dickensian* 85 (Spring 1989): 40–48.

Hacking, Ian. "Making Up People." *Reconstructing Individualism: Autonomy, Individuality, and the Self in Western Thought*. Ed. Thomas C. Heller, Morton Sosna and David E. Wellbery. Stanford: Stanford University Press, 1986, 22–36.

Rewriting the Soul: Multiple Personality and the Sciences of Memory. Princeton: Princeton University Press, 1995.

Haight, Gordon S., ed. *The George Eliot Letters*. 9 vols. New Haven: Yale University Press, 1954–78.

Harrington, Ralph. *The Railway Accident: Trains, Trauma and Technological Crisis in Nineteenth-Century Britain*. www.york.ac.uk/inst/irs/irshome/papers/rlyacc.htm (accessed April 25, 2009).

Hartman, Geoffrey. "On Traumatic Knowledge and Literary Studies." *New Literary History* 26:3 (1995): 537–63.

Herbert, Christopher. *War of No Pity: The Indian Mutiny and Victorian Trauma*. Princeton: Princeton University Press, 2008.

Hilton, Christopher. "Gaskell and Mesmerism: An Unpublished Letter." *Medical History* 39 (1995): 219–35.

Hogle, Jerrod E. The Cambridge Companion to Gothic Fiction. Cambridge: Cambridge University Press, 2002.

Holland, Henry. *Chapters on Mental Physiology*. London: Longman, 1852.

Holland, J. Gill. "George Henry Lewes and 'Stream of Consciousness': The First Use of the Term in English." *South Atlantic Review* 50:1 (1986): 31–39.

Hollington, Michael. "'To the Droodstone:' Or, from *The Moonstone* to *Edwin Drood* via *No Thoroughfare*." *Q/W/E/R/T/Y* 5 (1995): 141–49.

Houghton, Walter Edwards. *The Victorian Frame of Mind*. New Haven: Yale University Press, 1957.

Huxley, Thomas H. *Collected Essays of T. H. Huxley*. 9 vols. London: Macmillan, 1894–1908.

"On the Hypothesis that Animals are Automata and its History." *The Collected Essays of T. H. Huxley*, Volume 1. London: Macmillan, 1894, 199–250.

Hynes, Samuel. *The Edwardian Turn of Mind*. Princeton: Princeton University Press, 1968.

Jacobson, Wendy. *The Companion to the Mystery of Edwin Drood*. London: Allen and Unwin, 1986.

James, William. "Are we Automata?" *Mind* 4:13 (January, 1879): 1–22.

"Frederic Myers' Services to Psychology." *Proceedings of the Society for Psychical Research* (1901). Reprinted in William James. *Memories and Studies*. London: Longmans, 1911, 145–70.

"The Hidden Self." *Scribner's Magazine* 7 (1890): 361–73.

Review. *The Psychological Review* 1 (1894): 195–200.

Johnson, Edgar. *Charles Dickens: His Tragedy and his Triumph*. 2 vols. London: Gollancz, 1953.

Jolly, Emily. "An Experience." *All the Year Round* n.s. 2 (August, 1869): 256–64, 280–88.

Jones, Edgar, and Simon Wessely. "Case of Chronic Fatigue Syndrome after Crimean War and Indian Mutiny." *British Medical Journal* 319 (1999): 1645–47.

"Psychiatric Battle Casualties: An Intra- and Interwar Comparison." *The British Journal of Psychiatry* 178 (2001): 242–47.

Shell-Shock to PTSD: Military Psychiatry from 1900 to the Gulf War. Hove: Psychology Press, 2006.

Joseph, Gerhard. "Who Cares Who Killed Edwin Drood?, or, on the Whole, I'd Rather Be in Philadelphia." *Nineteenth-Century Literature* 51:2 (September, 1996): 161–75.

Kaplan, E. Ann. *Trauma Culture: The Politics of Terror and Loss in Media and Literature*. New Brunswick: Rutgers University Press, 2005.

Kaplan, Fred. *Dickens and Mesmerism: The Hidden Springs of Fiction*. Princeton: Princeton University Press, 1975.

Karbacz, Elsie, and Robert Raven. "The Many Mysteries of *Edwin Drood*." *The Dickensian* 90:1 (1994): 5–18.

Kinglake, Alexander. *The Invasion of Crimea: Its Origin, and an Account of its Progress Down to the Death of Lord Raglan*. 6 vols. New York: Harper & Brothers, 1880–88.

Lake, Colonel Atwell. *Kars and Our Captivity in Russia*. London: Richard Bentley, 1856.

Lazarus, Richard S. *Emotion and Adaptation*. New York: Oxford University Press, 1991.

Le Fanu, Sheridan. "Green Tea." *In a Glass Darkly*. Ed. Robert Tracy. Oxford: Oxford World's Classics, 1993, 5–40.

LeDoux, Joseph. *The Emotional Brain: The Mysterious Underpinnings of Emotional Life*. New York: Simon and Schuster, 1996.

Levine, George. *The Cambridge Companion to George Eliot*. Cambridge: Cambridge University Press, 2001.

Lewes, George Henry. *The Physiology of Common Life.* 2 vols. New York: Appleton, 1860.

Problems of Life and Mind. 5 vols. London: Trübner, 1874–79.

Leys, Ruth. *Trauma: A Genealogy.* Chicago: University of Chicago Press, 2000.

Luckhurst, Roger. *The Invention of Telepathy: 1870–1901.* Oxford: Oxford University Press, 2002.

The Trauma Question. London: Routledge, 2008.

Luddy, Maria, ed. *The Crimean Journals of the Sisters of Mercy: 1854–56.* Dublin: Four Courts Press, 2004.

Lytton, Edward Bulwer. "The Haunters and the Haunted, or The House and the Brain." *Blackwood's Edinburgh Magazine* 86 (August, 1859): 224–45.

A Strange Story. London: Routledge, 1887.

Maixner, Paul, ed. *Robert Louis Stevenson: The Critical Heritage.* London: Routledge and Kegan Paul, 1981.

Martineau, Harriet. *Letters on Mesmerism.* 2nd edn. London: Edward Moxon, 1850.

Martineau, James. "Mesmeric Atheism. Letters on the Laws of Man's Nature and Development. By Henry George Atkinson F. G. S., and Harriet Martineau. London: J. Chapman, 1851." *Prospective Review* 7:26 (1851): 224–62.

Marvin, Carolyn. *When Old Technologies Were New: Thinking About Electric Communication in the Late Nineteenth Century.* New York: Oxford University Press, 1988.

McDonagh, Josephine. *George Eliot.* Plymouth: Northcote House, 1997.

McNally, Richard. *Remembering Trauma.* Cambridge, Mass.: Harvard University Press, 2003.

Mendelson, Danuta. *The Interfaces of Medicine and Law: The History of the Liability for Negligently Caused Psychiatric Injury (Nervous Shock).* Aldershot: Ashgate, 1998.

Mengel, Ewald. *The Railway Through Dickens's World.* Frankfurt: Peter Lang, 1989.

"The Structure and Meaning in Dickens's 'The Signalman.'" *Studies in Short Fiction* 20:4 (1983): 271–80.

Menke, Richard. "Fiction as Vivisection: G. H. Lewes and George Eliot." *ELH* 67:2 (2000): 617–53.

Micale, Mark, and Paul Lerner, eds. *Traumatic Pasts: History, Psychiatry, and Trauma in the Modern Age, 1870–1930.* Cambridge: Cambridge University Press, 2001.

Mighall, Robert, ed. *The Strange Case of Dr Jekyll and Mr Hyde and Other Tales of Terror.* London: Penguin, 2002.

Milbank, Alison. "The Victorian Gothic in English Novels and Stories, 1830–1880." *The Cambridge Companion to Gothic Fiction.* Ed. Jerrold Hogle. Cambridge: Cambridge University Press, 2002, 145–65.

Morris, Edwin. *A Practical Treatise on Shock After Surgical Operations and Injuries: With Especial Reference to Shock Caused by Railway Accidents.* London: Hardwicke, 1867.

Myers, F. W. H. "Multiplex Personality." *The Nineteenth Century* 20 (Nov., 1886): 648–66.

"Obituary." *Journal of the Society for Psychical Research* 7 (January, 1895): 6–7.

Norquay, Glenda, ed. *R. L. Stevenson on Fiction: An Anthology of Literary and Critical Essays*. Edinburgh: Edinburgh University Press, 1999.

Nussbaum, Martha. *Upheavals of Thought: The Intelligence of Emotions*. Cambridge: Cambridge University Press, 2001.

Oatley, Keith. *Emotions: A Brief History*. Oxford: Blackwell, 2004.

Ochs, Sidney. *A History of Nerve Functions: From Animal Spirits to Molecular Mechanisms*. Cambridge: Cambridge University Press, 2004.

Oppenheim, Janet. *"Shattered Nerves": Doctors, Patients and Depression in Victorian England*. New York: Oxford University Press, 1991.

Otis, Laura, ed. *Literature and Science in the Nineteenth Century: An Anthology*. Oxford: Oxford University Press, 2002.

Page, Herbert. *Injuries of the Spine and Spinal Cord Without Apparent Mechanical Lesion, and Nervous Shock, in Their Surgical and Medico-Legal Aspects*. 2nd edn. London: Churchill, 1885.

Railway Injuries, With Special Reference to Those of the Back and Nervous System, in Their Medico-Legal and Clinical Aspects. London: Griffin, 1891.

"Shock from Fright." *A Dictionary of Psychological Medicine*, Volume II. Ed. Daniel Hack Tuke. Philadelphia: P. Blackiston, 1892, 1157–60.

Panksepp, Jaak. *Affective Neuroscience: The Foundations of Human and Animal Emotions*. Oxford: Oxford University Press, 1998.

Paroissen, David. Introduction to Charles Dickens, *The Mystery of Edwin Drood*. London: Penguin, 2002, xiii–xliii.

Penner, Louise. "Unmapped Country: Uncovering Hidden Wounds in *Daniel Deronda*." *Victorian Literature and Culture* 30 (2002): 77–97.

Persak, Christine. "Spencer's Doctrines and Mr. Hyde: Moral Evolution in Stevenson's 'Strange Case.'" *Victorian Newsletter* 86 (1994): 13–18.

Peterson, Audrey C. "Brain Fever in Nineteenth-Century Literature: Fact and Fiction." *Victorian Studies* 19:4 (1976): 445–64.

Petroski, Karen. "The Ghost of an Idea: Dickens's Uses of Phantasmagoria, 1842–44." *Dickens Quarterly* 16:2 (June 1999): 71–93.

Pick, Daniel. *Svengali's Web: The Alien Enchanter in Modern Culture*. New Haven: Yale University Press, 2000.

Picker, John. *Victorian Soundscapes*. Oxford: Oxford University Press, 2003.

Pinney, Thomas, ed. *Essays of George Eliot*. London: Routledge and Kegan Paul, 1963.

Poole, Adrian. "'Hidden Affinities' in *Daniel Deronda*." *Essays in Criticism* 33:4 (1983): 294–311.

Radstone, Susannah. "Screening Trauma: Forrest Gump, Film and Memory." *Memory and Methodology*. Ed. Susannah Radstone. Oxford: Berg Press, 2000, 79–107.

Rand, Nicholas. "The Hidden Soul: The Growth of the Unconscious in Philosophy, Psychology, Medicine, and Literature, 1750–1900." *American Imago* 61:3 (2004): 257–89.

Reddy, William. *The Navigation of Feeling: A Framework for the History of Emotions*. Cambridge: Cambridge University Press, 2001.

Reed, Edward. *From Soul to Mind: The Emergence of Psychology from Erasmus Darwin to William James*. New Haven: Yale University Press, 1997.

Ribot, Theodule. *Diseases of Memory: An Essay in the Positive Psychology*. 1881; trans. William Huntingdon Smith. New York: Appleton, 1887.

Richardson, Alan. *British Romanticism and the Science of the Mind*. Cambridge: Cambridge University Press, 2001.

Rosenwein, Barbara H. "Worrying About Emotions in History." *The American Historical Review* 107:3 (June, 2002): 821–45.

Rotenberg, Carl T. "George Eliot – Proto-Psychoanalyst." *The American Journal of Psychoanalysis* 59:3 (1999): 257–70.

Royle, Nicholas. *Telepathy and Literature: Essays on the Reading Mind*. Oxford: Blackwell, 1991.

Rylance, Rick. *Victorian Psychology and British Culture 1850–1880*. Oxford: Oxford University Press, 2000.

Ryle, Gilbert. *The Concept of Mind*. London: Hutchinson and Co., 1949.

Saposnik, Irving. *Robert Louis Stevenson*. New York: Twayne, 1974.

Schaumburger, Nancy E. "The 'Gritty Stages' of Life: Psychological Time in *The Mystery of Edwin Drood*." *The Dickensian* 86:3 (1990): 158–63.

Schivelbusch, Wolfgang. *The Railway Journey: The Industrialization of Time and Space in the Nineteenth Century*. Berkeley: University of California Press, 1986.

Schlicke, Paul, ed. *Oxford Reader's Companion to Charles Dickens*. Oxford: Oxford University Press, 1999.

Schnapp, Jeffery T. "Crash (Speed as Engine of Individuation)." *Modernism/Modernity* 6:1 (1999): 1–49.

Seed, David. "Mystery in Everyday Things: Charles Dickens' 'Signalman.'" *Criticism* 23:1 (1981): 42–57.

Seltzer, Mark. *Serial Killers: Death and Life in America's Wound Culture*. New York: Routledge, 1998.

"Wound Culture: Trauma in the Pathological Public Sphere." *October* 80 (Spring 1997): 3–26.

Showalter, Elaine. "Dr. Jekyll's Closet." *The Haunted Mind: The Supernatural in Victorian Literature*. Ed. Elton E. Smith and Robert Haas. London: The Scarecrow Press, 1999, 67–88.

The Female Malady: Women, Madness and English Culture: 1830–1980. New York: Pantheon Books, 1985.

Shuttleworth, Sally. "The Language of Science and Psychology in George Eliot's *Daniel Deronda*." *Victorian Science and Victorian Values: Literary Perspectives*. Ed. James Paradis and Thomas Postlewait. New York: New York Academy of Sciences, 1981, 269–98.

"'The Malady of Thought': Embodied Memory in Victorian Psychology and the Novel." *Memory and Memorials 1789–1914: Literary and Cultural Perspectives*. Ed. Matthew Campbell, Jacqueline M. Labbe and Sally Shuttleworth. New York: Routledge, 2000, 46–59.

Shuttleworth, Sally, and Jenny Bourne Taylor, eds. *Embodied Selves: An Anthology of Psychological Texts 1830–1890*. Oxford: Oxford University Press, 1998.

Small, Helen, ed. *Literature, Science and Psychology, 1830–1970: Essays in Honour of Gillian Beer*. Oxford: Oxford University Press, 2003.

Selected bibliography

Smith, Elton E., and Robert Haas, eds. *The Haunted Mind: The Supernatural in Victorian Literature*. Lanham: The Scarecrow Press, 1999.

Smith, Roger. "The Physiology of the Will: Mind, Body, and Psychology in the Periodical Literature, 1855–1875." *Science Serialized: Representations of the Sciences in Nineteenth-Century Periodicals*. Ed. Geoffrey Cantor and Sally Shuttleworth. Cambridge, Mass.: The MIT Press, 2004, 81–110.

Spencer, Herbert. *The Principles of Psychology*. 1855; 2nd edn. 2 vols. London: Williams and Norgate, 1870–72.

Stahl, John. "The Sources and Significance of the Revenant in Dickens's 'The Signalman.'" *Dickens Studies Newsletter* 11 (1980): 98–101.

Stanley, Edward. "Opening of the Liverpool and Manchester Railroad." *Blackwood's Edinburgh Magazine* 28 (1830): 823–30.

[Stephen, J. Fitzjames.] "A Letter to a Saturday Reviewer." *Cornhill Magazine* 8 (1863): 438–48.

Stiles, Anne. "Robert Louis Stevenson's *Jekyll and Hyde* and the Double Brain." *Studies in English Literature, 1500–1900* 46:4 (Autumn 2006): 879–900.

Stone, Carole. "George Eliot's *Daniel Deronda*: The Case of Gwendolen H." *Nineteenth Century Studies* 7 (1993): 57–68.

Stone, Harry, ed. *Dickens' Working Notes for his Novels*. Chicago: University of Chicago Press, 1987.

Stoneman, Patsy. *Elizabeth Gaskell*. Sussex: Harvester Press, 1987.

Sully, James. Preface to George Henry Lewes, *The Physical Basis of Mind*. London: Kegan Paul, Trench, Trübner, 1893, v–viii.

Swearingen, R. G. *The Prose Writings of Robert Louis Stevenson: A Guide*. London: Macmillan Press, 1980.

Tambling, Jeremy. *Dickens, Violence and the Modern State: Dreams of the Scaffold*. Houndmills: MacMillan, 1995.

Taylor, Jenny Bourne. *In the Secret Theatre of Home: Wilkie Collins, Sensation Narrative, and Nineteenth-Century Psychology*. London: Routledge, 1988.

  "Obscure Recesses: Locating the Victorian Unconscious." *Writing and Victorianism*. Ed. J. B. Bullen. London: Longman, 1997, 153–58.

"The War." *The Lancet* (January 21, 1871): 98–99.

Thomas, Ronald. *Dreams of Authority: Freud and the Fictions of the Unconscious*. Cornell: Cornell University Press, 1990.

Thomson, Mathew. "Neurasthenia in Britain: An Overview." *Cultures of Neurasthenia: From Beard to the First World War*. Ed. Marijke Gijswijt-Hofstra and Roy Porter. Amsterdam: Rodopi, 2001, 77–95.

Thomson, Mowbray. *The Story of Cawnpore*. London: 1859.

Thurschwell, Pamela. "George Eliot's Prophecies: Coercive Second Sight and Everyday Thought Reading." The Victorian Supernatural. Ed. Nicola Brown, Carolyn Burdett and Pamela Thurschwell. Cambridge: Cambridge University Press, 2004, 87–105.

  Literature, Technology and Magical Thinking: 1880–1920. Cambridge: Cambridge University Press, 2001.

Tromp, Marlene. "Gwendolen's Madness." *Victorian Literature and Culture* 28:2 (2000): 451–67.

Trotter, David. "The Invention of Agoraphobia." *Victorian Literature and Culture* 32:2 (2004): 463–74.

Tuke, Daniel Hack, ed. *A Dictionary of Psychological Medicine.* 2 vols. Philadelphia: P. Blackiston, 1892.

Illustrations of the Influence of the Mind upon the Body in Health and Disease: Designed to Elucidate the Action of the Imagination. 1872; 2nd edn. Philadelphia: Henry C. Lea's Son & Co., 1884.

Uglow, Jenny. *George Eliot.* London: Virago, 1987.

Veeder, William. "Collated Fractions of the Manuscript Drafts of Strange Case of Dr Jekyll and Mr Hyde." *Dr Jekyll and Mr Hyde after One Hundred Years.* Ed. William Veeder and Gordon Hirsch. Chicago: University of Chicago Press, 1988, 14–56.

Vrettos, Athena. "Defining Habits: Dickens and the Psychology of Repetition." *Victorian Studies* 42:3 (1999/2000): 399–426.

Somatic Fictions: Imagining Illness in Victorian Culture. Stanford: Stanford University Press, 1995.

Ward, Andrew. *Our Bones are Scattered: The Cawnpore Massacres and the Indian Mutiny of 1857.* New York: Henry Holt, 1996.

Ward, T. O. "Case of Double Consciousness Connected with Hysteria." *Journal of Psychological Medicine and Mental Pathology* 2 (1849): 456–61.

Webb, Alisa. "Constructing the Gendered Body: Girls, Health, Beauty, Advice, and the *Girls' Best Friend*, 1898–99." *Women's History Review* 15:2 (April 2006): 253–75.

Weisser, Susan Ostrov. "Gwendolen's Hidden Wound: Sexual Possibilities and Impossibilities in *Daniel Deronda*." *Modern Language Studies* 20:3 (Summer 1990): 3–13.

Whyte, L. L. *The Unconscious Before Freud.* London: Tavistock, 1962.

Wilde, Oscar. "The Decay of Lying." *The Nineteenth Century: A Monthly Review* 25 (January–June, 1889): 35–56.

Wilson, Edmund. "Dickens: The Two Scrooges." *The Wound and the Bow: Seven Studies in Literature.* New York: Oxford University Press, 1965, 3–85.

Winslow, Forbes. *On Obscure Diseases of the Brain, and Disorders of the Mind: Their Incipient Symptoms, Pathology, Diagnosis, Treatment, and Prophylaxis.* London: John Churchill, 1860.

Winter, Alison. *Mesmerized: Powers of Mind in Victorian Britain.* Chicago: University of Chicago Press, 1998.

Wood, Mrs. Ellen. "Lease, the Pointsman." *The Argosy* (January 1, 1869): 49–65.

Wright, Terence. *Elizabeth Gaskell: "We are not Angels": Realism, Gender, Values.* Houndmills: Macmillan Press, 1995.

Yonge, Charlotte. *The Daisy Chain, or, Aspirations: A Family Chronicle.* London: Macmillan, 1881.

Young, Robert. *Darwin's Metaphor: Nature's Place in Victorian Culture.* Cambridge: Cambridge University Press, 1985.

Index

CAMBRIDGE STUDIES IN NINETEENTH-CENTURY
LITERATURE AND CULTURE

General editor
Gillian Beer, *University of Cambridge*

Lightning Source UK Ltd.
Milton Keynes UK
UKOW051856020212

186549UK00001B/5/P